Looking at Linlithgow

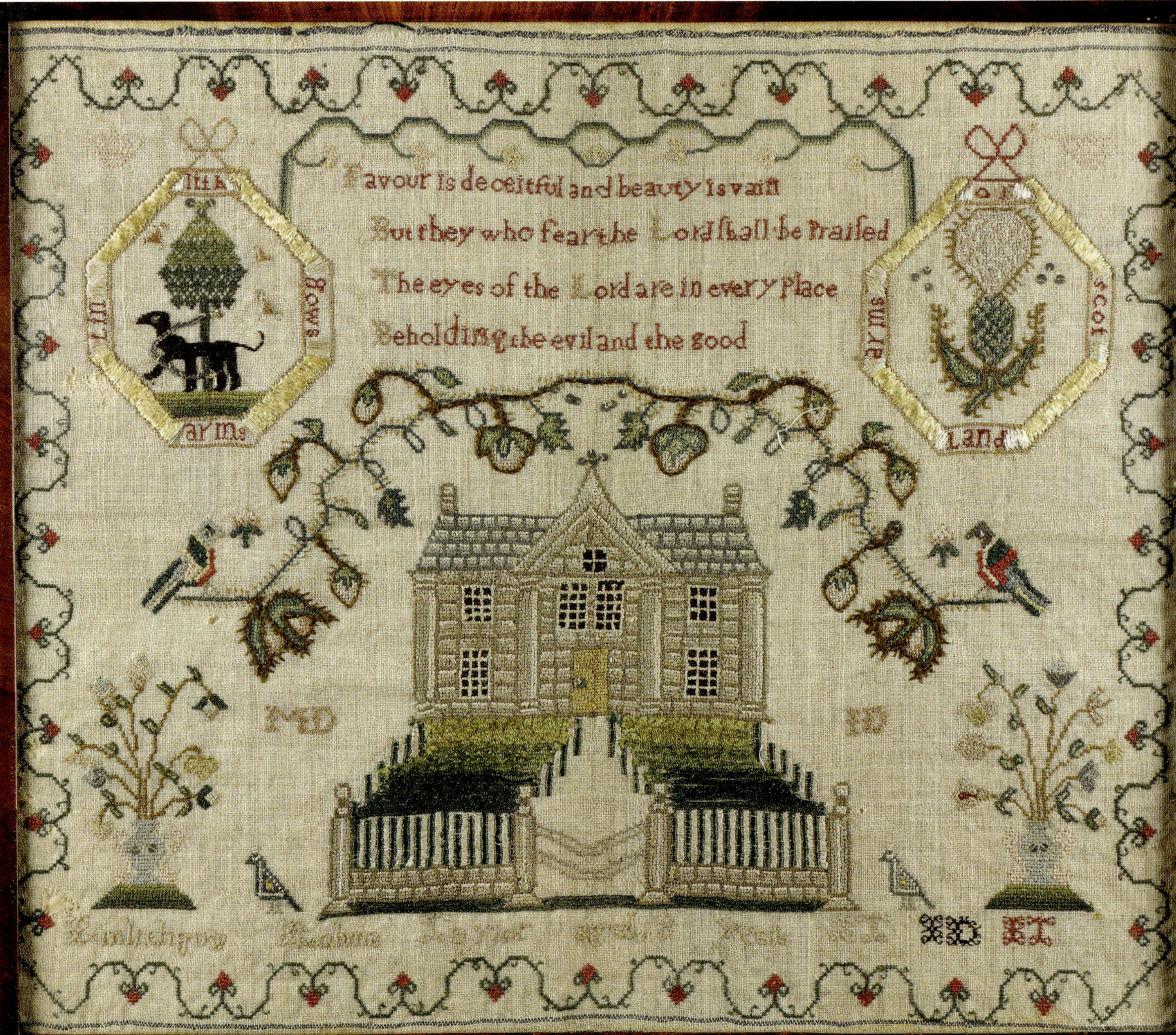
Favour is deceitful and beavty is vain
But they who fear the Lord shall be Praised
The eyes of the Lord are in every Place
Beholding the evil and the good
Lin lith Bows arms
arms of scot land
MD
ID
ID ET

Looking at Linlithgow

The Royal Burgh in Art
Through the Centuries

Christopher Long
Linlithgow Civic Trust

Linlithgow Civic Trust is part of Linlithgow Burgh Trust
Scottish Charity No. SC047211

On the cover are illustrated the the representation of the Cross fountain drummer in sculpture,
© Christopher Long
and in tile
© Douglas Watson Studio

Sampler embroidered by Robina Taylor circa 1792
© National Museums Scotland
(Opposite title page)

Published by Linlithgow Civic Trust
First published in 2018

Printed by JMK, Linlithgow Bridge
ISBN 978 09537047 5 0
www.lbt.scot

Linlithgow Civic Trust is a part of Linlithgow Burgh Trust, Scottish Charitable Incorporated Organisation Scottish Charity No. SC047211

Foreword

Certain places draw artists to them. The Royal Burgh of Linlithgow between Edinburgh and Stirling in Scotland is one such place. Dating back to the 12th century it has history aplenty, including being the birthplace at Linlithgow Palace of Mary, Queen of Scots.

It is not surprising, therefore, that artists have been drawn to the town over many centuries and still are today. This book for the first time shows how artists have portrayed Linlithgow as it has evolved from a royal residence through a centre of trade and industry to being an important tourist and commuting town.

Well-known artists such as J.M.W. Turner and John Abraham Slezer and more recently Mary Louise Coulouris have produced works inspired by Linlithgow and are covered in this book. However, the book also covers images of the town and its people, textiles, sculptures and more quirky illustrations such as that of Linlithgow Palace on the lid of a pot of jam! It is also pleasing to see that the work of current young artists is included in the book.

It requires a huge amount of effort and skill to bring together the material for an ambitious publication like this one. Immense credit must therefore go to the author, Christopher Long, who has spent three years researching all the artworks, getting copyright consent and writing a unique book that uses artwork to illustrate all aspects of Linlithgow now and in the past. It has taken Christopher on a journey of discovery from the Palace of Westminster, the National Trust for Scotland's Alloa Tower, to the vaults of the West Lothian archives in Livingston.

Credit is also due to Linlithgow Civic Trust, a charity, for taking on such an ambitious project and raising the funds to publish this book. I am sure that it will be enjoyed not only by those interested in Linlithgow but also anyone who is interested in Scottish history and art history.

Sir John Leighton
Director-General
National Galleries Scotland

Sponsors and Subscribers

Corporate and Private Sponsors

Pollock Hammond Ltd, Architects and Conservation Consultants, Linlithgow
Dianne Lamont, Linlithgow
Allan Robertson Consulting Limited, Property and Construction Consultants, Linlithgow
Ron & Myra Smith, Rivaldsgreen Crescent, Linlithgow
Gavin & Averil Stewart, Linlithgow
Alan Steel Asset Management, Nobel House, Linlithgow
Gordon and Kathryn Young, Lochend, Linlithgow

Subscribers

Cafébar 1807, Linlithgow
Jack & Christine Adair, Linlithgow
Elizabeth Aitken, Lanark
John and Lyn Aitken
Chris Beetham, Ashstead, Surrey
Gordon and Liz Beetham, Laverock Park, Linlithgow
Paul Beetham, Little Sandhurst, Berkshire
Gordon and Jess Blair, Linlithgow
Sybil Cavanagh
M. & T. Duncan, Rivaldsgreen Crescent, Linlithgow
Peter Fairweather
Ian and Eleanor Fyfe
Mrs H. Gray, Linlithgow
Ferelith and Niall Green, Linlithgow
Trish & Brian Lightbody, Clarendon Mews, Linlithgow
Jim and Nuala Lonie
David Long, Glasgow
Jean Long, Linlithgow
Jim McAdam, Sheriffs Park, Linlithgow
John and Alison Mason, Kettil'stoun Mains, Linlithgow
Mr & Mrs N. A. Middleton, Linlithgow
Angela & Mike Moran, Kettil'stoun Crescent, Linlithgow
Thom & Clare Pollock, Beinn Castle House, 293 High Street, Linlithgow
Mary & Anton Shelton, Linlithgow
Morag Stevenson, Strawberry Bank, Linlithgow
Councillor David Tait, Beechwood, Linlithgow
David Timperley, Bailielands, Linlithgow
Martyn and Anne Wade, Beechwood, Linlithgow
Gordon Wallace, Linlithgow

Acknowledgements

This book would not have been possible without a great deal of support from a wide range of people.

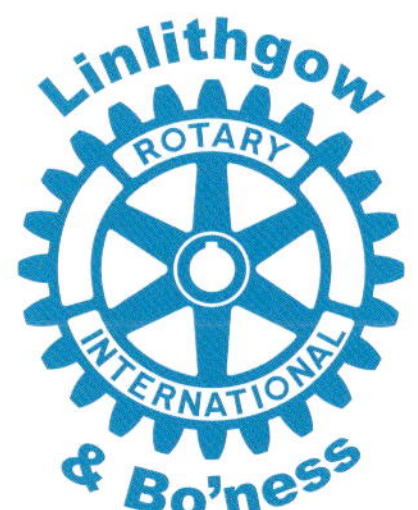

I am grateful to those who have supported the publication financially, including: West Lothian Community Arts Fund, the three local councillors: Tom Conn, Tom Kerr and David Tait, the Historic Environment Scotland Support Fund, Linlithgow Town Centre Business Improvement District and the Rotary Club of Linlithgow and Bo'ness. I would also like to thank all the corporate and private sponsors who have helped with this publication.

My heart-felt thanks are owed to the following for their work as proof readers and for their constructive comments: Laurie Alexander, Sybil Cavanagh, Bruce Jamieson, Nicholas Leonard, Roddy Simpson and Gordon Young as well as other commentators.

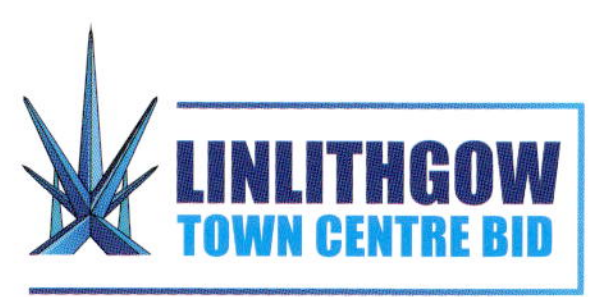

Thanks are due to photographers Calum Smith, Gordon Young and Roddy Simpson and also to the following: Fiona Hyslop MSP, Jim Hay, Michael McVeigh, William Cadell, Gail Boardman, Andrew Mylne, Gordon Wallace, Graham Galloway, Rosie McCaig at JMK, Sandy Wood, Yvonne Sherratt, Valerie Spence, David Long, John Cunningham, Ross McIntosh, Sally Pattle and Steve Parlanti for all sorts of help.

I also want to thank the numerous local artists including Douglas Cook, Lorna Pirrie, Sarah Fenton Lewis, Morag Stevenson and Leo du Feu. Sir John Leighton, Director-General of the National Galleries Scotland, the kirk session of St Michael's Parish Church and the congregation of St Peter's Episcopal Church, Linlithgow must also be thanked for their contributions. I hope this list is inclusive and that I have not forgotten anyone.

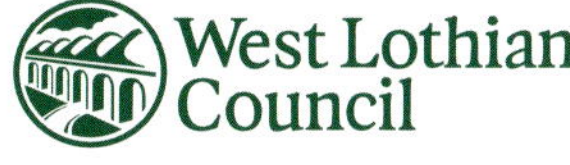

Thanks are also due to the following: Camille Archer, Arts Officer, West Lothian Council, Emma Peattie, Museums Officer, West Lothian Council, Patricia McIntosh, the highly professional indexer, Chantal Hamill, Gordon Wallace, members of the Linlithgow Heritage Trust as well as the members of Linlithgow Burgh Trust, including, in particular Marilyne McLaren, John Mason CBE, Ron Smith, Allan Robertson, John Aitken and of course to Jean, my wife, my personal proof reader and organiser with whom I will be keen to renew acquaintance after the launch!

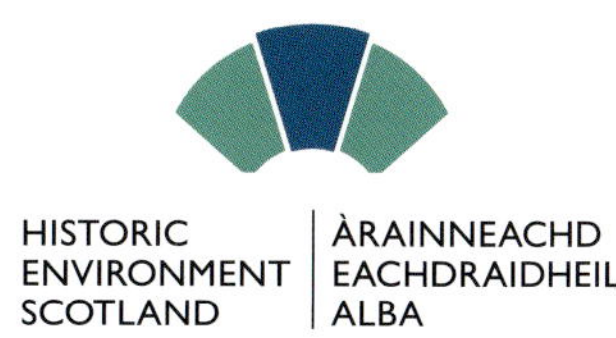

Christopher Long

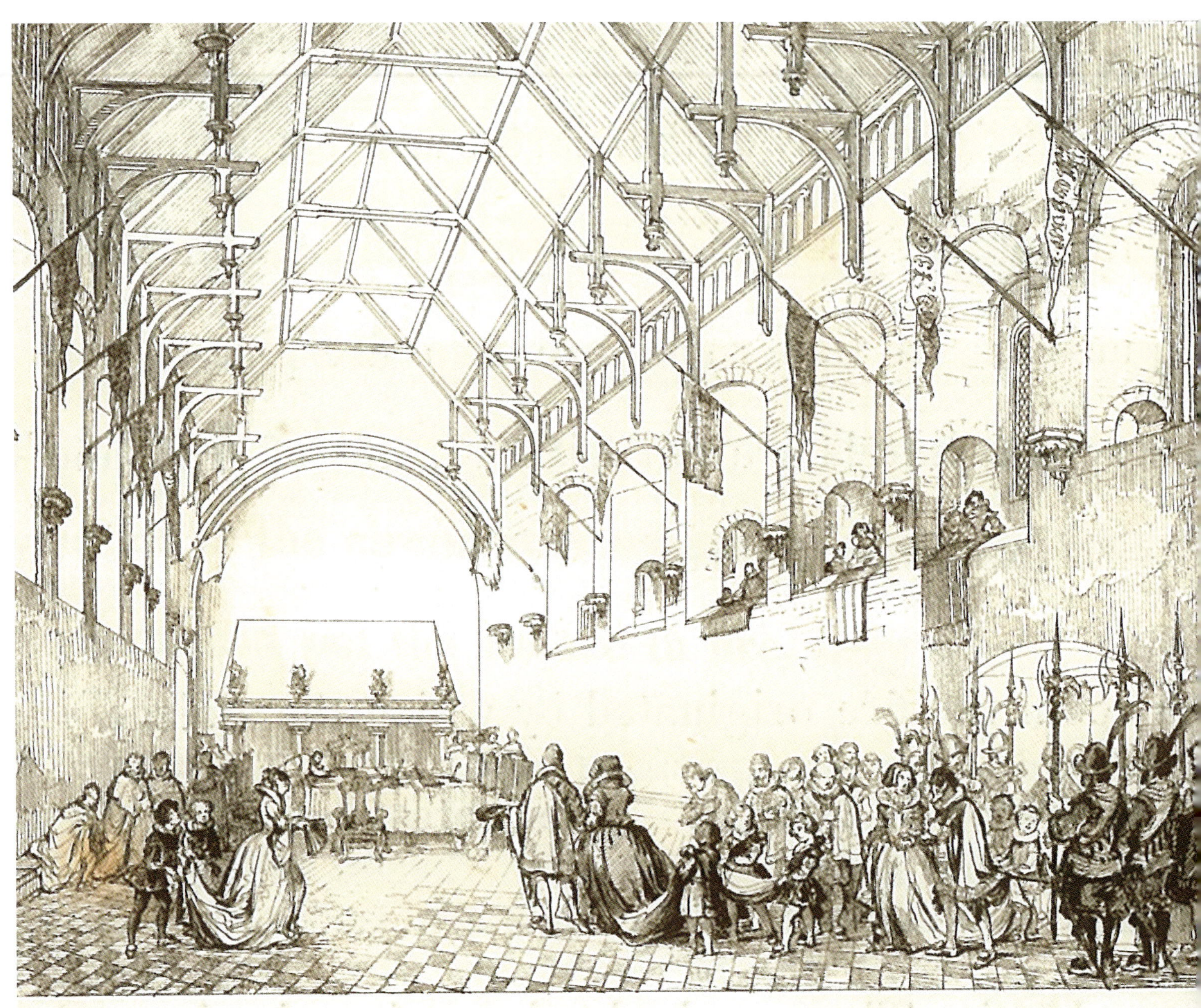

PARLIAMENT HALL.

Contents

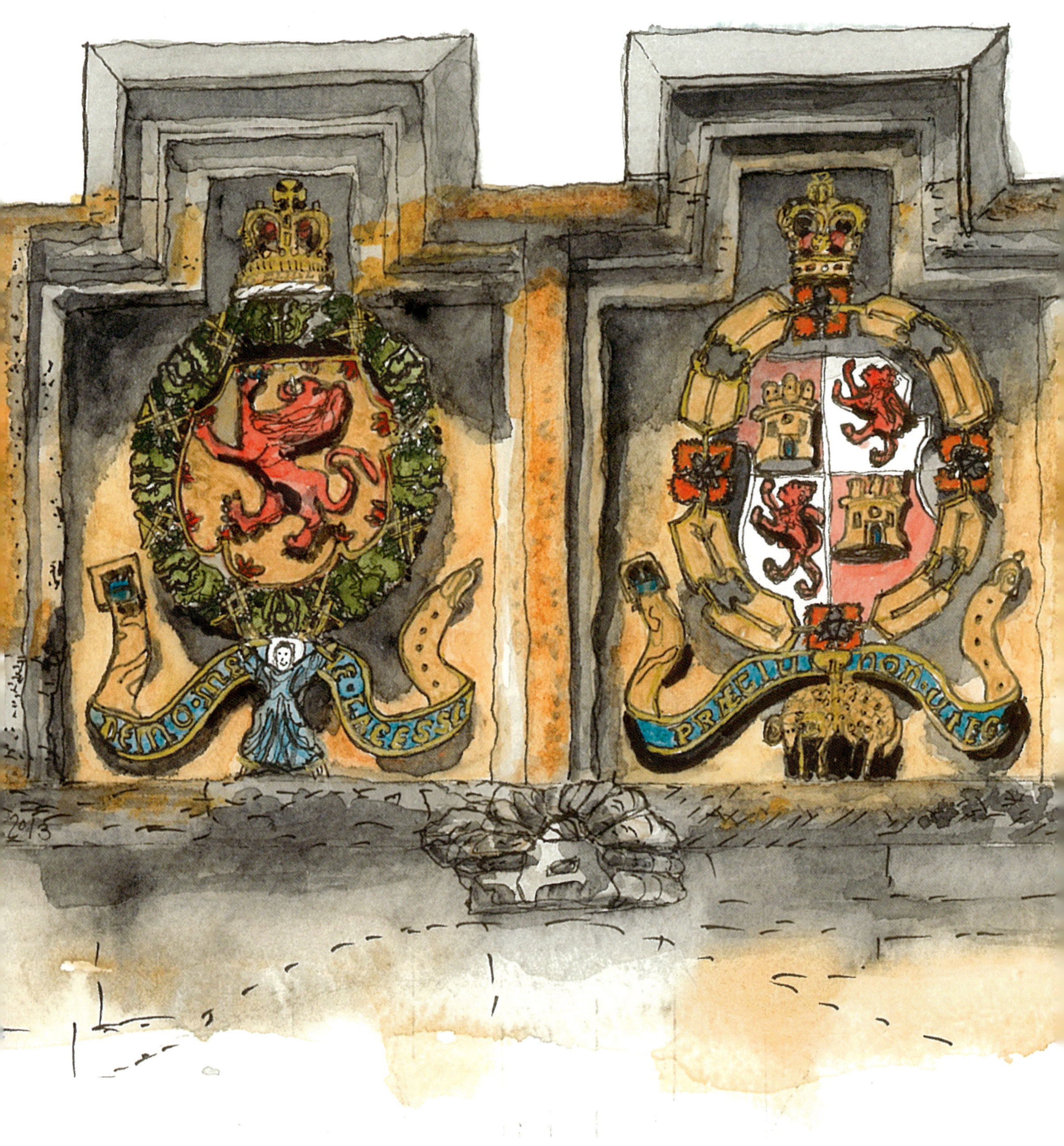

Introduction

Parliament Hall by James Collie
From 'The Royal Palace of Linlithgow' by James Collie, 1847
Private collection
(On page 6)

Detail of two of the orders of chivalry, on the Palace Gateway by Christopher Long
© Christopher Long
(Opposite)

Linlithgow is located 17 miles west of Edinburgh and lies on the Edinburgh to Glasgow railway line making it suitable as a commuter town. Its current population is around 14,000 having doubled in size since 1970, expanding to east and west.

Linlithgow has an illustrious but often tumultuous history. St Michael's Parish Church was consecrated in May 1242, though a church existed on the site for centuries before that but not always peacefully, as evidenced by Edward 1 of England requisitioning the church in 1301 as a store for war provisions. Linlithgow Palace was a favourite of the Stuart monarchs who were mostly responsible for its development into one of the foremost palaces of Europe. The Palace was the birthplace of Mary, Queen of Scots and of her father, James V, but the town was also the site of the assassination of the Earl of Moray, regent for James VI. However, it was with the Union of the Crowns in 1603 that the Palace lost its place as a pleasant retreat for the Stuarts and subsequently never recovered its status. The loss of revenue from royal patronage was replaced by trades such as shoemaking, linen-bleaching and papermaking. Eventually these too declined to be replaced by mainly small and medium businesses. Linlithgow was presented with its Royal Charter in 1389 by Robert II and in 1369 it became one of the Court of Four Burghs and was given custody of the standard grain measures. It was the county town until local authority reorganisation in 1975. Today its history, its fine buildings, its attractive setting and its vibrant population make it a popular place in which to live, and to visit.

This publication is not a history of Linlithgow. It is intended as a collection of some of the notable artwork inspired by the town and its people. The artwork covers a range of genres such as painting, sculpting, cartography and textile art. I have given some background information about the artists included and some key information about their works but I do not set myself up as an art critic. The book is divided into five parts: art related to Linlithgow's history; art of the 19th century; art of the contemporary era; art to show the work and play of the community and its individuals; and art to show how Linlithgow, its history and its icons have been used by businesses and organisations to promote their products or services.

Many gifted artists and photographers have captured the landscape and townscapes of the beautiful Royal Burgh of Linlithgow. Their paintings, sketches and photographs are held in many UK and international museums, libraries and galleries. This book brings together, for the first time in print, many of these fascinating images. Each is a unique memorial to the many people who, through the centuries, have contributed to the reputation of Linlithgow as one of the most attractive towns in the United Kingdom.

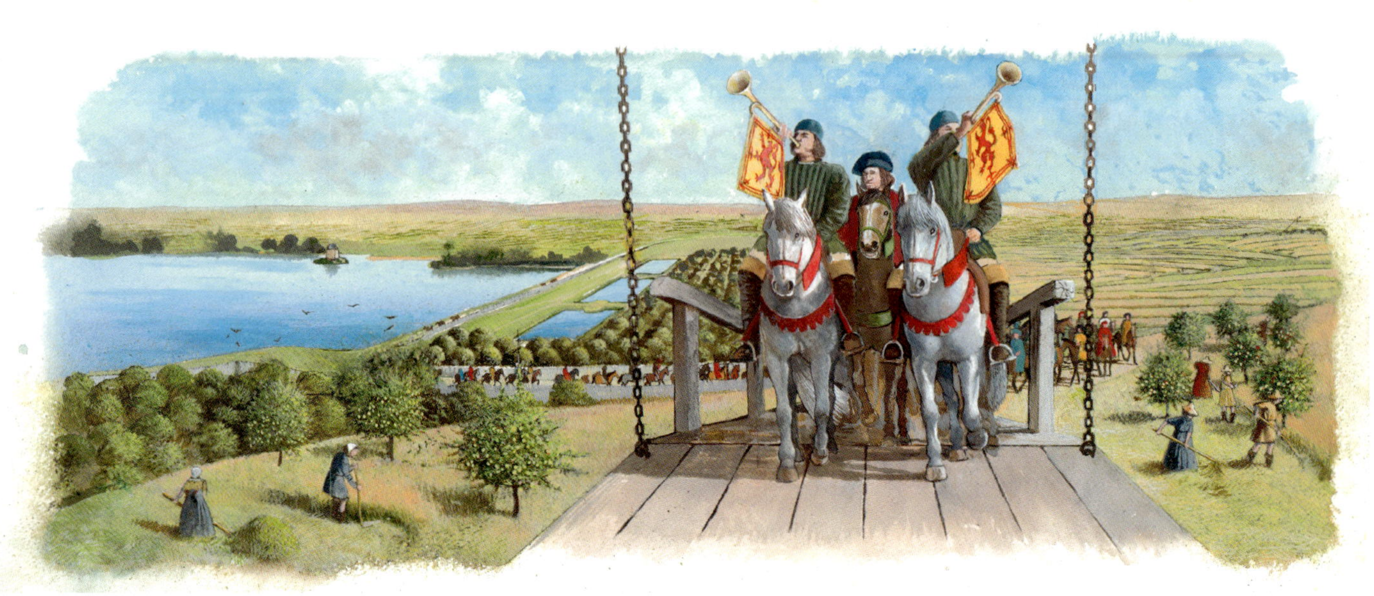

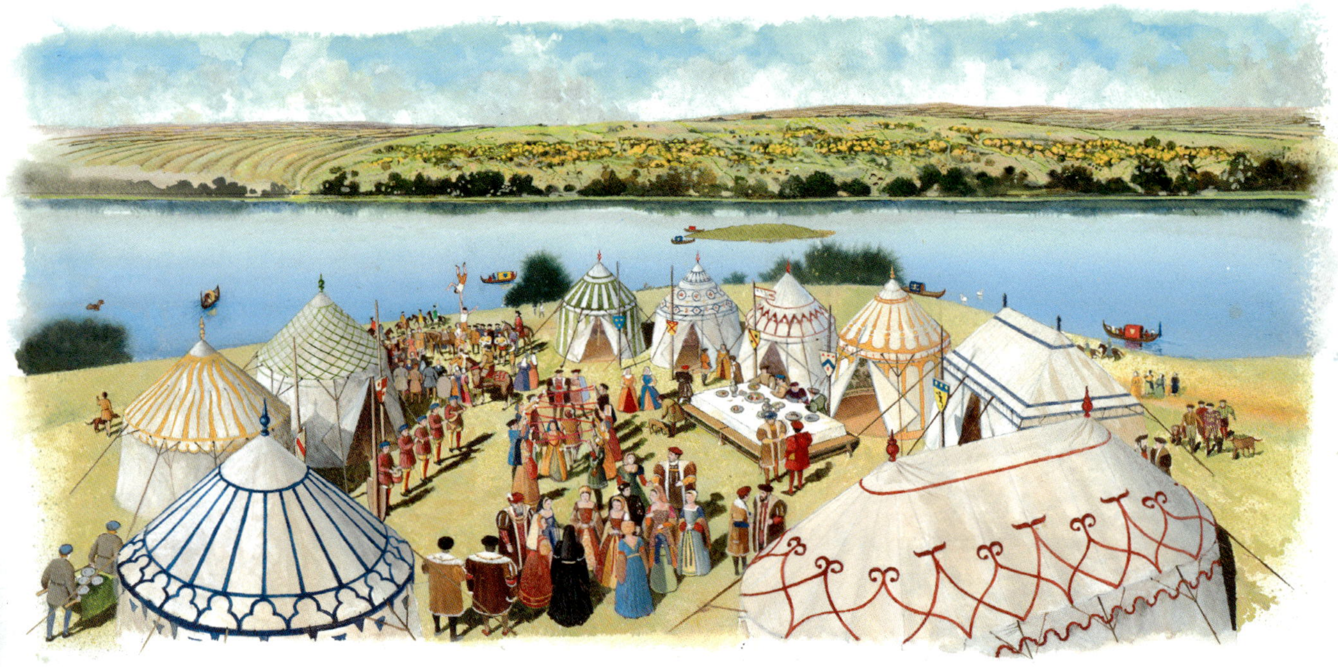

ONE

Linlithgow and its 'Princely Palace'

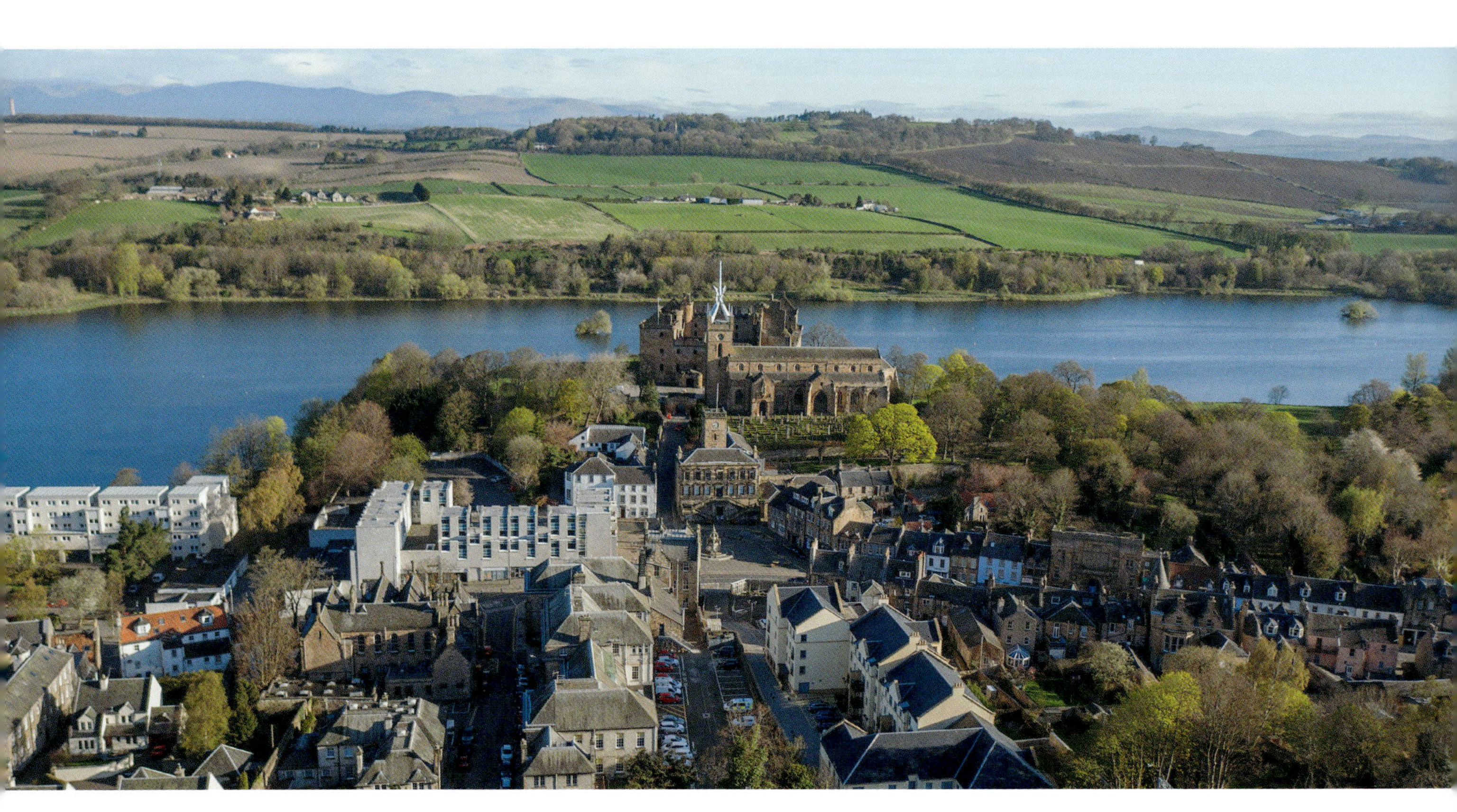

Outlook to the east and west of Linlithgow Palace by David Simon
© Historic Environment Scotland
(On page 10)

View of Linlithgow from a drone
© Images Above Ltd
(Opposite)

Linlithgow town sign
© West Lothian Council
(Below)

From a height of fifty metres above Rosemount Park, in Linlithgow, using a drone, Alan Corrie looked down, towards the north, at Linlithgow.

Linlithgow runs from east to west with the main thoroughfare being the High Street. Previously the High Street residences had long, narrow rigs – plots of land – which ran behind to provide space for agricultural purposes. The town's shape is dictated by the loch to the north side and high land to the south so most development, as demand grew, has occurred east and west with some on the south side. The south side is also bisected by the Union Canal and the Edinburgh railway. The north of the town is now bounded by the M9.

This 'bird's eye view' indicates the prominence of the palace and the church of St Michael, both bordered by Linlithgow Loch. Beyond, the fields rise to Parkhead Holdings, Grange and Airngarth Hill. Beyond again, lie the Firth of Forth and the Ochil Hills. In front, the line of the High Street is visible passing from west to east punctuated by the presence of the Burgh Halls and the Cross Well.

Road signs at each of the entrances to Linlithgow read:

'Welcome to the Royal Burgh of LINLITHGOW'

Below this is a representation of the ancient double-sided town seal showing St Michael killing a dragon and a dog chained to a tree. The sign continues with:

'Birthplace of Mary, Queen of Scots. Twinned with Guyancourt'

This book looking at Linlithgow examines these themes, and many more, through the eyes of artists over the centuries.

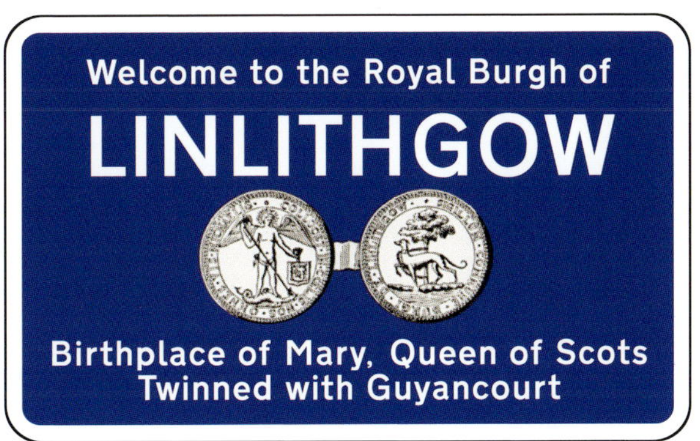

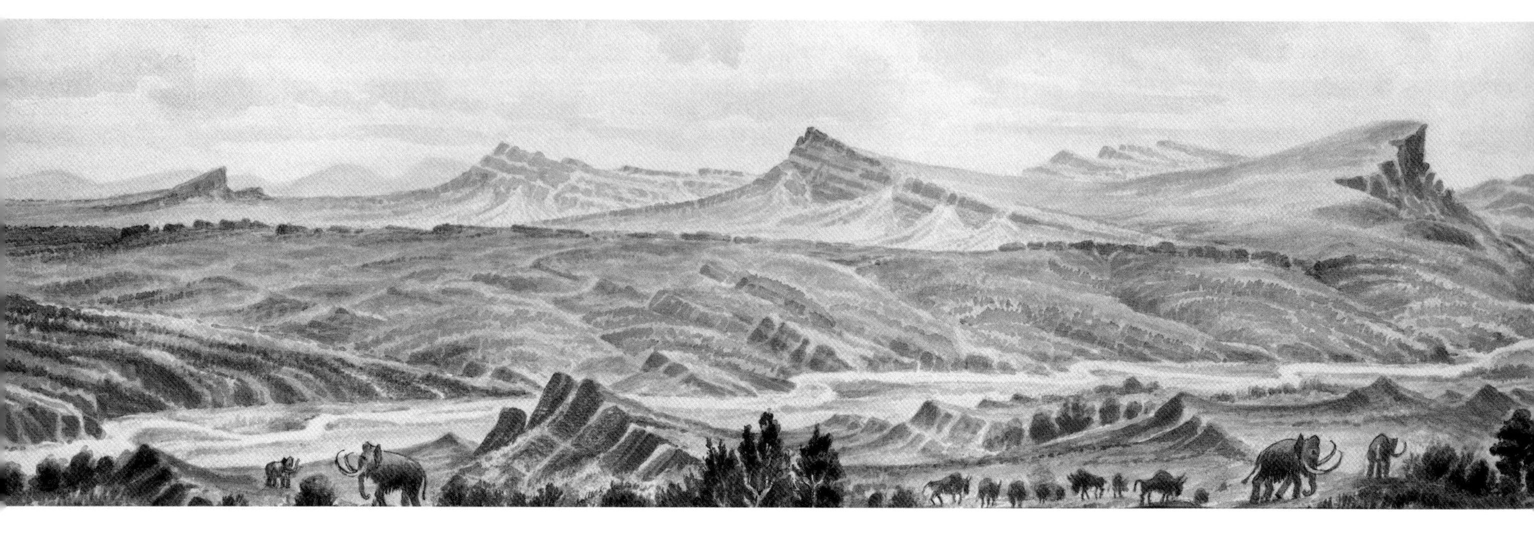

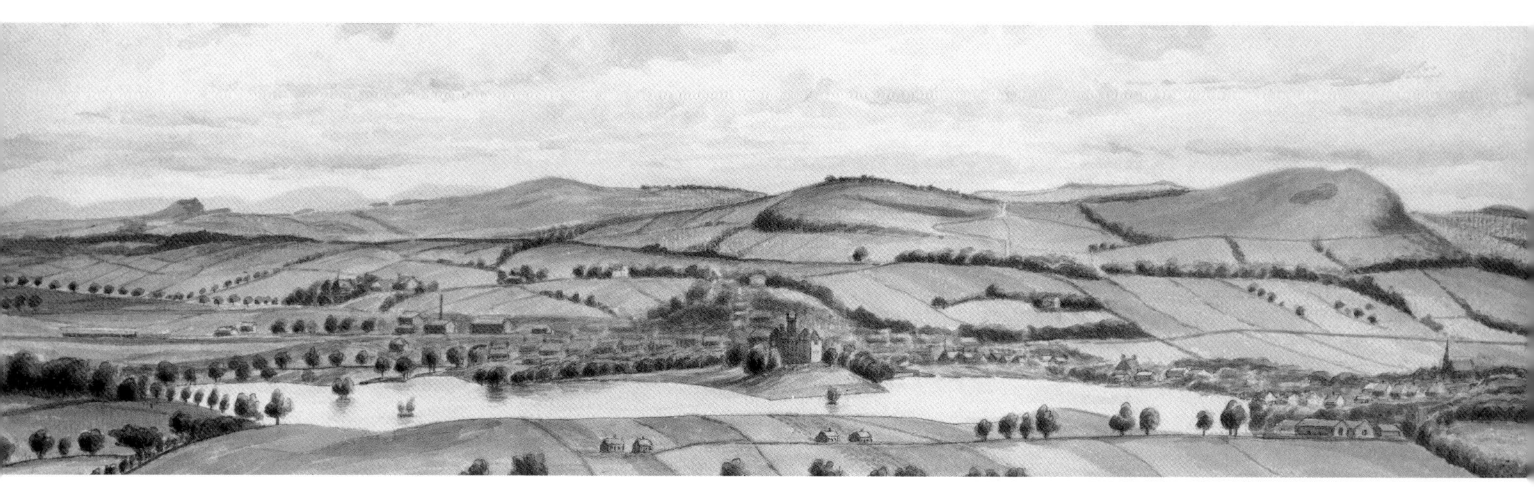

The Linlithgow valley before the Ice Age by H. M. Cadell

(Opposite, top)

The Linlithgow valley after the Ice Age, by H. M. Cadell

(Opposite, lower)

There were, of course, no artists in Linlithgow, sketchbook in hand, recording how the landscape looked before the last ice age. Born in the second half of the 19th century, a remarkable geologist, Henry M. Cadell, of Grange, (1860-1934) indulged a lifelong passion for geology and a fascination for understanding how the landscape of the Scottish highlands was formed. This curiosity extended to the valley of the Forth where he lived. Educated at Edinburgh University, under Professor Geikie, Cadell served on the first ordnance survey of Sutherland with the geologists Peach and Horne. His vivid watercolours of the Highlands can be viewed online and are archived by the British Geological Survey.

In 1925, H.M. Cadell published 'The Rocks of West Lothian'. He included sketches of how he imagined the landscape around Linlithgow may have looked, before the last ice age. He populated the scene with woolly mammoths in an environment free of man's influence. He then compared the scene from the same point in modern times, without the mammoths! He states that: 'the (upper) sketch shows what may have been the pre-glacial appearance of the old river at Linlithgow, and the one below the modern view of the 'dry' valley with the loch and the palace in the centre seen from Airngarth Hill.'

Many inhabitants of Linlithgow feel a connection with Mary Stuart, Queen of Scots - Linlithgow's most famous 'native'. Mary has over the centuries featured in operas, films and numerous biographies as well as prominently in the town. But, undoubtedly, her detractors have been as numerous as her supporters.

'This bewitching Princess ... abandoned by her son, confined by her Cousin, abused, reproached & vilified by all ... firm in her Mind, Constant in her Religion; & preparing herself to meet the cruel fate to which she was doomed, with a magnanimity that could only proceed from conscious Innocence.' (Jane Austen, as quoted in the Guardian newspaper, by Sarah Gristwood.)

Some historians view her as totally incompetent. 'Mary, Queen of Scots. A Study in Failure' is the title of the 1988 book by Jenny Wormald, a former lecturer in Scottish History at the University of Stirling.

Antonia Fraser aimed to test the truth or falsehood of the many legends about Queen Mary in her 1969 book 'Mary, Queen of Scots' and to set her in the context of the age in which she lived. Fraser stressed what she saw as Mary's main virtues but believed that the Scotland of that time required a strong ruler to pull the nobles into line.

The town signs may proclaim that Mary Stuart was born in Linlithgow, at the palace. However, today the palace is far from palatial. Modern visitors to Linlithgow Palace see bare stone walls as high as cliffs and holes in the walls where fireplaces once warmed the occupants, which give few clues to how grand it once was. The ruins of the palace

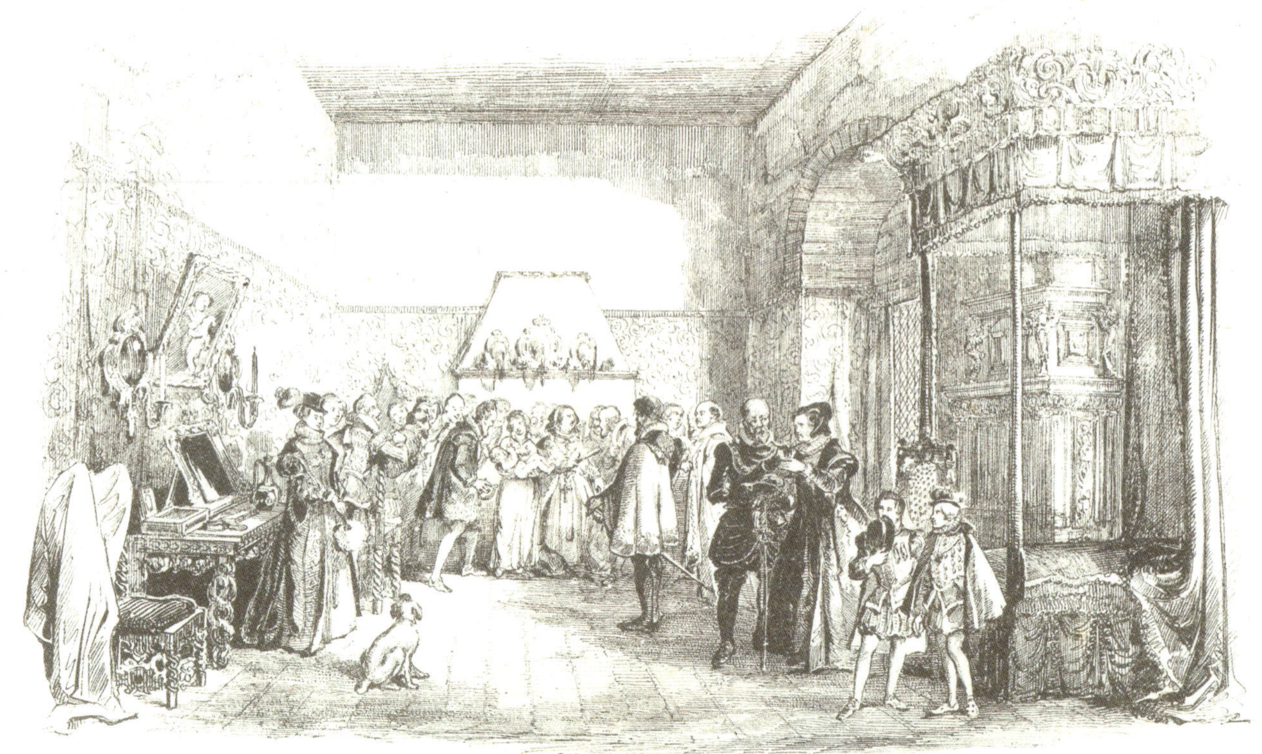

Mary's birthplace, by James Collie, 1847
From 'The Royal Palace of Linlithgow' by James Collie 1847
Private Collection
(Above)

have been managed by many custodians over the years up to Historic Environment Scotland today. Guidebooks have engaged the imagination of visitors over the years and contributed new visions of how the palace might have been. The Historic Scotland guidebook published in 2010 gives three possible locations where Mary Stuart may have been born. The Victorian imagination of artist and architect James Collie, in 1847, envisaged the 'room in which Queen Mary was born' full of family, courtiers and even a dog.

The oldest surviving view of Linlithgow was drawn by a cartographer named Timothy Pont in the late 16th century. Working between 1583 and 1614, Pont produced drawings, now digitally archived, which are intriguing. He drew what is an extensive diagram of the towns, villages and estates of Scotland, a combination of illustrations and maps. The section that looks at Linlithgow is recognisable today and records names still familiar, four hundred years later.

His map shows an area of the south coast of the Firth of Forth between Blackness and Bo'ness and inland which includes the town of Linlithgow. There is a very clear and detailed depiction of the royal palace, loch and park of the royal burgh of Linlithgow. The viewpoint is from the north. The loch, including a wooded island, and palace are

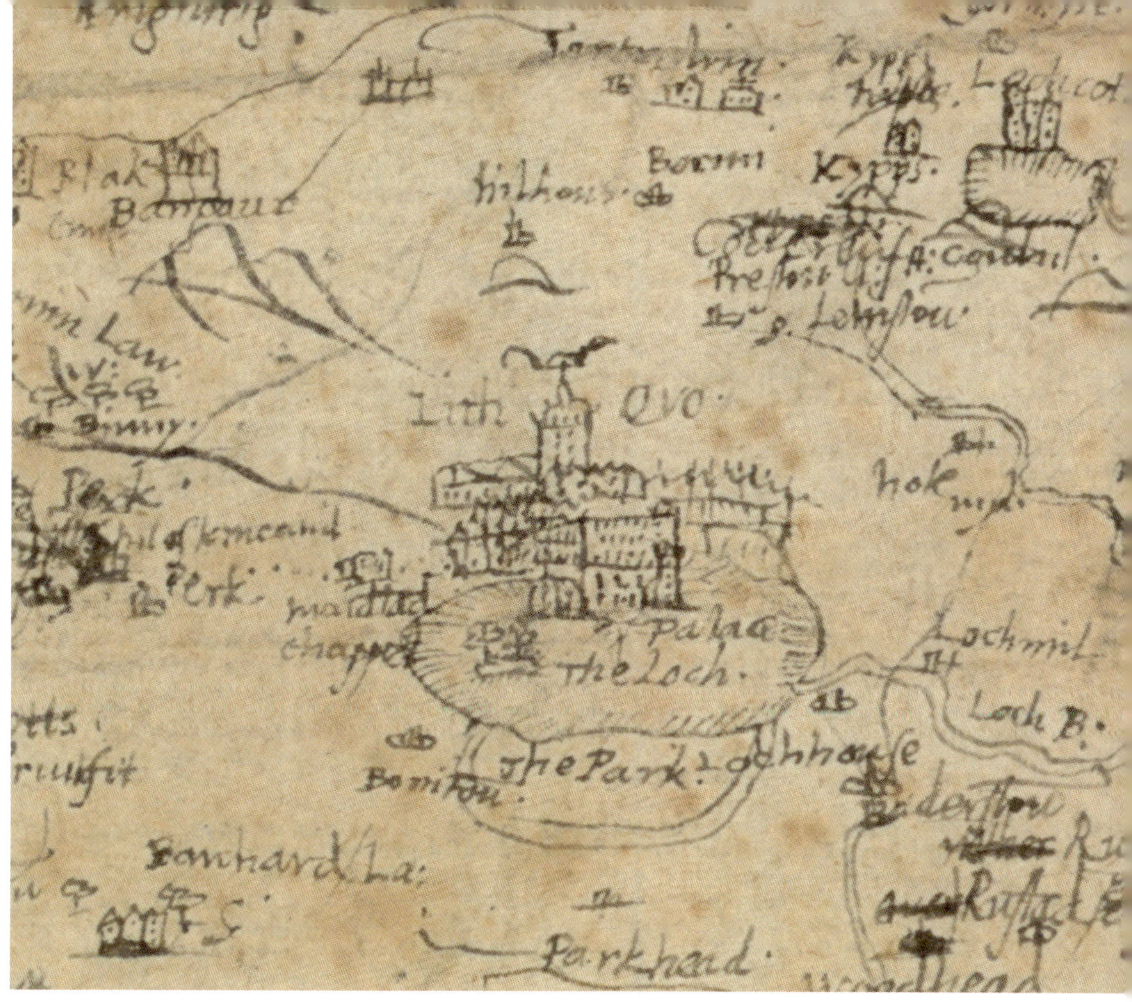

Pont's map of Linlithgow, 1630 Reproduced by permission of the National Library of Scotland (Above)

clearly visible. 'The Park' below the loch is the area now known as Parkhead which was then used for hunting. A double enclosure round the park is clearly visible. The buildings of the High Street and the Town House are clearly drawn as is the Town House's weather vane cockerel on top, now in the town museum.

No contemporary pictures survive to assist us to appreciate how grand the palace must have been. The closest we can achieve is by visiting the palace at Falkland and Stirling Castle, now faithfully restored. Despite repeated proposals over the years, the palace at Linlithgow has remained a ruin, if a 'well-preserved ruin'.

Recent academic research by Ian Campbell, Emeritus Professor at the University of Edinburgh, indicates that: 'James III and James IV transformed James I's French-inspired palace into a Scoto-Italian palazzo, unparalleled in northern Europe, and hence, worthy of imitation in some of the most significant buildings in 16th and early 17th century France, Denmark and Germany.'

A banquet in the Great Hall in the days of James VI by David Simon
© Crown Copyright HES
(Opposite)

Local historian, Bruce Jamieson, conjured up a vision of a 15th century Christmas at Linlithgow Palace in a newspaper article:

'On arrival the palace staff set to work. The dichter (cleaner) o' the king's palace organised the removal of the accumulated cobwebs of the autumn. The weschell gardener carefully supervised the unloading of the kitchen utensils and the pewter and silver vessels for the feasts to come. The master brewster, the yeoman of the larder and the king's cook each found their way to their own domains and set about their tasks.

'Up in the Great Hall the tapissier was hanging the beautiful wall coverings – elegant products from the looms of France and Flanders depicting scenes from the Bible or from mythology. One work was given pride of place – above the magnificent hooded, triple fireplace. This enormous tapestry came from Bruges and showed the lion rampant emblem of Scotland: giving to the hall its name – the 'Lyon Chalmer.' In this chamber the glessin wrycht (glazier) was also hard at work fixing the precious panes of glass into the six square-headed clerestory windows along the west side.

'Eventually all was made ready. In the banqueting hall the torches flickered in their stone sconces around the walls – illuminating the solid hammer beam roof above. Down the turnpike staircase the kitchen fires were lit and the spit-boys – the turnbrochies - were busy turning the roasting meat. All the ewers, trenchers, methers, lavers and cauldrons were stored in their wall-aumbries. All the officials were waiting.

'They had visited the local Saturday market and purchased the Christmas fare: a whole seal for 5/-; 16 swans; herons and bitterns; from the Bass Rock they had brought solan geese (gannets) and from the king's own traps in the loch – pike, perch and eels. Venison from the late summer hunts hung from the rafters and the storerooms were well filled with local taxes - paid in kind.

'The king's cavalcade had arrived. At the East High Port, the town gates were thrown open and the horses drummed up the frost-hardened clay of the 'King's High Street.' Turning right at the Market Cross, past the Old Tolbooth, the procession swung into the Kirkgait and then almost immediately right again to skirt round the kirkyaird and the vicar's garden.

'This old route to the palace – the Palisgait – then arrived at the east face where the drawbridge was lowered onto its pier and ramp. The troop of riders clattered over through the massive oaken doors and beneath the raised portcullis of this 'auld entrie.' In the courtyard they were greeted by a fanfare of trumpets. The king had arrived in his palace of Linlithgow, in time for Christmas Eve.

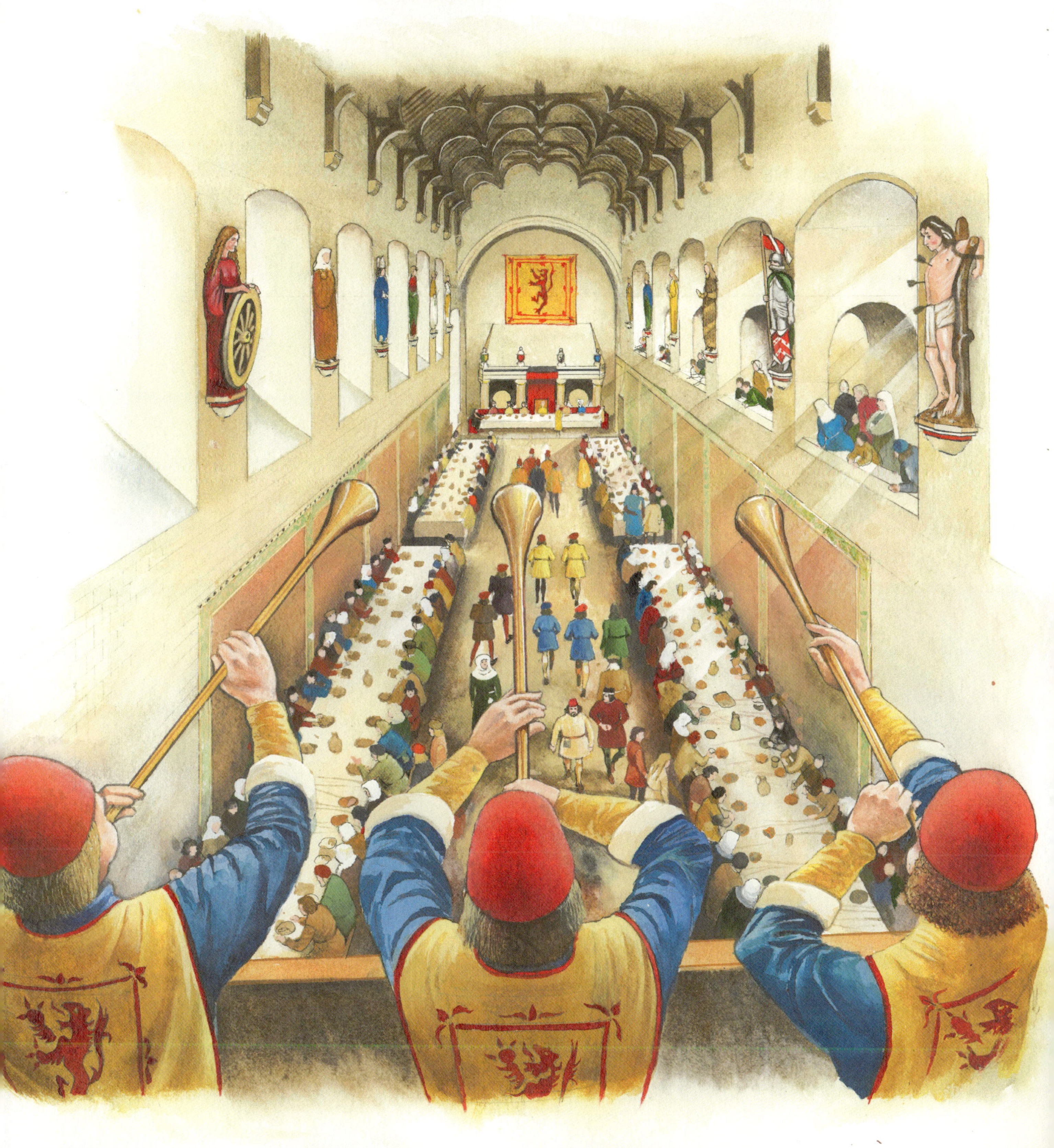

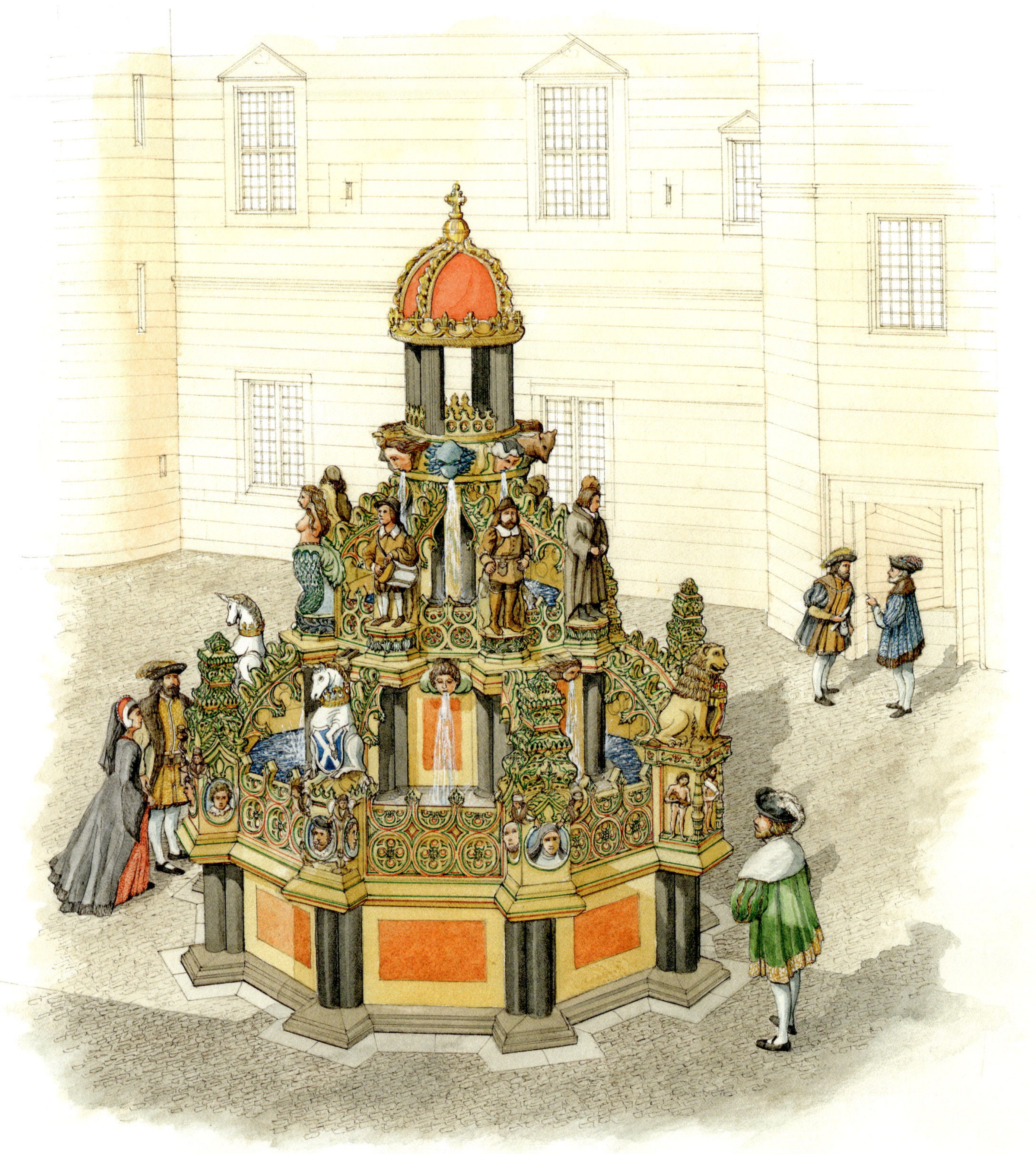

How the fountain may have looked when painted in the times of James V of Scotland, by Stephen Conlin

(Opposite)

'The horses were led off to their stables in the outer close and the king and his attendants ascended the flight of stairs leading directly from the courtyard to the great hall. There the raised dais had been prepared for the king's table - the high board. Beneath and below it stretched two rows of linear trestle tables for the lesser guests - their backs to the walls so that they could be served from the centre of the room. Before the meal, servants came round carrying napkins and basins of water - fresh drawn from the kitchen well - and everyone washed their hands.

'On Christmas Day itself the morning began with a procession of chapel clerks singing a carol. After attending church, James presented gifts to the assembled company. Usually he gave money or perhaps clothes or material – carefully allocated because, by law, each rank of person was only allowed to wear a particular type of cloth. The lords might wear mantles of red lined with silk or trimmed with fur in grey, purple or green. The labourers and townsfolk might only wear white or grey on ordinary days or light blue, green, or red on holidays.

'After church the Christmas entertainments began. Patrick Johnson and his Linlithgow Players might perform some nativity play. A choir of women singers might entertain or Currie, the Court Fool, might amuse in his jester's outfit of red and yellow. Watschod, the tale teller, would captivate his audience with his tales of Scotland's heroic past.

'The choir boys from St Michael's delighted in parodying the chants and psalms which they sang so solemnly for the rest of the year. In his chair of red velvet fringed with gold silk, King James watched the proceedings – occasionally suggesting a game of cards or dice or demanding another tune from the musicians up in their gallery to the north of the hall, while guests nibbled on gingerbread, liquorice or almonds.

'This lasted until the 5th of January. On that night a Twelfth Night cake was baked. In it was hidden a bean and whoever chose the slice with the bean in became the King of the Bean – able to choose and preside over the final days festivities – the real king 'abdicating' for that day.

'Then it was all over. Linlithgow returned to normal – and the king to the hard tasks of governing the kingdom, until next Christmas time.'

In the centre of the palace courtyard is the magnificent fountain constructed around 1538 for King James V, imagined in its fully painted glory by illustrator Stephen Conlin. His work is based on documentary evidence and is intended to enhance the understanding and appreciation of buildings such as Linlithgow Palace. The talents of historical illustrators, commissioned for guidebooks such as the official guidebook to Linlithgow Palace published by Historic Environment Scotland, are evident in lavish illustrations by modern artists such as Stephen Conlin and David Simon.

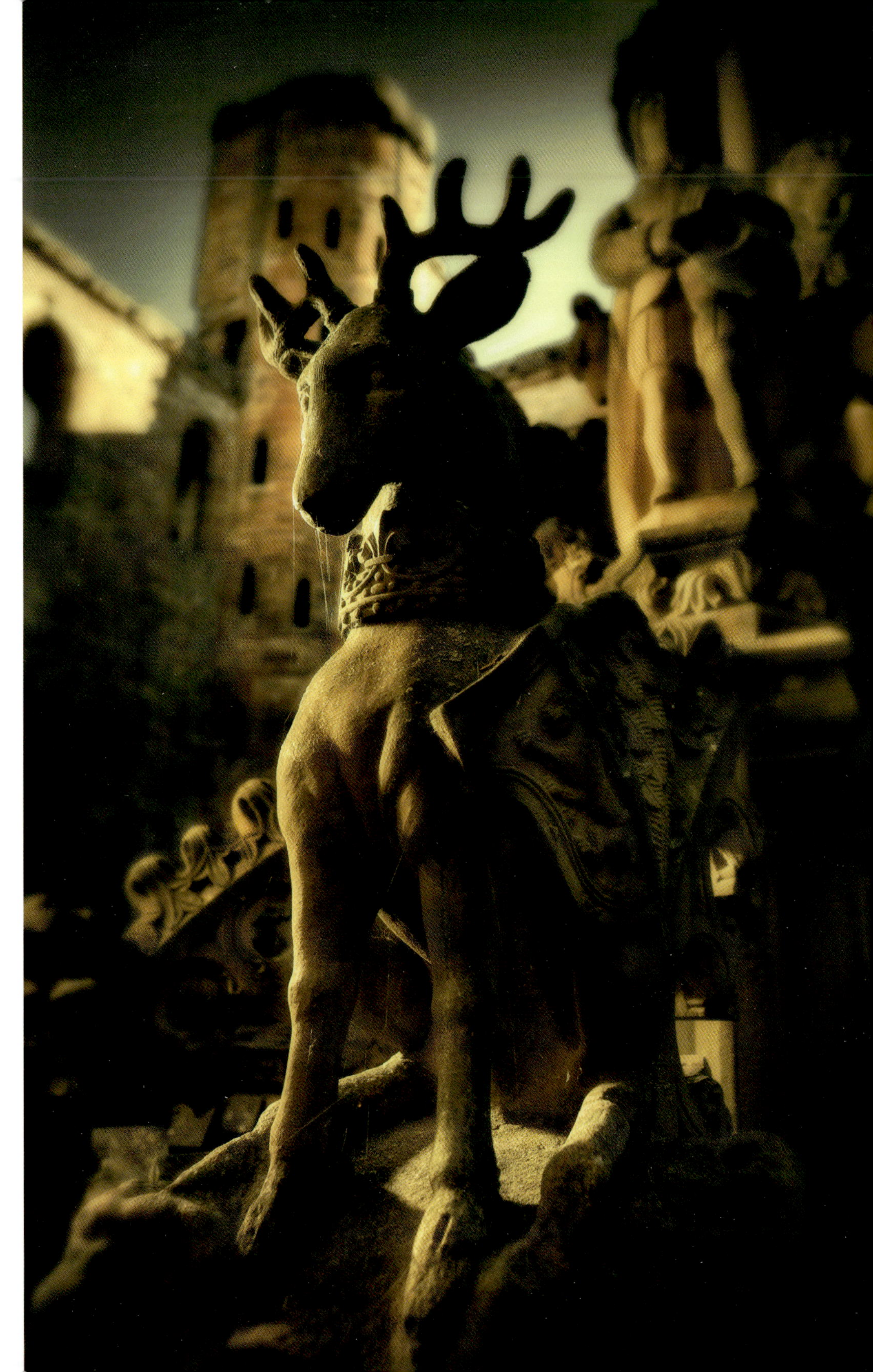

A view of the stag in the renovated Palace fountain
© Laurence Winram Photography
(Opposite)

Details of the Palace fountain
© Calum Smith photographer
(Right)

Professional photographer, Laurence Winram, captured the fountain stag, cobwebs and all, in an atmospheric photograph reproduced on these pages. This picture is included in the Saatchi Art Collection.

A selection of images of the palace and its handsome central fountain sculpture, recently renovated, have been captured by local photographer Calum Smith.

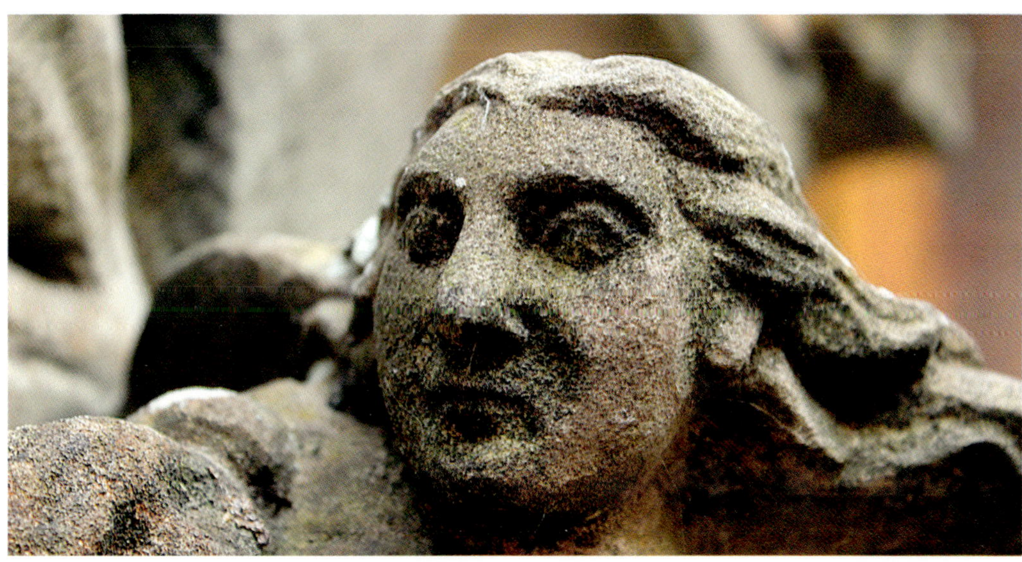

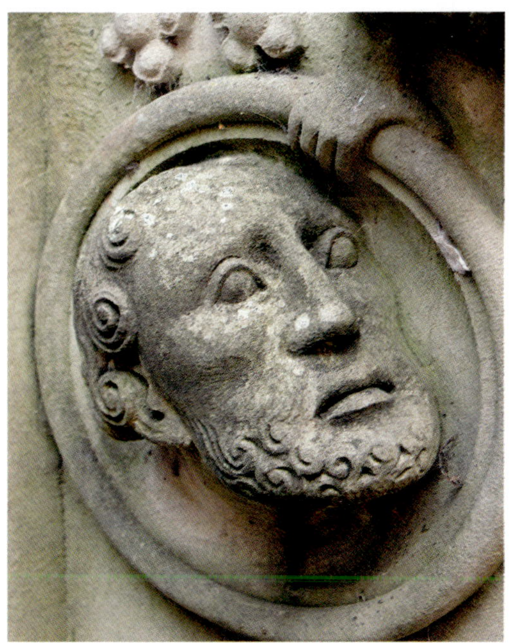

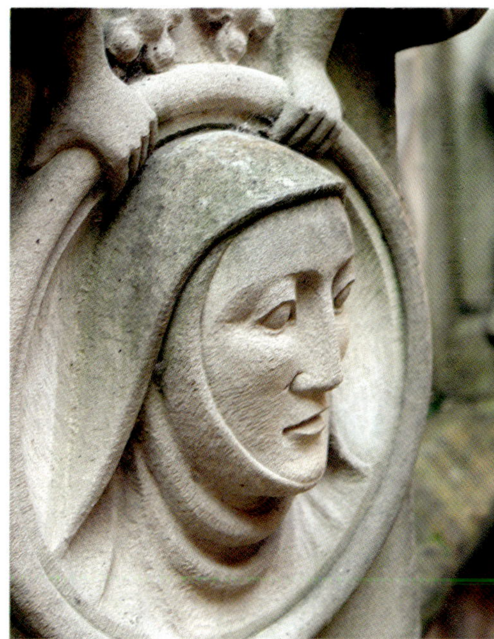

The wall hanging in St Michael's Parish Church titled 'Fire and Bells'
© Gordon Young photographer
(Opposite left)

The wall hanging depicting Mary, Queen of Scots
© Gordon Young photographer
(Opposite right)

There is a long-established tradition in Linlithgow of telling stories through textile art. This still flourishes today.

A series of tapestries was planned in 1990, to mark 700 years of St Michael's Parish Church. Over eight years, a team designed and crafted eight fine hangings, one for each century. Measuring 120cm by 75cm they hang on the walls and columns of the church. They depict the consecration of St Michael's, the town charter, the destruction by fire, Mary Stuart, the establishment of the communion chalice, town trades, church music, and peace and hope in the 20th century. Perhaps the parishioners will rise to the challenge to look at Linlithgow in the 21st century in textile art!

The descriptions below come from notes prepared by the late Iris McGowran MBE, one of the textile artists. Two of the tapestries are illustrated here.

The first panel illustrates the consecration of the church by Bishop de Bernham in 1242.

The next panel covers the 14th century and illustrates the founding of the town by charter. The tapestry shows a herald proclaiming the royal charter on the church steps accompanied by nobility and watched by townspeople. Wild flowers, fruit and berries, used in local potions, are depicted in the side panels.

Fire broke out in the roof of the nave of St Michael's Church in 1424 and this is covered in the panel depicting fire and bells in the 15th century (illustrated). This panel shows the beams, masonry, slates, rubble and ashes on the floor of the nave with flames still rising from the ruins. St. Michael's was restored and extended and at the end of the 15th century, three bells were installed in the tower - Alma Maria, embossed with a crown, is shown on the left, Santo Michael Archangelo, embossed with St. Michael, and the smaller Meg Duncan embossed with a black hound. The last two bells were recast during the 18th century. Masons' marks are recorded at the four corners of the panel.

The church tapestry group considered that there could be only one theme to illustrate the 16th century - Mary Stuart - so often dressed in black. The group were excited to find a portrait showing her in the colourful dress pictured in this tapestry (illustrated). The panel shows the young queen with auburn hair, feathered cap and wearing pearls. Entwined on the side panels are the symbols of her ancestry – the Tudor rose, and the Scottish thistle surmounted by the fleur-de-lys of France. The jewel on the rosary is depicted in two of the corners. The legend, 'Scotiæ Piissima Regina,' is translated as 'the most pious queen of Scotland'.

The 17th century is represented by the church communion chalice. The vessels sit on the communion table which has a fine linen cloth, as made in Linlithgow and bleached

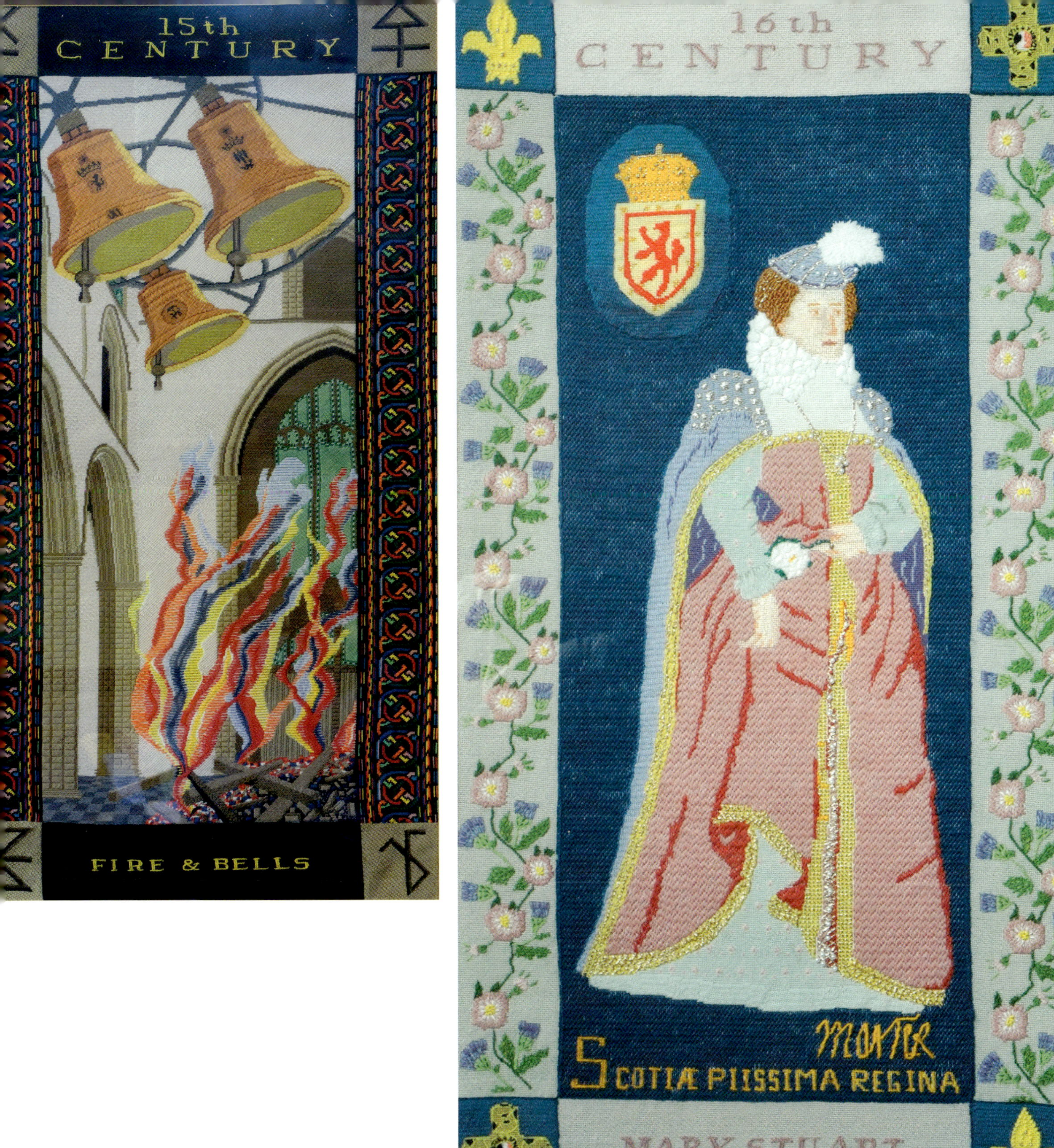
15th
CENTURY
FIRE & BELLS
16th
CENTURY
SCOTIÆ PIISSIMA REGINA
MARY STUART

South Porch, St Michael's Parish Church, Linlithgow, 2000
© Roddy Simpson photographer
(Opposite)

on the lochside bleaching green. In the 17th century, plague was rife elsewhere and Linlithgow was a haven where the parliament, illustrated by the quill and scrolls, and the University of Edinburgh, represented by books, took sanctuary temporarily in St Michael's Church. The flags at the top are Cromwell's personal banner. He housed his army and cavalry in the church, resulting in great damage.

'Princes & Trades' covers the central panel of the 18th century tapestry depicting the people busy about their weekly market day, with stalls and hawkers selling vegetables, poultry, fish, breads, as well as the products of the looms. Cabbages, kittens and chickens are visible. The building on the right was once a fire station as was the back of the Burgh Halls, which also housed a jail. In the background is seen St. Michael's Parish Church with the old stone crown on the tower. Above this panel is a representation of the palace well, flanked by the Jacobite roses of 1715 and 1745. The bottom panel shows a map of the town as it appeared towards the end of the 18th century. In the side panels and corners are depicted the old trades of the town: baxters (bakers), cordiners (shoemakers) and hammermen (blacksmiths and metalworkers). Other illustrations include birds, ribbons and foliage.

Kirk music is used to represent the 19th century. An organ was installed in St. Michael's Parish Church during this time of refurbishment. St Cecilia is shown holding a hand-pumped organ with Michaelmas daisies. The side panels are full of flowers, birds and vine leaves as well as staves of music.

In a departure from the conventional style of preceding panels, the tapestry depicting the 20th century shows a highly stylised representation by Graham Galloway of a view of St. Michael's Parish Church from the west. There are children playing on the Peel and overhead are swans in flight while on the loch is shown some of the bird life which is so noticeable a feature of the area. Sheep quietly grazing and tilled fields recall the smallholdings which existed to the north of the loch before the motorway was built.

The subject matter for each of the panels was conceived and created by a team consisting of Denise Bain, Frances Baker, David Brown, Graham Galloway, Ann Hogg, Catherine Irvine, Valerie Lynch, Iris McGowran, Ella Sutherland, Margaret Turnbull and Elma Webster.

On the south side of the church, local writer and lecturer, Roddy Simpson has captured the south door of St Michael's Parish Church in Linlithgow, with priest's room above, in black and white photography. In his book 'Thresholds', Roddy says: 'My introduction to the history of photography was Thomas Keith's Scotland by John Hannavy. From the beginning, what captivated me was the quality of the image-making of early photographers and Thomas Keith was an exceptional exponent and this photograph is in homage.'

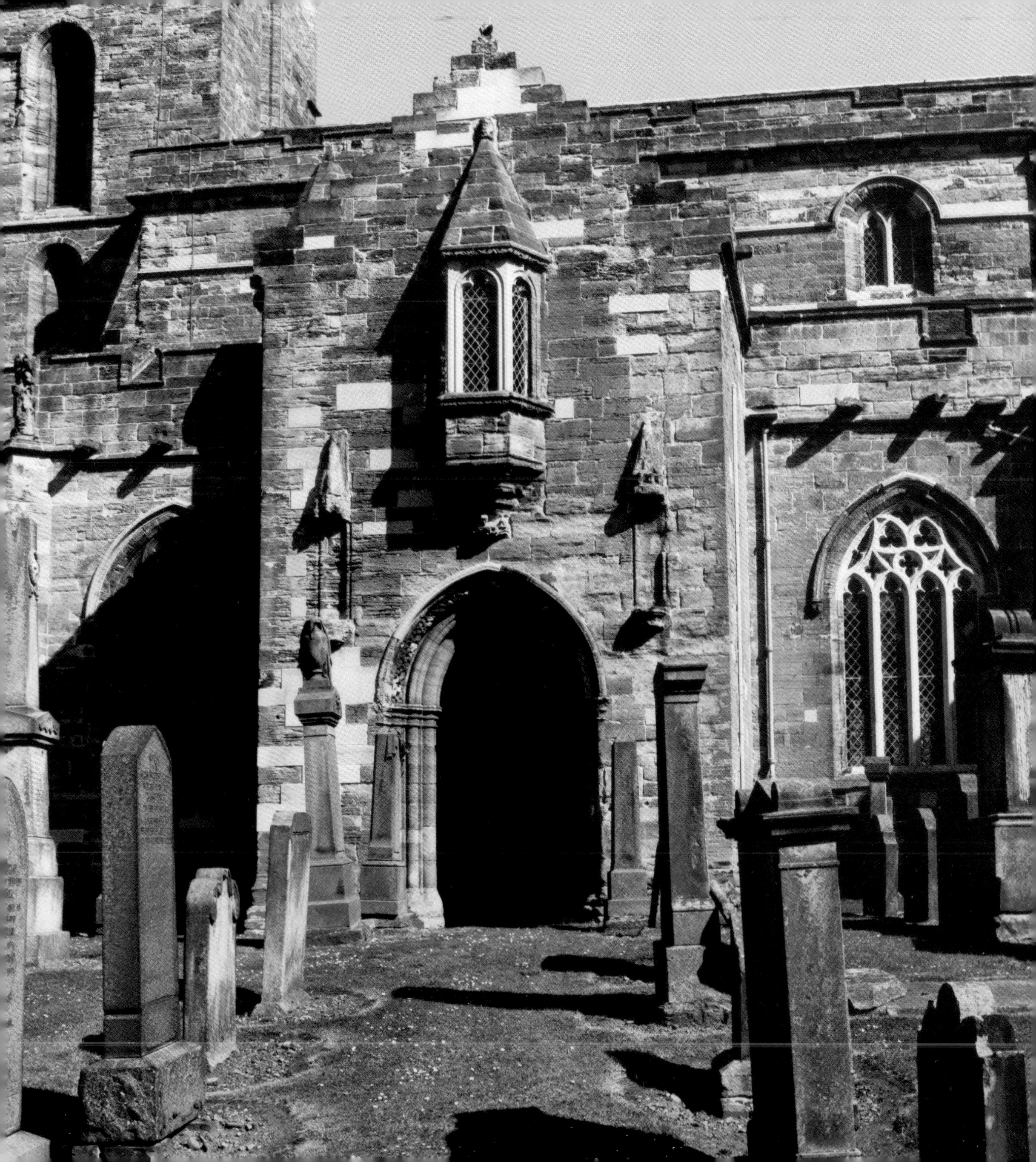

The present oak pulpit was erected in 1896 to a design by the Glasgow architect John Honeyman, and was constructed by the fine cabinet makers, John Taylor and Son in Edinburgh. It was a gift from J. Millar Richard who lived in Clarendon House in Linlithgow. A representation of Mary, Queen of Scots in the parish church is in one of four small corner statues around the pulpit. Three other female monarchs include Queen Margaret, Queen Victoria and, added very recently, Queen Elizabeth II. Mary wears a full-length, high-necked dress, with a ruff. Her right hand holds a crucifix which hangs around her neck.

Mary, Queen of Scots, one of four queens depicted in the pulpit at St Michael's Parish Church
© Gordon Young photographer
(Below)

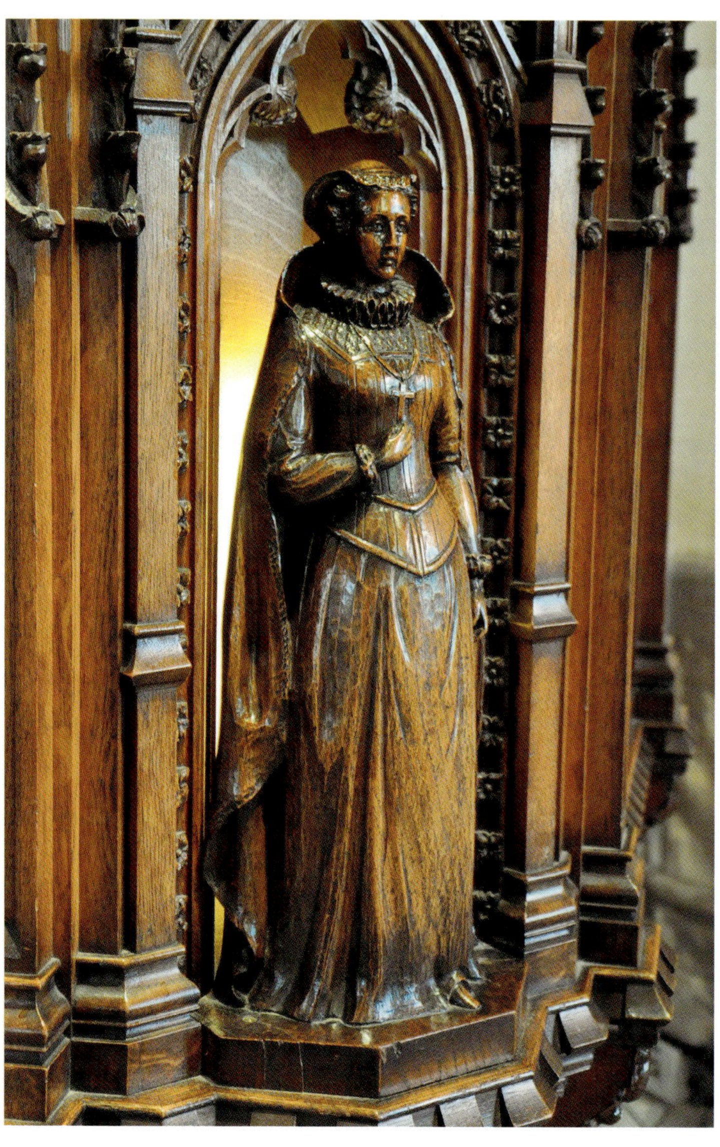

Mary, Queen of Scots, sculpted by Alan Herriot in 2002
© Alan Herriot
Commissioned by Linlithgow Heritage Trust.
© Christopher Long photographer
(Below left)

Mary, Queen of Scots, sculpted by David Annand in 2015
© David Annand
Commissioned by the Marie Stuart Society
(Below right)

Apart from a statue on the east façade of the Scottish Portrait Gallery in Edinburgh, Mary, Queen of Scots featured in no public statues in Scotland. However in 2002 the Linlithgow Heritage Trust commissioned a statue of her to recognise the work of Tom McGowran OBE, founding secretary of the Trust. The statue of resin and cold bronze was unveiled by Tom's widow, Iris McGowran, in the garden of the former museum, Annet House, Linlithgow, in 2002. Now displayed in Tam Dalyell House, Mary holds a merlin, the traditional hunting bird, on her right arm.. The work was by the Scottish figurative sculptor, Alan Herriot, who graduated from the Johnstone College of Art in 1974 and is now one of Scotland's most successful figurative sculptors. Alan Herriot also sculpted the small drummer boy on the war memorial in the nearby village of Winchburgh.

Outside the church is a statue of Mary gazing towards her birthplace, holding a bible in her left hand and a crucifix in her right. The two-metre high bronze was sculpted by David Annand. The St Andrews-based Marie Stuart Society raised funds for this project in 2015.

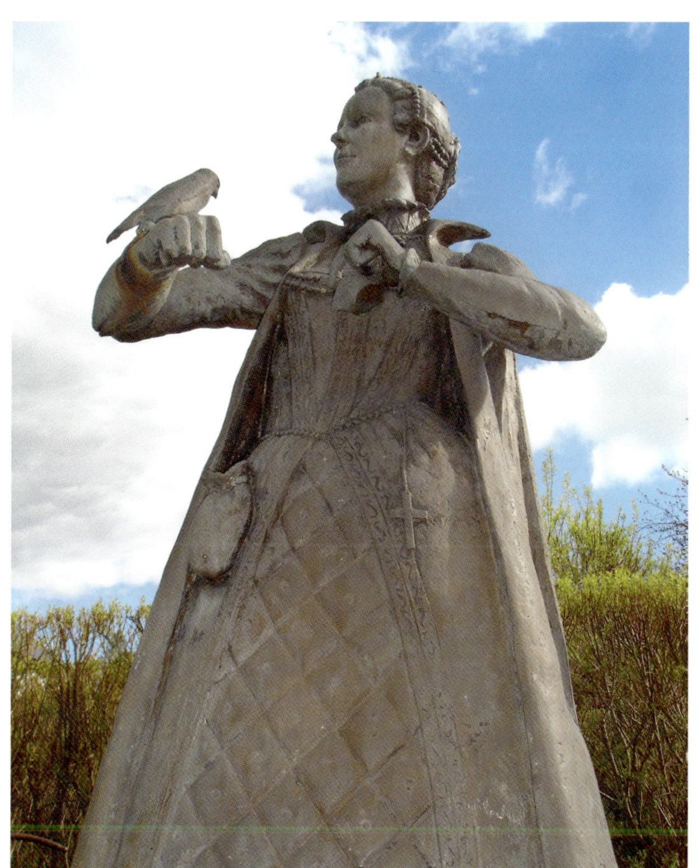

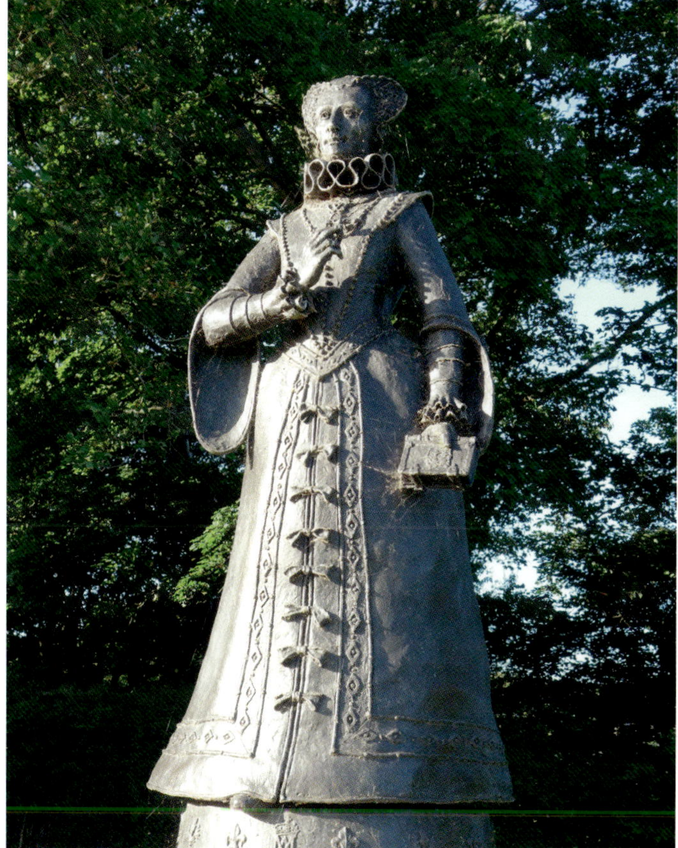

Dudley, the canal-side cat, sculpted by David Annand in 2018
© David Annand
Commissioned by Burgh Beautiful Linlithgow
© Ron Smith photographer
(Right)

More recently, David Annand has been commissioned by Burgh Beautiful Linlithgow to sculpt Dudley, a bronze cat, located at the Union Canal Basin. It is mounted on a granite pedestal, broadly similar in nature to Greyfriars Bobby in Edinburgh and commemorates the life of a founder member of the local environmental group, Burgh Beautiful Linlithgow.

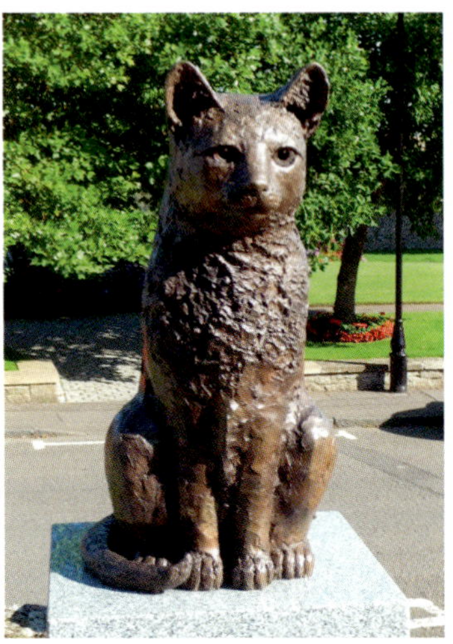

The Guyancourt Vennel Screen, by David Ogilvie, 1977
© David Ogilvie
Commissioned by West Lothian Council
© Calum Smith photographer
(Opposite)

The 16th century palace gateway displays the four sets of insignia representing the European orders of chivalry borne by King James V of Scotland, father of Mary, Queen of Scots. They are the orders of the Garter, the Thistle, the Golden Fleece and St Michael. Two of these are illustrated on page 8. The gateway, giving access to the outer enclosure of the palace, was the work of Sir James Hamilton of Finnart and constructed circa 1533.

As you descend the Kirkgate there is a series of plaques fixed on the churchyard wall which display the line of descent from Mary, Queen of Scots to the present monarch, Elizabeth II. The series is not a direct line of succession but is the blood-line between Mary Queen of Scots and the present monarch. The plaques, which intrigue passing tourists, were erected by Linlithgow District Girl Guides as their contribution to the coronation of Queen Elizabeth II in 1953.

The Guyancourt Vennel screen, illustrated opposite, features a view of the Kirkgate in wrought-iron, fabricated by David Ogilvie Engineering in 1997. It hangs on a wall in Guyancourt Vennel to the west of the Kirkgate and depicts the entrance to the palace with two birds of peace flying overhead and a five-pointed star at its apex. The artwork was originally designed to form part of a larger nativity scene proposed by Councillor Jimmy McGinley as a centrepiece to the town's Christmas celebrations. The centre panel now forms a tribute to that hard-working local councillor.

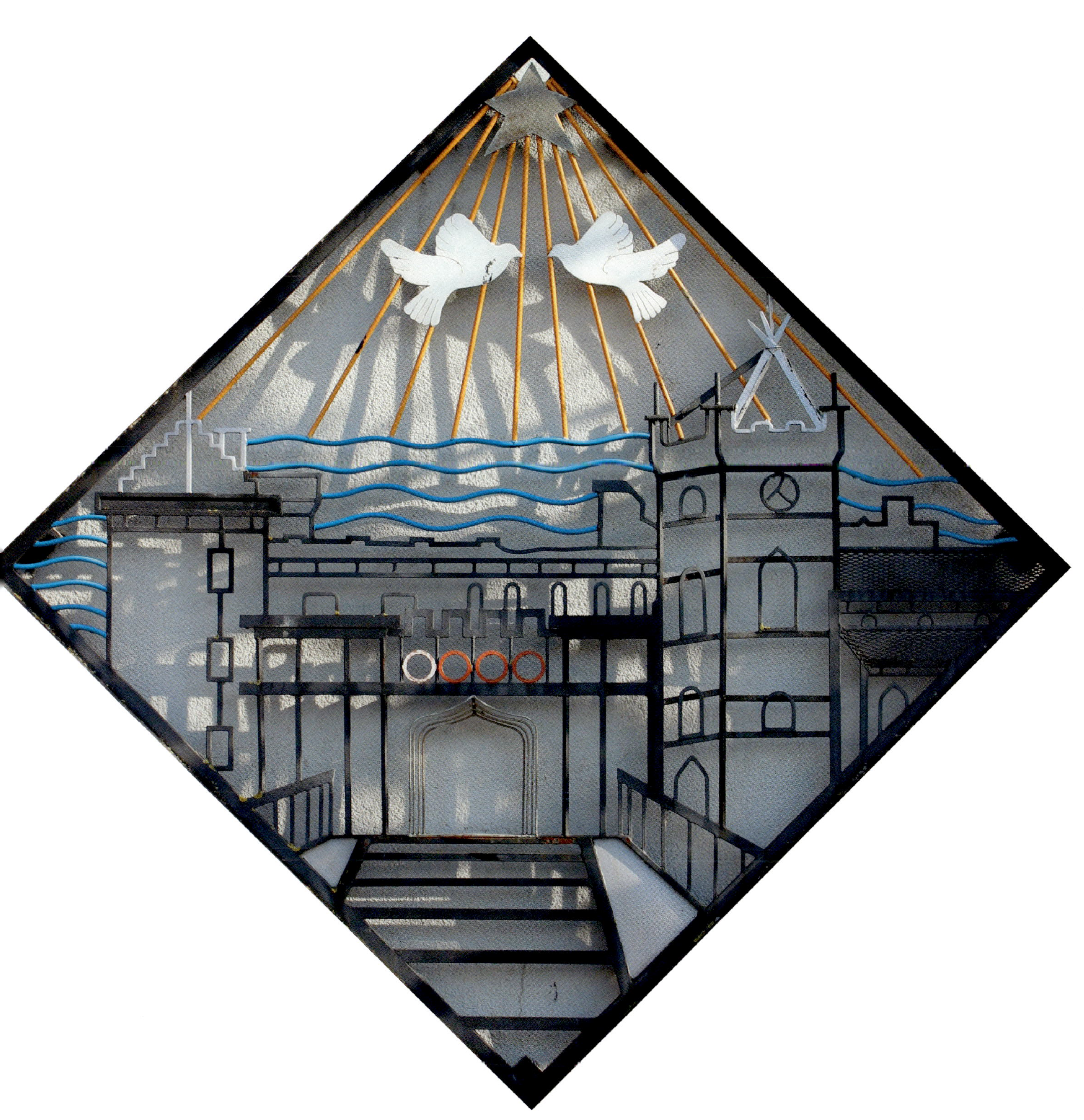

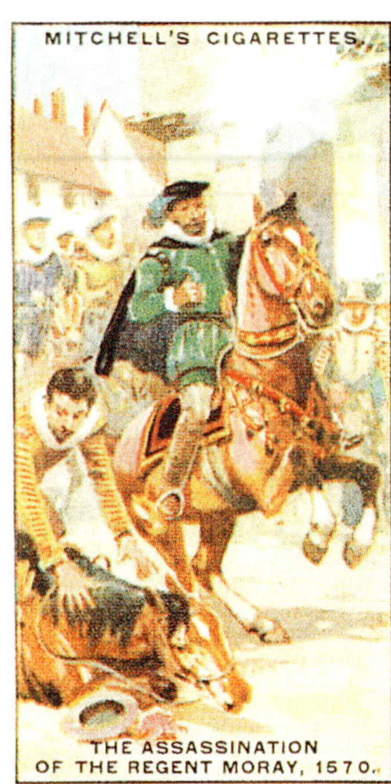

The Assassination of the Regent Moray, Linlithgow, 1570
Mitchell's Cigarette Card, 1929
Private Collection
(Above)

The Assassination of the Regent Moray celebrated in glass in the Holy Blood Aisle in St Giles' Cathedral
© Jarrold Publishing & St Giles' Cathedral
(Opposite)

Linlithgow High Street is infamous as the location, in January 1570, of the first recorded assassination using a firearm. The victim was the half-brother of Mary, Queen of Scots, James Stewart, Regent Moray. He was acting as regent to the infant James VI of Scotland and was shot as he passed along the High Street. The assassin was James Hamilton of Bothwellhaugh.

No brass plaque in the road marks where the atrocity took place. The buildings of the time have long been swept away and it is difficult to imagine the contemporary scene. However, various artists have attempted to picture the event, in etchings, water colours, oils and stained glass.

Mitchell's Cigarettes published a series of 50 cigarette cards entitled 'Scotland's Story' in 1919. Number 28 featured the event. 'James Stewart, Earl of Moray, had reluctantly accepted the Regency on the abdication of his half-sister Mary, Queen of Scots, and in 1570 he was negotiating with Queen Elizabeth for the return of Mary as a prisoner to Scotland. In that year, however, he was murdered by Hamilton of Bothwellhaugh, chiefly in revenge for private injuries to his family. The assassin, hiding behind a curtained window, carbine in hand, shot the Regent as he was leaving Linlithgow. Assisted by his kinsmen the murderer escaped from the back of the house and sailed for France.' The card was issued originally for the cigarette manufacturers, Stephen Mitchell & Son, whose Linlithgow premises were at 150 High Street, not far from the scene of the crime.

The Regent Moray was buried in St Giles' Cathedral, Edinburgh, in a service conducted by his friend, John Knox. The assassination and the funeral are commemorated in the windows of what is known as the Holy Blood Aisle in the cathedral. The window, manufactured by James Ballantine and Sons in 1881, was financed by the 14th Earl of Moray as part of a Victorian restoration. The glass illustrates how Victorians thought Linlithgow might have looked at that time with half-timbered buildings. The assassin is shown framed in a timber window with his smoking gun, leaving the mortally injured victim slipping off his horse.

Just over 300 years later, a bronze plaque by Sir Noel Paton, commemorating the assassination of the Regent Earl of Moray, was unveiled, mounted on the wall of the new sheriff court, now Court Residence. It overlooks the scene of the murder. The memorial plaque included a fine relief bust of the victim by Amelia Robertson Hill, wife of the pioneering photographer, David Octavius Hill. The plaque reads:

'ON THE STREET OPPOSITE THIS TABLET
JAMES STUART EARL OF MURRAY* REGENT
OF SCOTLAND WAS SHOT BY JAMES HAMILTON
OF BOTHWELLHAUGH ON 20** JANUARY 1570.
ERECTED IN 1875'

*The spelling of 'Murray' was one used by the earl himself. **The actual date was 23rd January 1570.

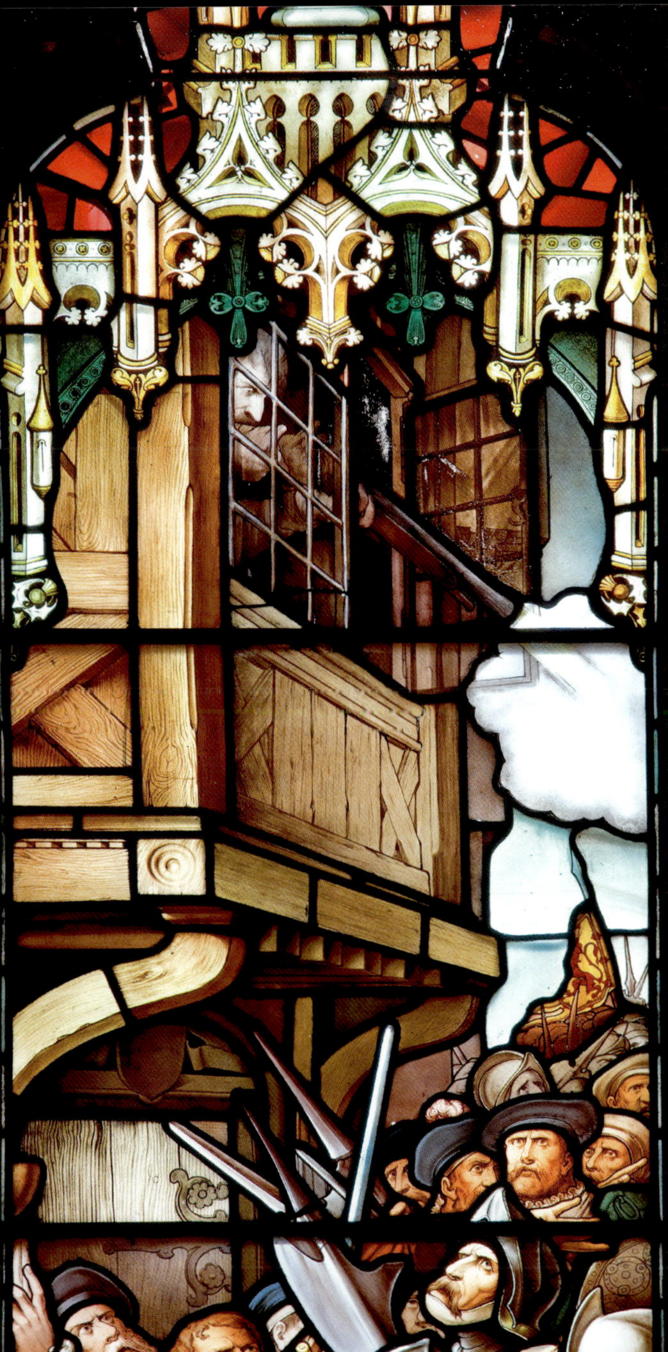

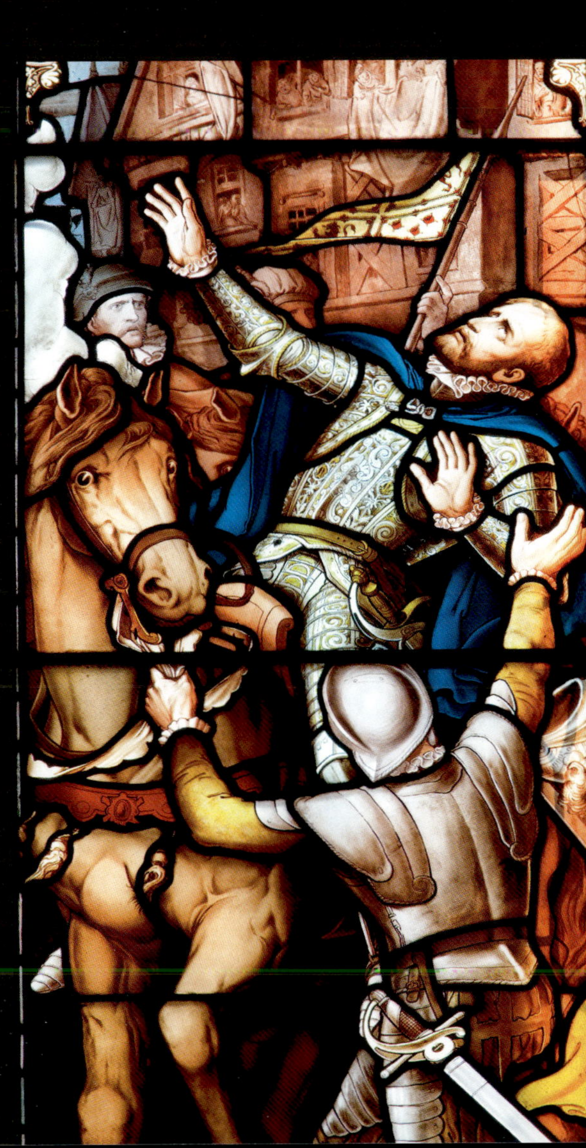

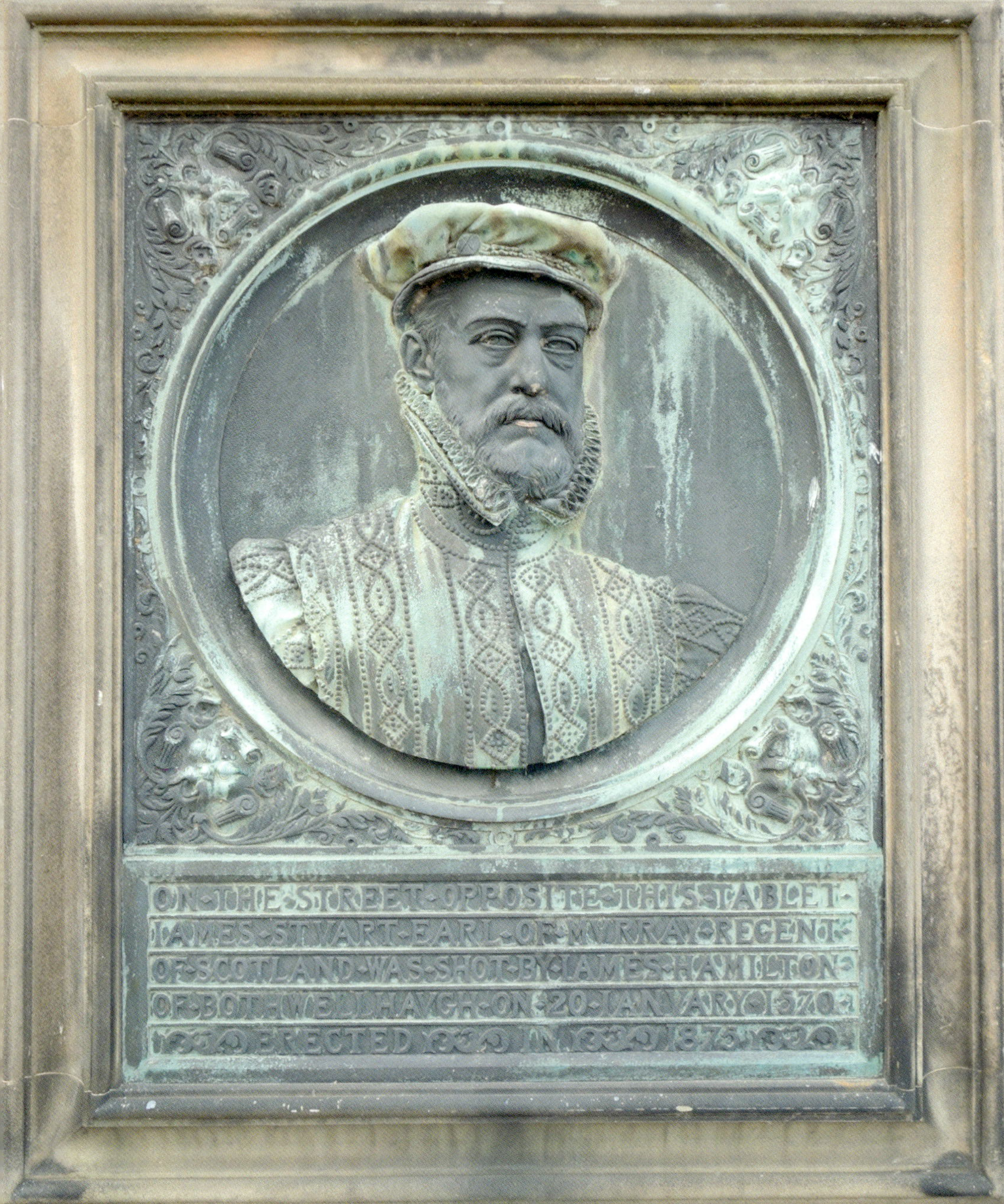
ON THE STREET OPPOSITE THIS TABLET
IAMES STVART EARL OF MVRRAY REGENT
OF SCOTLAND WAS SHOT BY IAMES HAMILTON
OF BOTHWELLHAVGH ON 20 IANVARY 1570
ERECTED IN 1875

Bronze plaque by Sir Noel Paton of James Stuart, Regent Moray
© Christopher Long photographer
(Opposite and right)

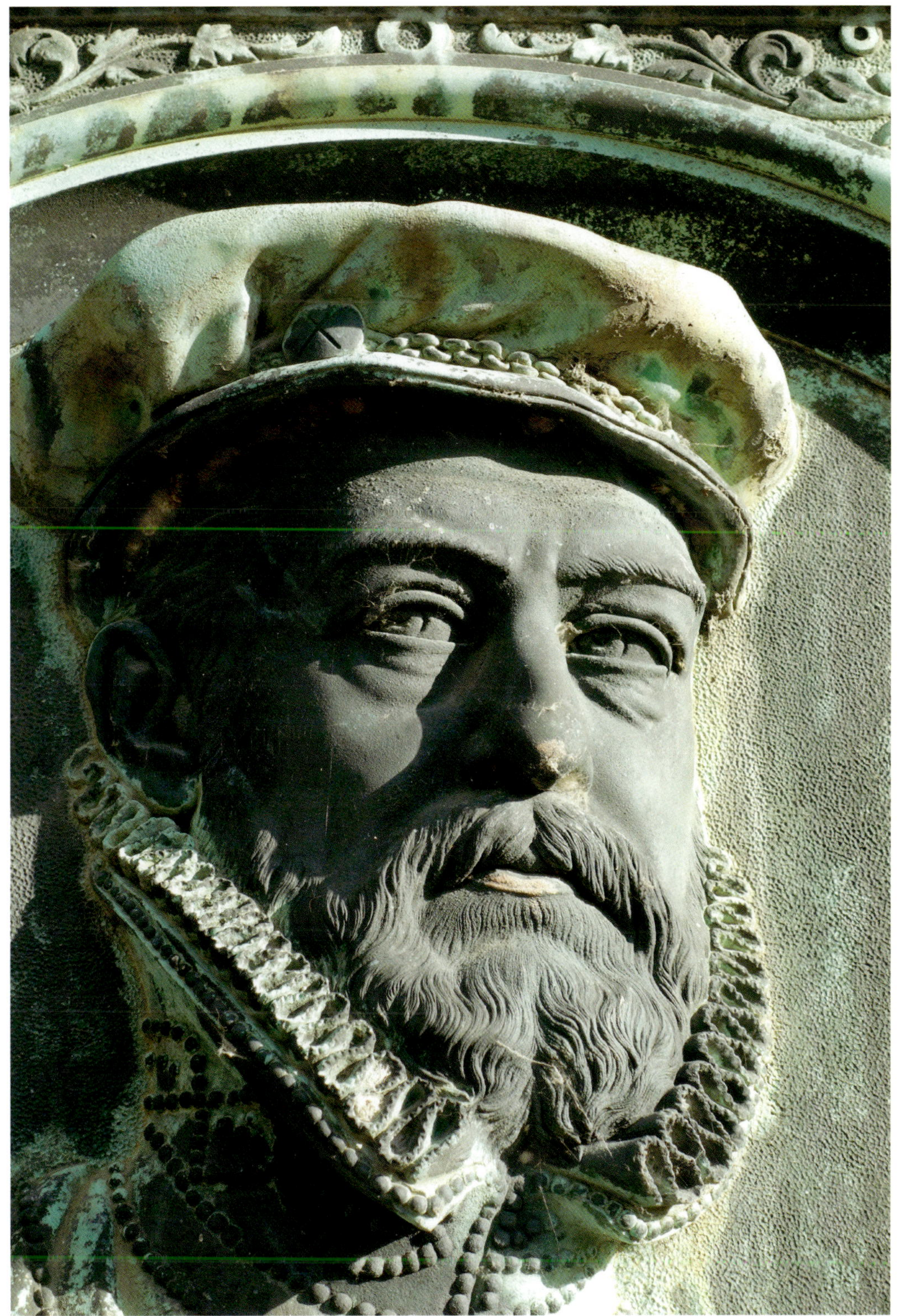

The inner court of the Palace on fire by Thomas Allom, engraved by Henry Wallis
© Courtesy of HES
(Below)

Burning of the Palace by James Collie from 'The Royal Palace of Linlithgow' by James Collie, 1847
Private collection
(Opposite)

The palace was destroyed on 1st February 1746 during the occupation by the Duke of Cumberland's forces, marking the end of the princely palace. Two accompanying pictures imagine the devastating event. The first, an etching from about 1838, shows smoke coming from the windows of the west wing. The artist was Thomas Allom and the engraver Henry Wallis.

The other view of destruction of the palace is by James Collie, illustrator and architect. It was lithographed by MacLure and Macdonald and published in 'The Royal Palace of Linlithgow Illustrated' by James Collie around 1850. Collie practised architecture in Glasgow, surveying Glasgow Cathedral and publishing 'An Historical Account of the Cathedral of Glasgow' in 1835. This was followed by his illustrated book about the Royal Palace of Linlithgow. He remained in practice as a civil engineer in Edinburgh and in Bridge of Allan.

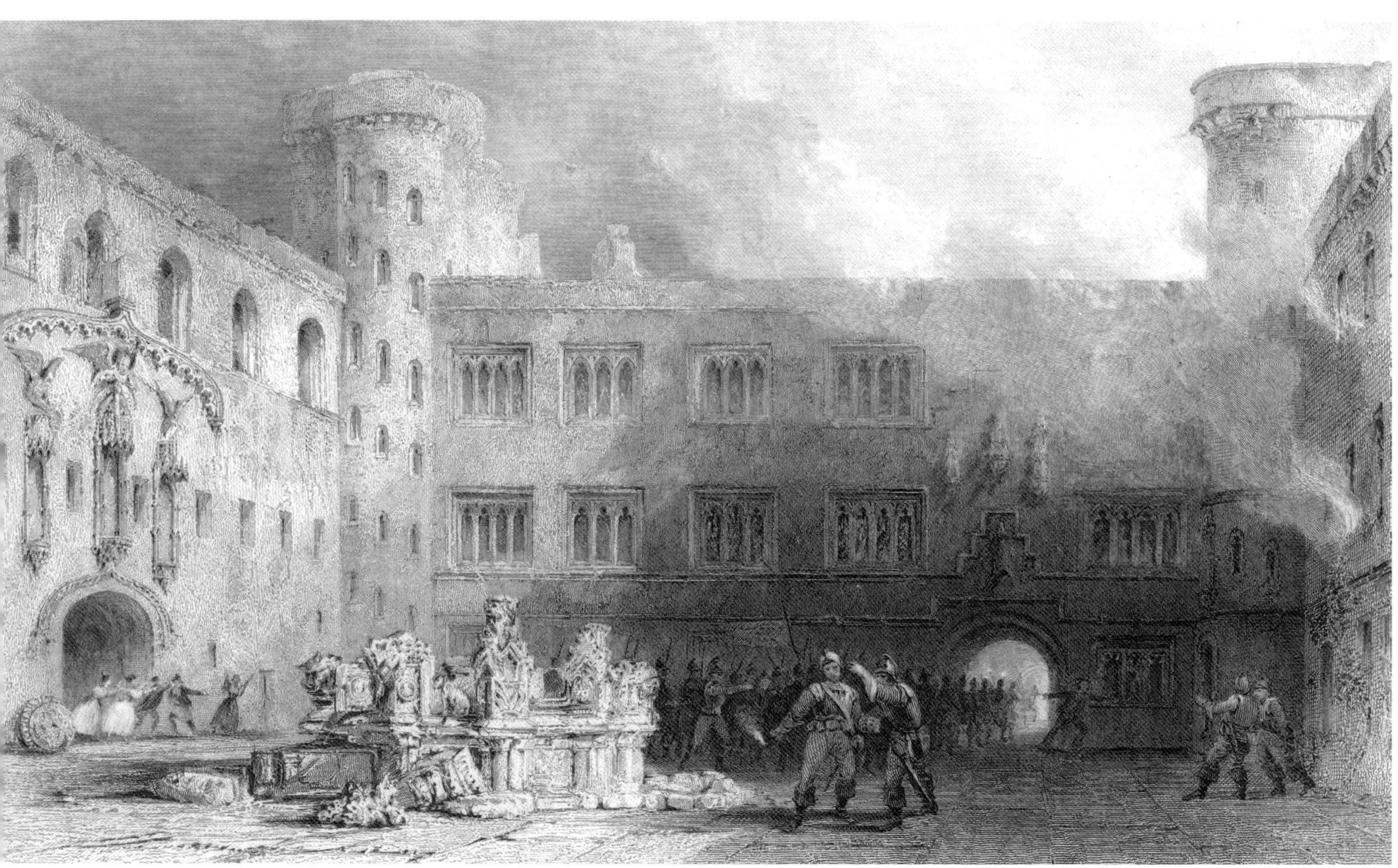

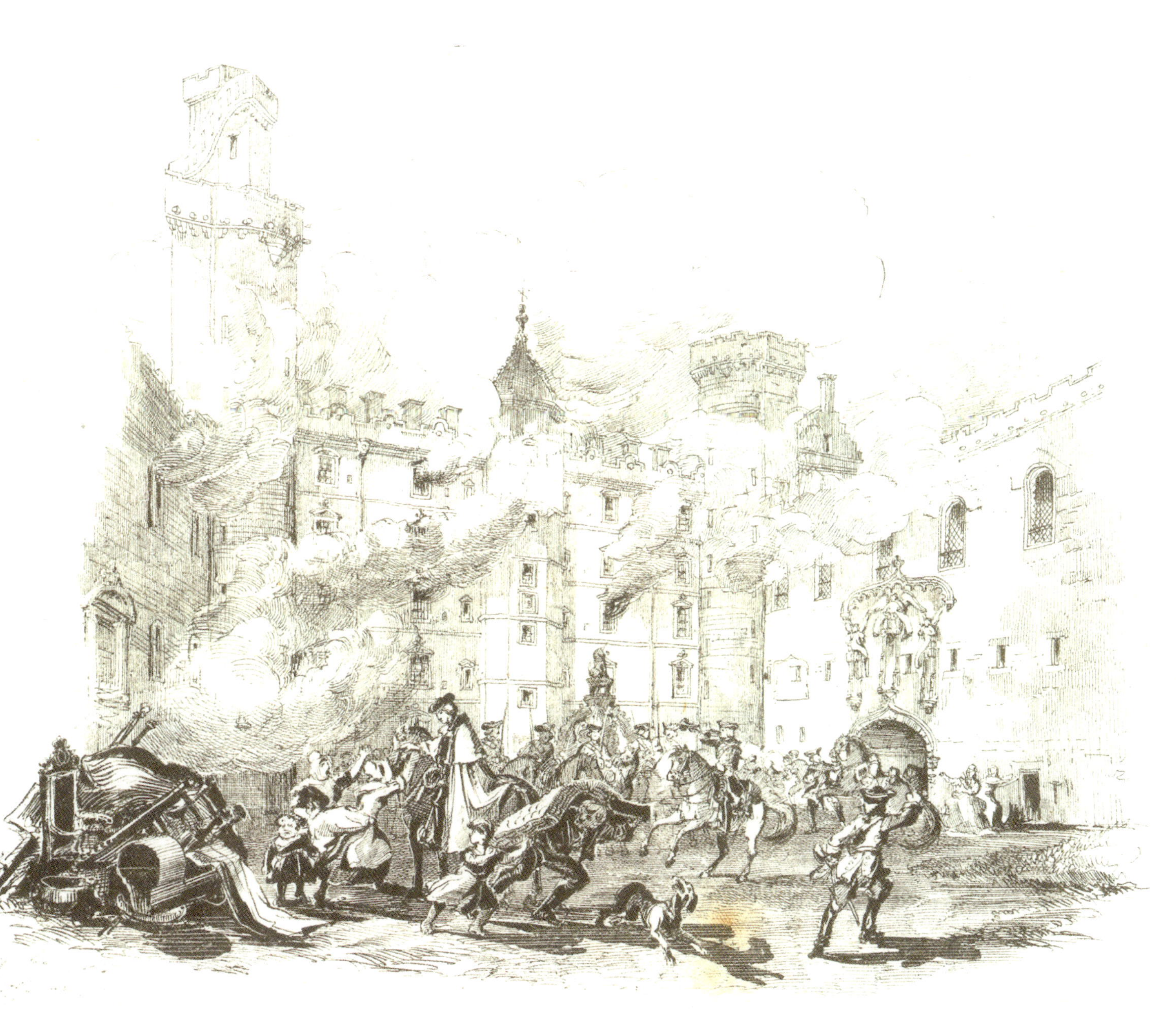

'The Prospect of their Maj'ties Palace of Linlithgow' by J.A. Slezer
Reproduced by permission of the National Library of Scotland
(Opposite top)

'The Prospect of the Town of Linlithgow' by J.A. Slezer
Reproduced by permission of the National Library of Scotland
(Opposite lower)

Two views or prospects of Linlithgow were drawn in the 1670s. John Abraham Slezer, of Dutch or German extraction, was born in 1650. He was a military engineer who travelled round Scotland surveying defences and fortifications. He produced numerous views of the places he visited across Scotland and published the results in 'Theatrum Scotiae' in 1693. It was the first time anyone had made a pictorial record of an entire nation. Original copies are archived in the National Library of Scotland and can be viewed online.

The first view, 'The Prospect of their Maj'ties Palace of Linlithgow', shows the palace almost surrounded by the waters of the loch, with few trees present, unlike now. St Michael's Parish Church sports its crown spire, one of a few in Scotland. A wall divided the palace grounds from the town and extended as far as the loch. It is likely that the painter, John Wyck, touched up the drawings. The figures and boats are slightly out of scale with the image they have been added to. The ancient Town House, topped by its cockerel, already seen in the Pont map, towers above the surrounding town buildings. The detail appears accurate, yet distortions are apparent. I am indebted to the detective work of Laurie Alexander, retired architect and local historian, who has closely examined where the palace view was taken from. Laurie's work indicates that the prospect is a combination of views from two nearby areas of high ground to the west of the loch: Jocks Hill and the Roundel. It is likely that Slezer used an optical device known as a camera obscura to achieve accuracy, but a certain amount of artistic licence crept in.

The second view, 'The Prospect of the Town of Linlithgow' is taken from the southeast, 150 years before the cutting of the canal. The low town wall is evident as are the dovecote in Learmonth Gardens, the buildings along the High Street, including Hamilton's Land, and the tower of the Knights Hospitaller of St John's complex, often referred to as the Mint. Above them all is the palace, shown still largely roofed, together with the tombstones and the old manse in the graveyard in front of St Michael's Parish Church.

Today the palace comprises only high walls of stone. Holes in the walls reveal where fireplaces once were and rows of chimneys indicate where there must have been rooms. What did Linlithgow Palace look like in its heyday? In the past many schemes have been proposed to renovate the shell of the palace, but to no effect.

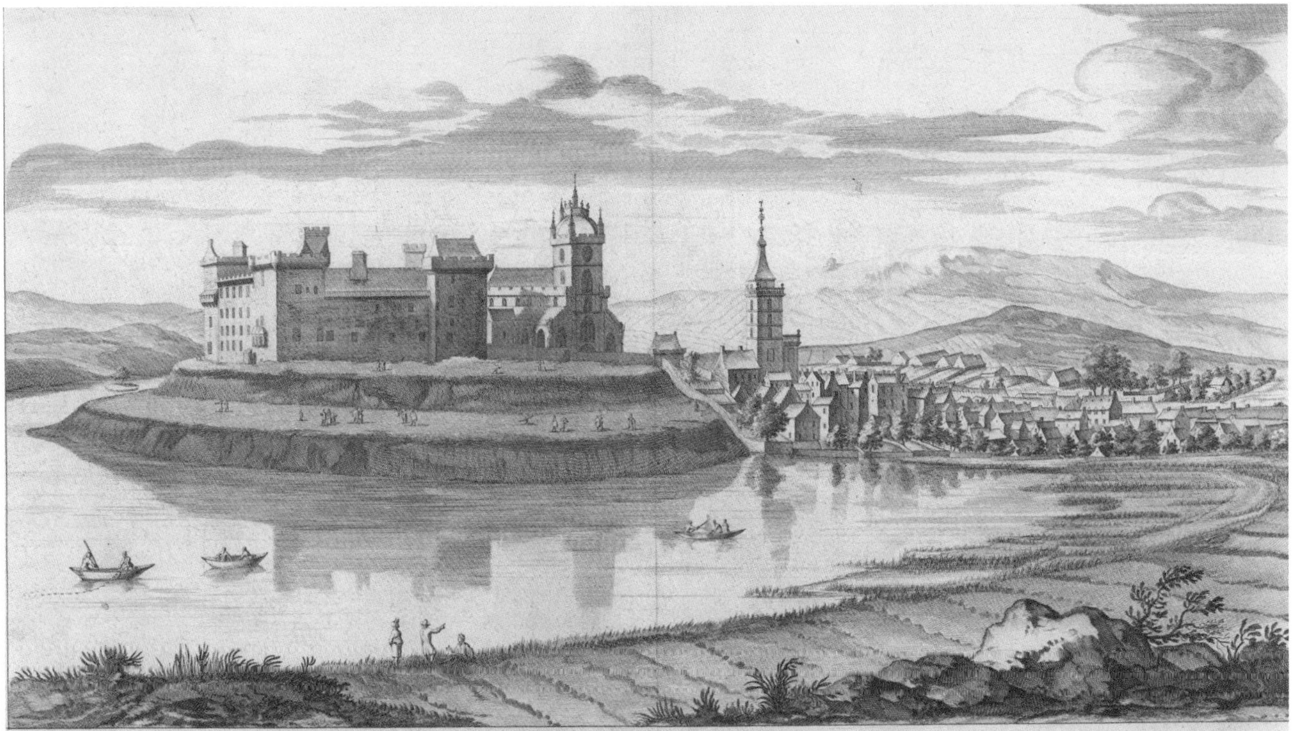

Prospectus Regis Palatis LIMNUCHENSIS. The Prospect of Their Maj:ties Palace of LINLITHGOW.

10

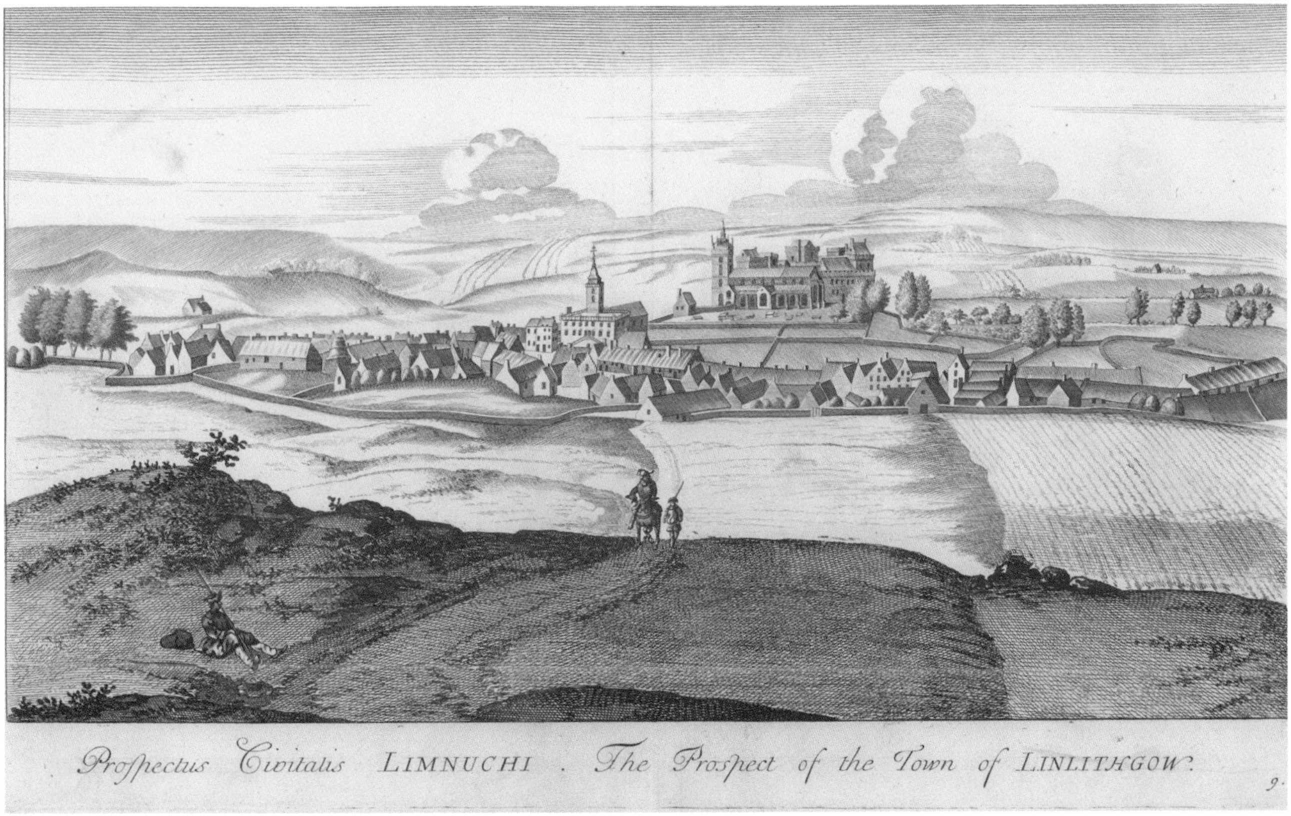

Prospectus Civitatis LIMNUCHI. The Prospect of the Town of LINLITHGOW.

9.

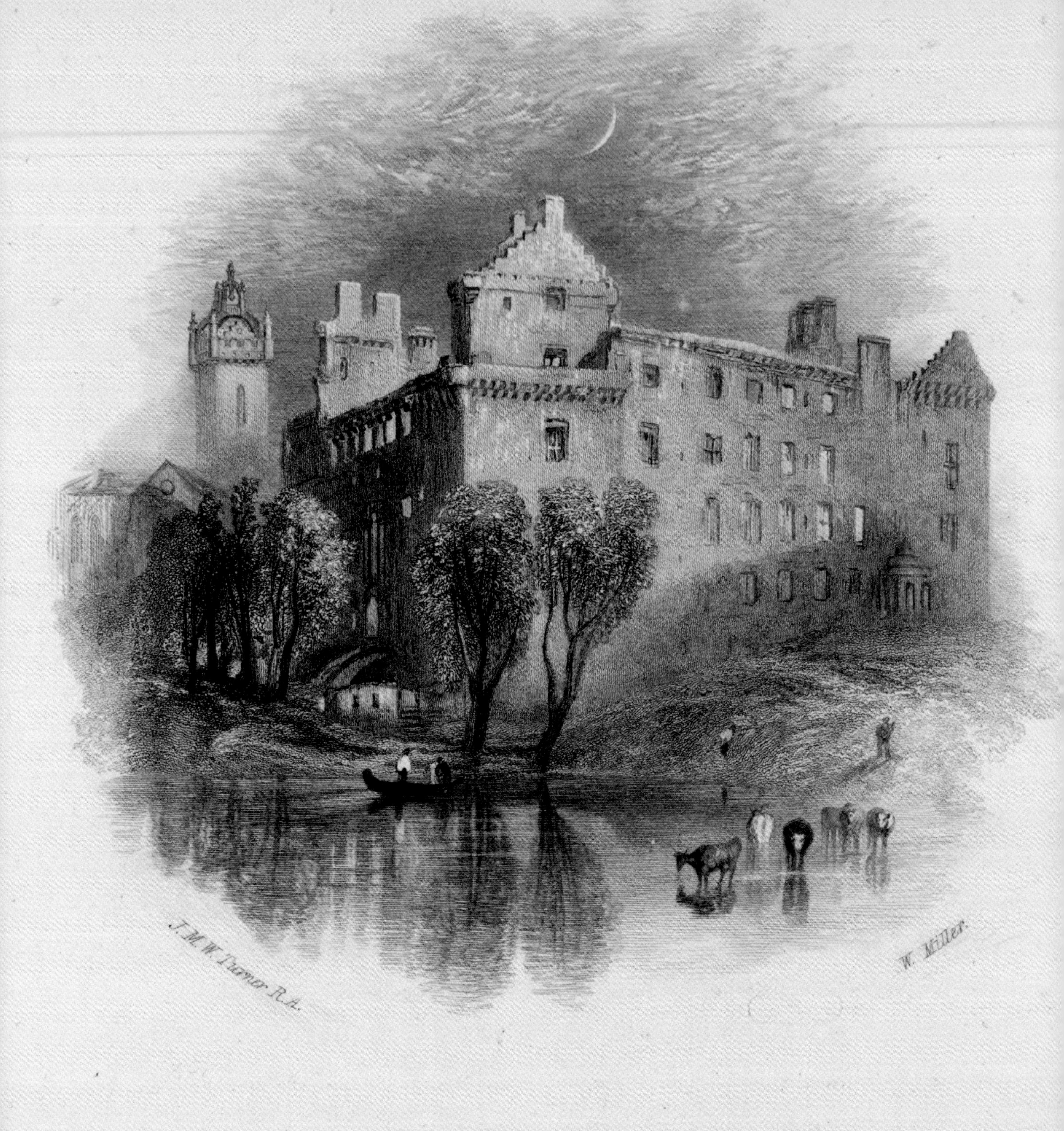
J. M. W. Turner R.A.
W. Miller.

TWO

Linlithgow - The Victorian View

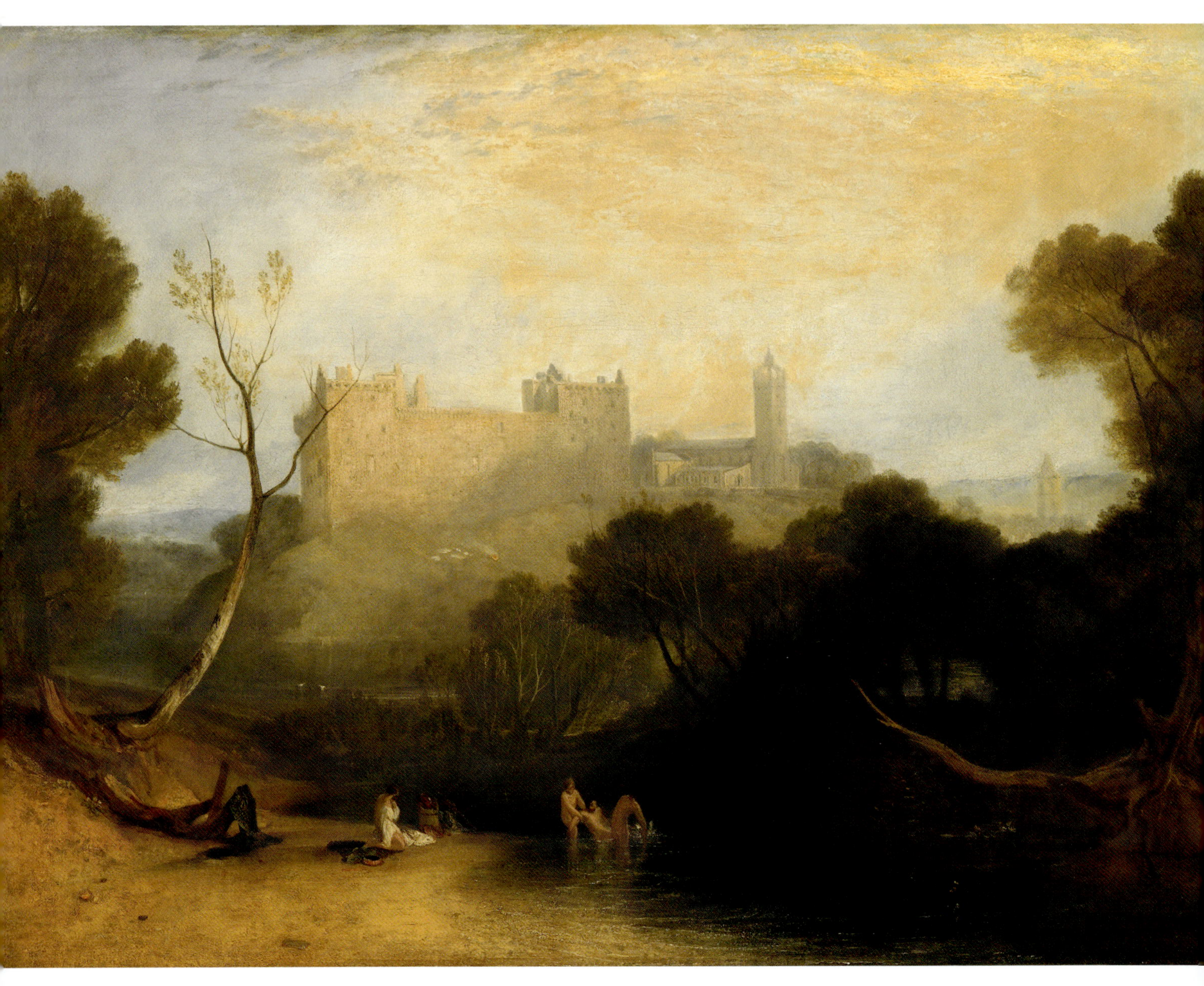

Engraving of Linlithgow Palace by William Miller, after J.M.W. Turner
Scott's Prose Works, Linlithgow. 1834-36. William Miller after J.M.W. Turner (1775-1851) (T04755)
Photo credit: ©Tate, London 2018
(On page 40)

In the late 18th and early 19th centuries Linlithgow became a popular location for artists to visit and to record what they saw, primarily the romantic ruins of the splendid palace with its moat of water. Many are on view in galleries in the UK and abroad while some are hidden in gallery storerooms.

Cartographers, too, continued to map the town. Linlithgow developed with the growth of industries such as linen bleaching, distilleries, shoemaking, and papermaking. Progress brought water transport in the early 19th century and Linlithgow, geographically sandwiched between two areas of high ground, was divided by the Union Canal which opened in 1822. Twenty years later it was divided again by the railway lines of the Edinburgh and Glasgow Railway Company which opened in 1842.

One of Britain's most prolific and innovative artists was J.M.W. Turner. Born in London in 1775, he travelled widely throughout his life, undertaking extensive tours of Europe as well as visiting distant parts of the United Kingdom sketching wherever he went. Travelling from his studio in London must have been physically exhausting prior to the construction of railways and metalled roads. To get to Edinburgh, from London, it could take horse-drawn coaches 60 hours to arrive, stopping frequently along the way.

Linlithgow Palace, by J.M.W. Turner
Courtesy National Museums Liverpool, Walker Art Gallery
(Opposite)

When painting in Scotland, in the early 19th century, it is likely that Turner based himself in Edinburgh, travelling by gig for day trips to nearby places such as Lanark or Linlithgow. He filled numerous sketchbooks of the scenes he saw with marvellous line drawings. His travels round Linlithgow Loch, sketchbook in hand, can be traced; even the time of day may be deduced from his pictures. His sketchbooks can be viewed online and the originals are in Tate Britain. His sketchbooks formed the basis for later watercolours and oil paintings.

His first, rather sombre, painting of Linlithgow, not illustrated, dated 1802, is now in the National Gallery of Victoria in Melbourne. It was taken from the north of the loch with the palace in the centre. Turner was 26 at the time and returned to the same scene later in his life.

Undoubtedly his finest picture of the palace, titled 'Linlithgow Palace, Scotland,' was first exhibited in 1810. The oil painting is large (91cm by 122cm) and is on view at the Walker Art Gallery in Liverpool. The gallery's online guide referring to the painting states that: 'Linlithgow Palace, birthplace of Mary, Queen of Scots, was a romantic and picturesque ruin by 1807. Turner added naked nymphs and evenly balanced trees to the composition. Such details elevated the picture above a simple landscape into something closer to a classical history painting in the manner of Claude Lorrain. The thickly impastoed sunlit clouds, however, betray Turner's fundamental love of depicting strong natural effects.'

Engraving of Linlithgow Palace, by R. Wallis, after J.M.W. Turner 1822. After J.M.W. Turner (1775-1851) (T06065). Photo credit: ©Tate, London 2018 (Below)

Earthenware plate, depicting Linlithgow Palace, manufactured by William Mason Private collection (Opposite)

In 1818, at the age of 43, Turner contributed views to Walter Scott's 'Provincial Antiquities and Picturesque Scenery of Scotland.' This twelve-part publication included an image of Linlithgow, but the book was not a commercial success. Turner was often a guest of Walter Scott at Abbotsford House, near Melrose. Several of Turner's watercolours hung for many years in the house. An interesting sideline is that the Abbotsford entrance porch was modelled on that of Linlithgow Palace.

A further picture of Turner's, 'Linlithgow Palace,' was painted in 1821 and now hangs in Manchester City Galleries. This depicts a kilted fisherman and his dog sitting on the north side of the loch. Walter Scott was said to have been irritated by what he considered the excessive use by Turner of tartan. This image was subsequently engraved by R. Wallis and used commercially. It was also used as the basis for a fine earthenware plate, 24cm in diameter, decorated in a beaded frame with roses and other flowers, made around 1824 by William Mason, England.

William Miller (1796 – 1882), a Scottish Quaker, line-engraver and watercolourist from Edinburgh, used Turner's works for 'Provincial Antiquities and Picturesque Scenery of Scotland' and had a great respect for Turner. See his work at the start of this section.

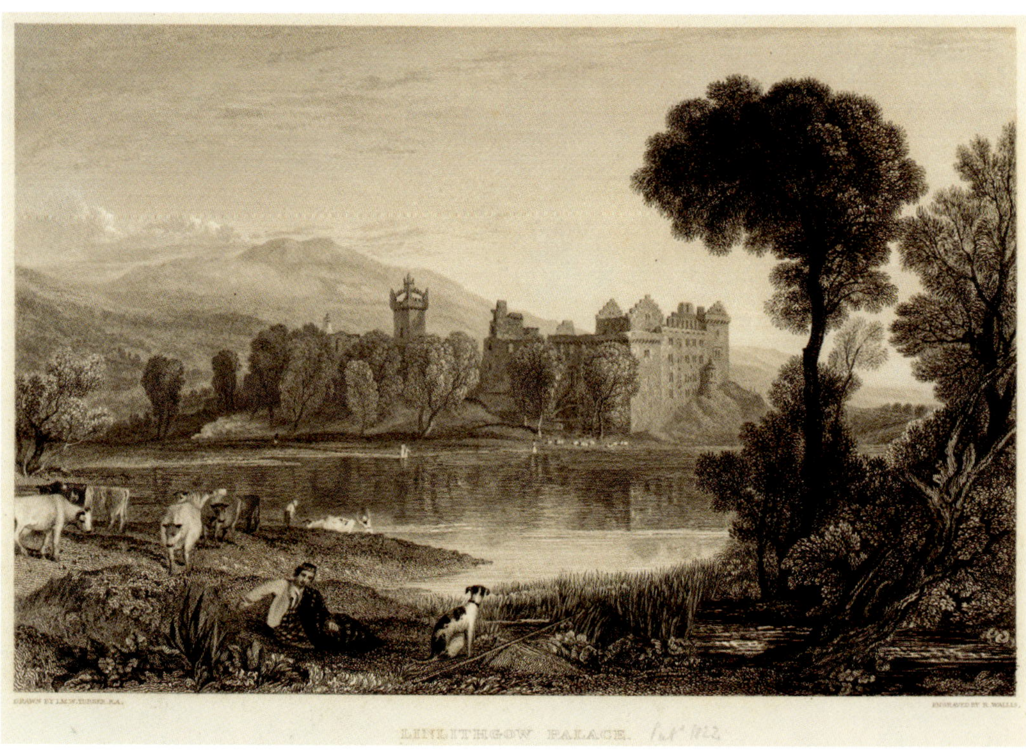

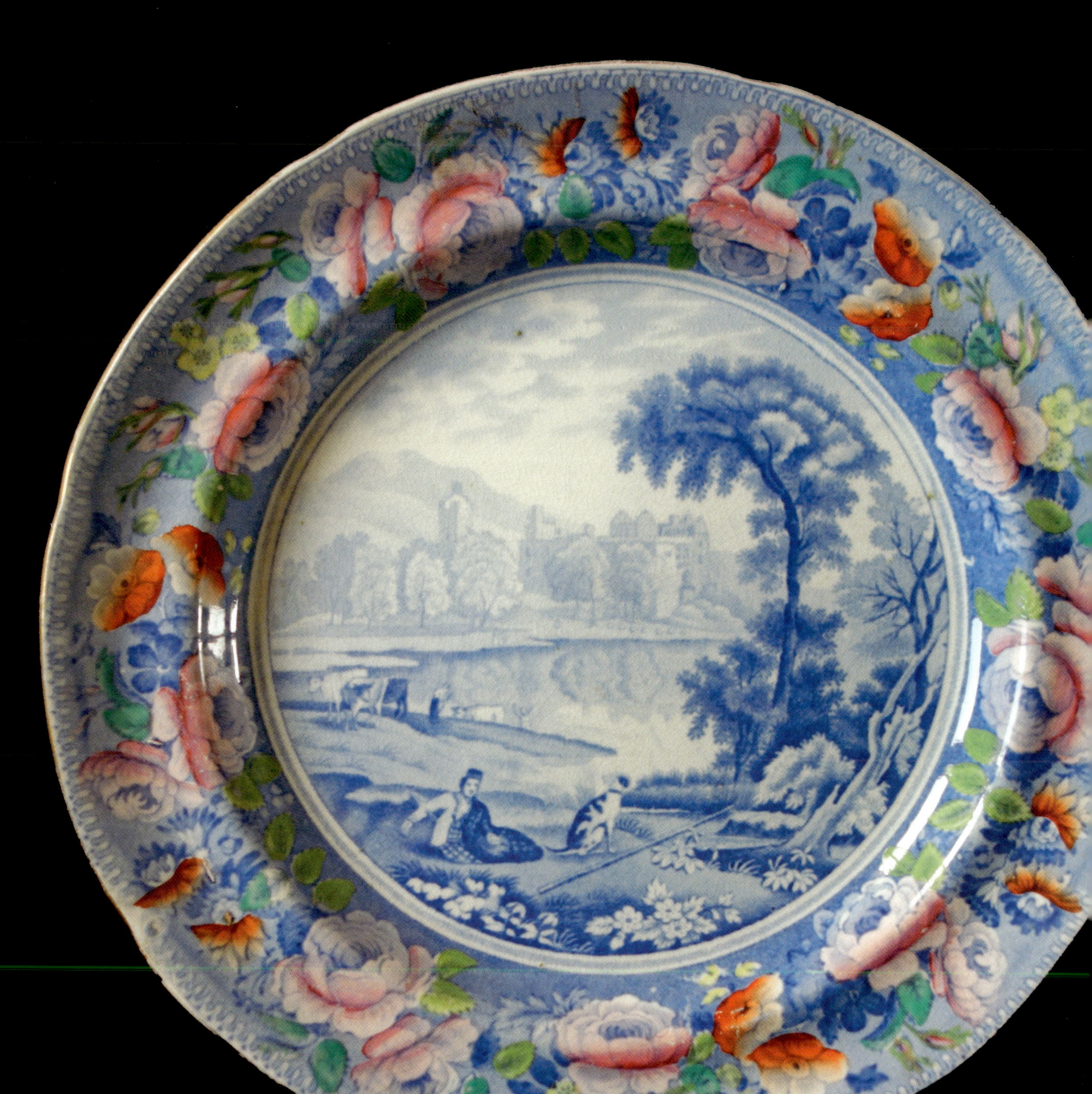

Part of the plan of the Town of Linlithgow by John Wood, 1820 Reproduced by permission of the National Library of Scotland (Below)

An annotated plan of the town was drawn by John Wood and was dated 1820. The original is in the National Library of Scotland. Wood was an important surveyor of Scottish towns who published fifty plans of them between 1818 and 1826, many based on his own original surveys. He published the Town Atlas of Scotland in 1828. The map shows in great and accurate detail buildings and ownership along the High Street and the names of the occupants. The palace is marked as a void or 'in ruins'. It is possible that the change in direction of the High Street to the west was drawn perhaps to better fit the page.

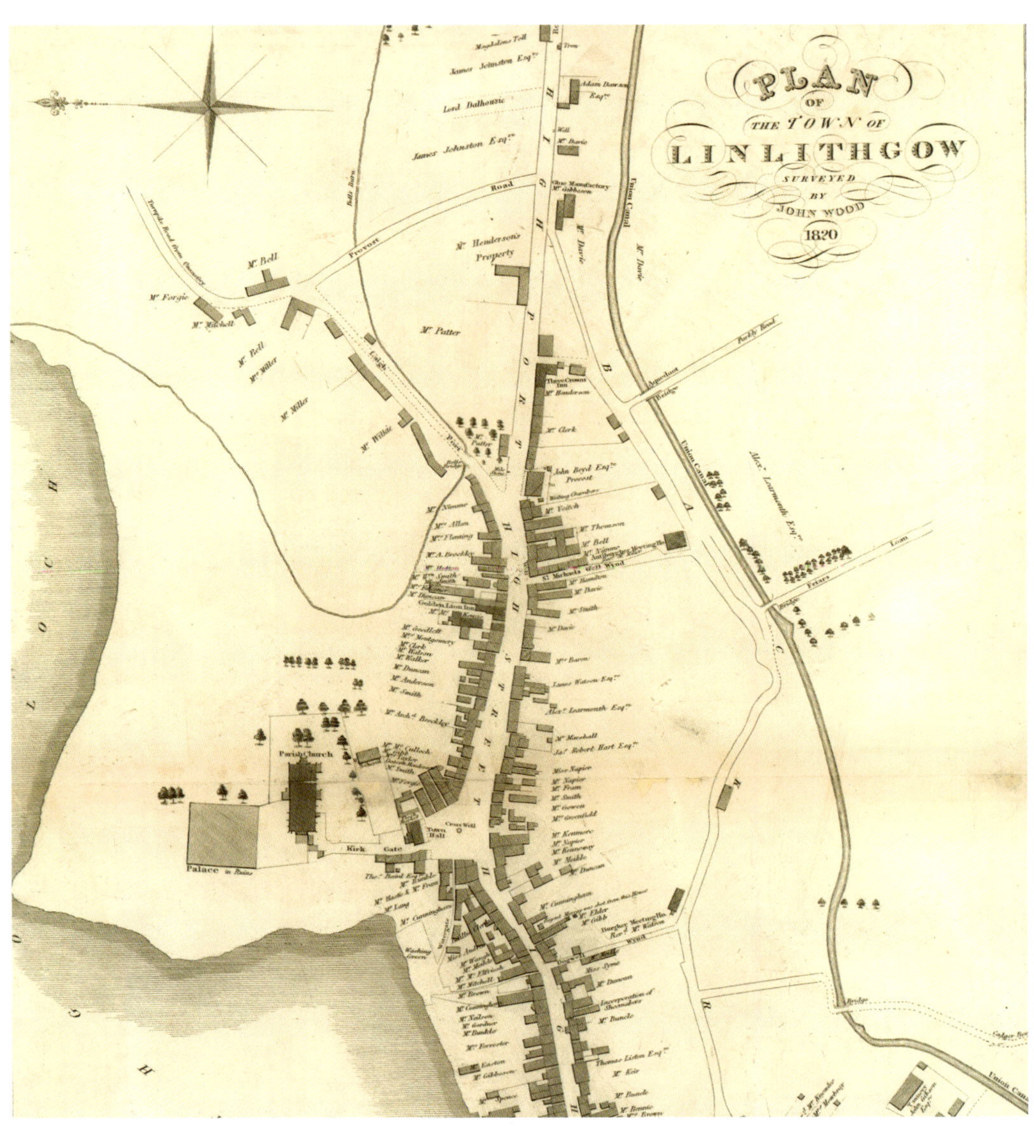

Aerial view of Linlithgow, by Ivan Lapper
© Ivan Lapper. Commissioned by Linlithgow Heritage Trust (Below)

Ivan Lapper, a figurative and landscape artist, is a successful 'reconstruction artist' who has produced dramatic historical scenes from around the UK. He was commissioned by Linlithgow Heritage Trust to produce work to be displayed at Annet House, the then local museum.

Ivan Lapper tried to imagine how Linlithgow looked in the early 1820s when the local workmen and Irish navvies were constructing a waterway along the 73 metre (240 feet) contour right through the town to form the Union Canal. The original of Ivan's imaginative reconstruction, in oil on handmade paper, now hangs in Tam Dalyell House and it graphically illustrates the numerous tanneries, boot and shoe factories, the forge and the horse and flesh markets which operated in the town. To the east lay the St Magdalene Distillery. It is an intriguing bird's eye view of the town and it is interesting to compare it with Alan Corrie's drone view from a similar position on page 12.

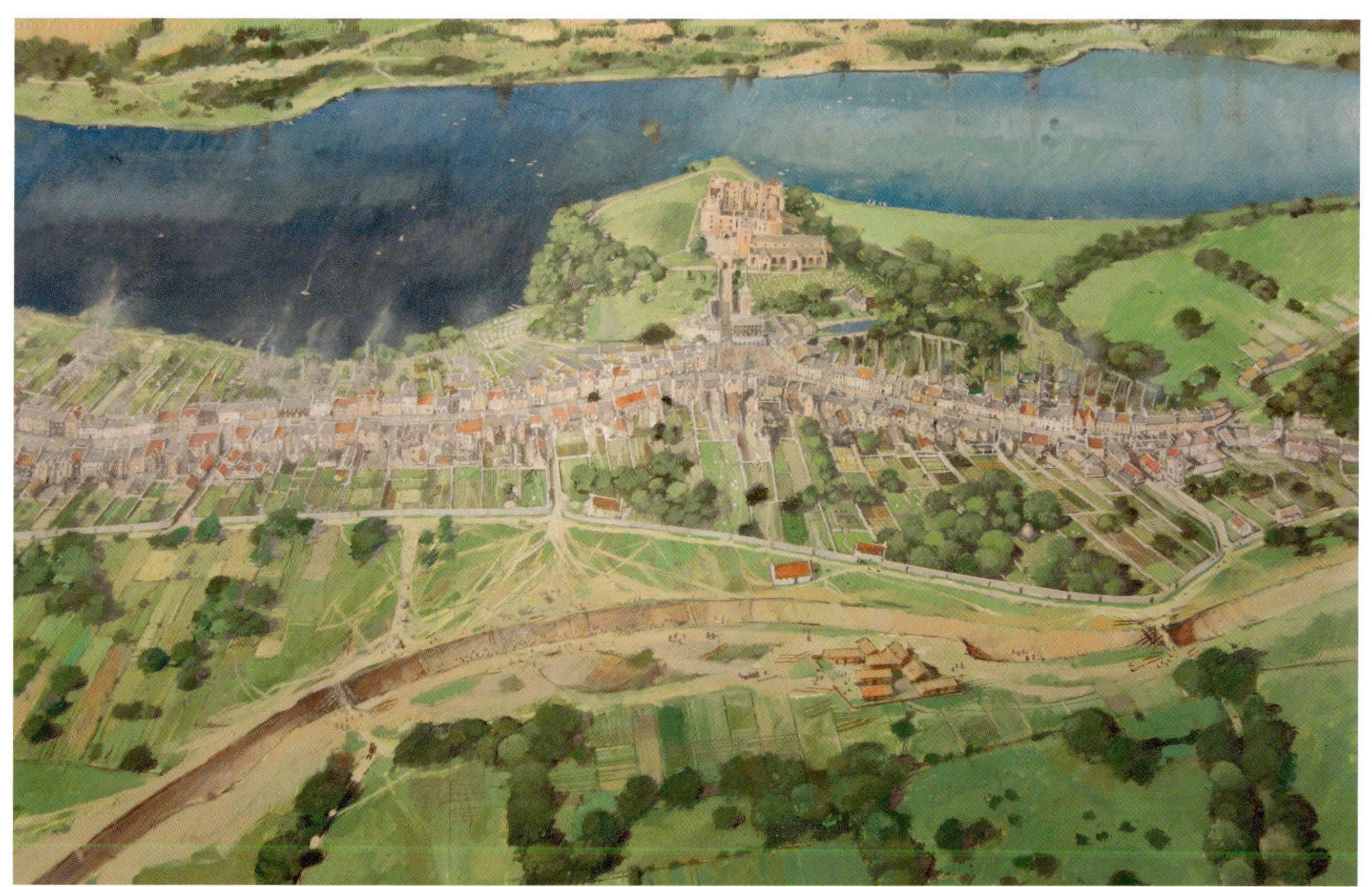

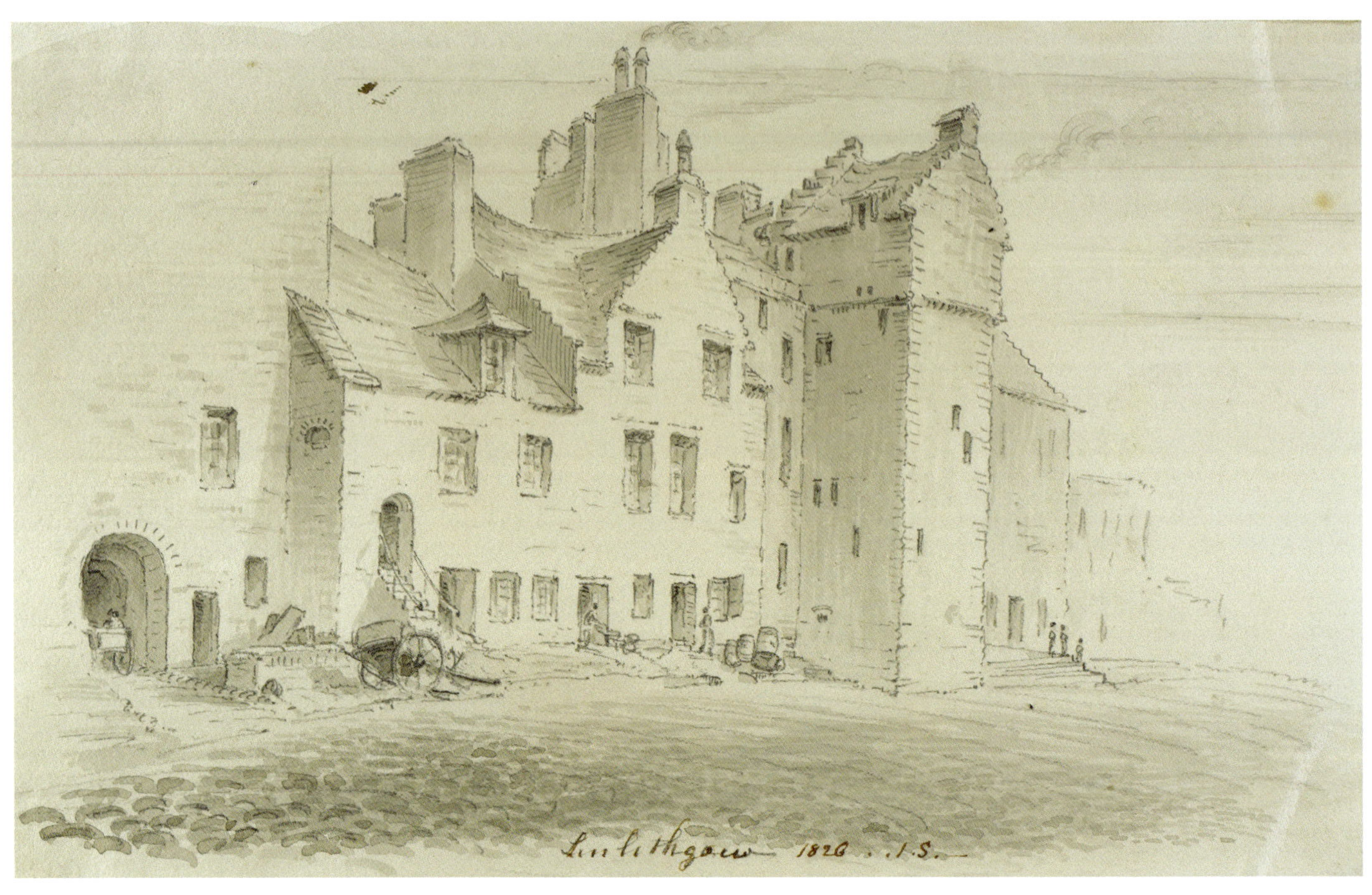

Away from the faded grandeur of palace scenes so favoured by 19th century artists, James Skene looked at Linlithgow differently and drew the prosaic dwellings and cobbled streets around what is today 129 High Street. His delicate sketches show a square towered building with crow-stepped gables sticking out across the pavement in a quiet street scene. The picture shows a cart waiting outside one of the buildings and a man on a horse. Barrels and sacks sit at the entrance of another of the buildings. Smoke rises from the chimneys. These drawings can be viewed in the Art and Design Library, George IV Bridge, in Edinburgh.

James Skene was born in Aberdeen in 1775 and died in 1864. He was an amateur artist and etcher and professionally a lawyer. He became a friend of Sir Walter Scott who described him as 'an amiable and accomplished young man, and for a gentleman the best draughtsman I ever saw.' Scott continued to encourage Skene's talent for illustration, intending to publish a descriptive volume on Edinburgh. Skene and Scott toured the Borders for scenes to illustrate the Waverley Novels.

Two drawings of Linlithgow High Street in 1826 by James Skene

(Opposite and right)

The spire of St Michael, Linlithgow, pre-1821
From the 'The Master Masons to the Crown of Scotland And Their Works' by the Rev. Robert Scott Mylne
Private Collection
(Below)

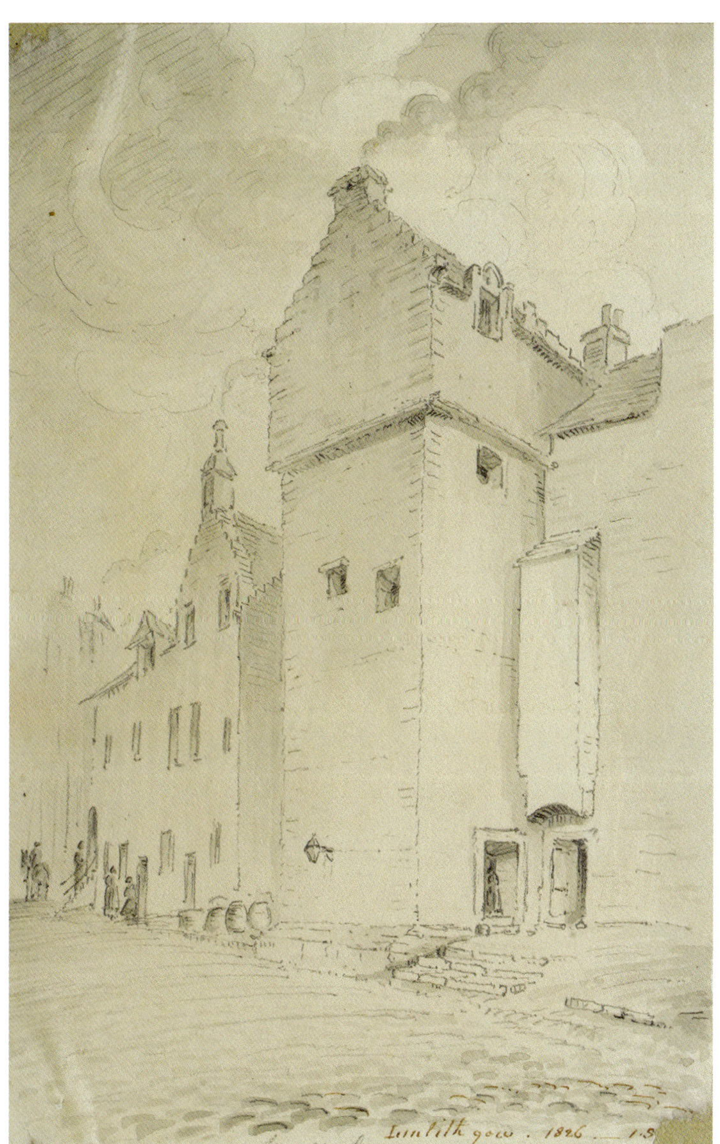

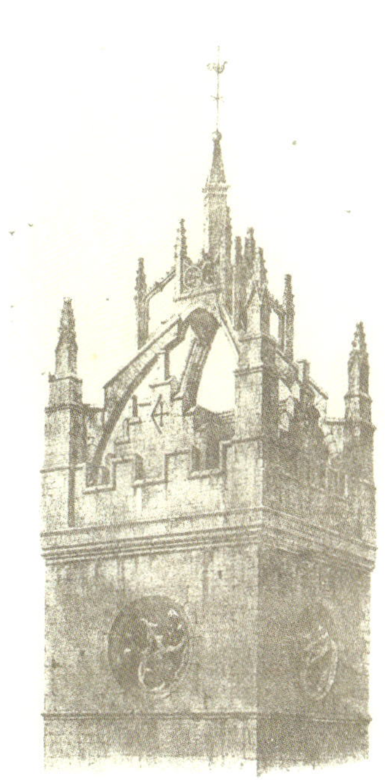

ST. MICHAEL, LINLITHGOW.

(Taken down in 1820)

The Mylne family has long played an active role in the design and construction of notable buildings in Linlithgow, such as the church spire and the palace. The Rev. Robert Scott Mylne in the 'The Master Masons to the Crown of Scotland And Their Works' describes how crown steeples were erected at St Giles', Edinburgh; St Nicholas, Newcastle; Kings College, Aberdeen, as well as at St Michael's, Linlithgow, in about AD 1500. The characteristic shape of the crown spire in Linlithgow was lost in 1821 when the stonework was deemed unsafe and at imminent risk of collapse, resulting in the removal of the construction.

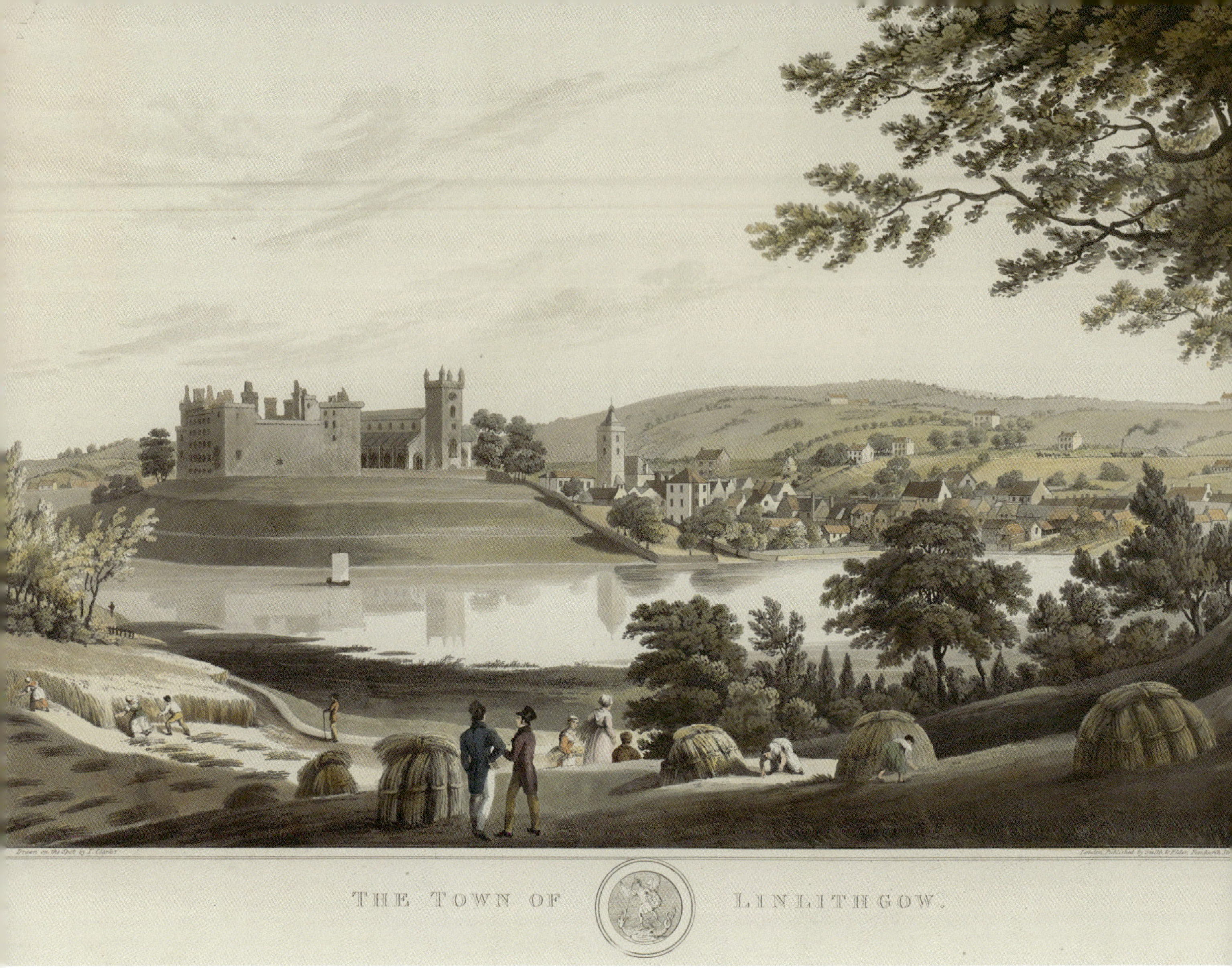

The Town of Linlithgow, 1824
by John Clark
© Crown Copyright: UK Government Art Collection
(Above)

Watercolourist and engraver, John Clark, toured Scotland during the summer of 1823 and made sketches for his series of aquatints (copper-plate etchings) entitled 'Views in Scotland' which were published between 1824 and 1825, under the patronage of King George IV. Little is known of the artist other than the fact that he specialised in topographical, sporting and marine views.

His outstanding 1824 aquatint of 'The Town of Linlithgow' shows men and women working in the fields to the north-west of Linlithgow Loch, while two gentlemen admire the peaceful, idyllic view of the town. To the left is Linlithgow Palace, and to the right is St Michael's Parish Church, now without its spire, as well as the spreading town of Linlithgow. The Burgh Halls, Cross House, the dovecot at Learmonth Park, the Canal House are all clearly recognisable, as are the canal boat and horses. The roundel in the title contains an image of St. Michael killing the dragon. This was plate number nine of 39 plates, drawn on the spot and engraved by John Clark as part of his 'Views in Scotland'.

Historic Environment Scotland maintains a valuable online resource of Scottish engravings on 'Canmore' the National Record of the Historical Environment. This rural engraving shows a distant view of the town, entitled 'Linlithgow'. It was drawn by A. W. Callcott, R.A., engraved by W. B. Cooke and published by Charles Tilt of Fleet Street in 1833. The view is from the east just below the Union Canal. The town is in the distance, with its distinctive skyline and the loch.   Agricultural workers are sitting down in the foreground eating their lunch, while a man on horseback appears to supervise proceedings. The height of the cereal crop was greater in those days before plants were bred for distinctive qualities such as shorter straw.

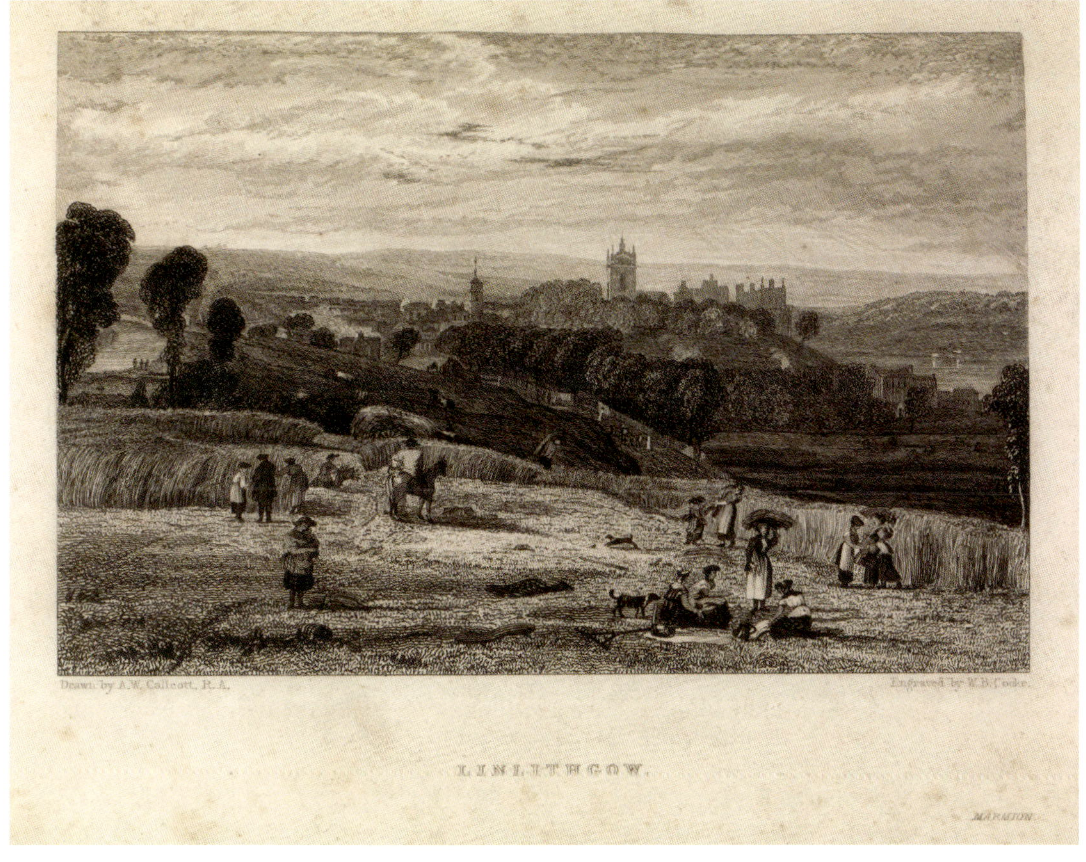

Linlithgow by A. W. Callcott,1833, engraved by W.B. Cooke

(Below)

Linlithgow Palace by W. Herdman, 1854

(Below)

William Herdman painted the delightful watercolour entitled 'Linlithgow Palace' in about 1854. Light floods in over the loch from the west onto a bucolic scene of locals enjoying music from a fiddler while sitting on a very hilly Peel. Sunshine highlights St Michael's Parish Church which is clearly defined while rooks fly above the ruins of Linlithgow Palace. The painting forms part of the Government Art Collection and can be viewed online.

William Gawin Herdman was born in Liverpool in 1806, the son of a corn merchant. He enrolled at the Liverpool Academy in 1824 and later worked as an art teacher. He exhibited at the Royal Academy, the Royal Society of British Artists and the Liverpool Academy. He helped found the Liverpool Society of Fine Arts. Herdman wrote on subjects as diverse as cosmology and skating, and he composed hymns and poetry. He died in Liverpool at the age of 77.

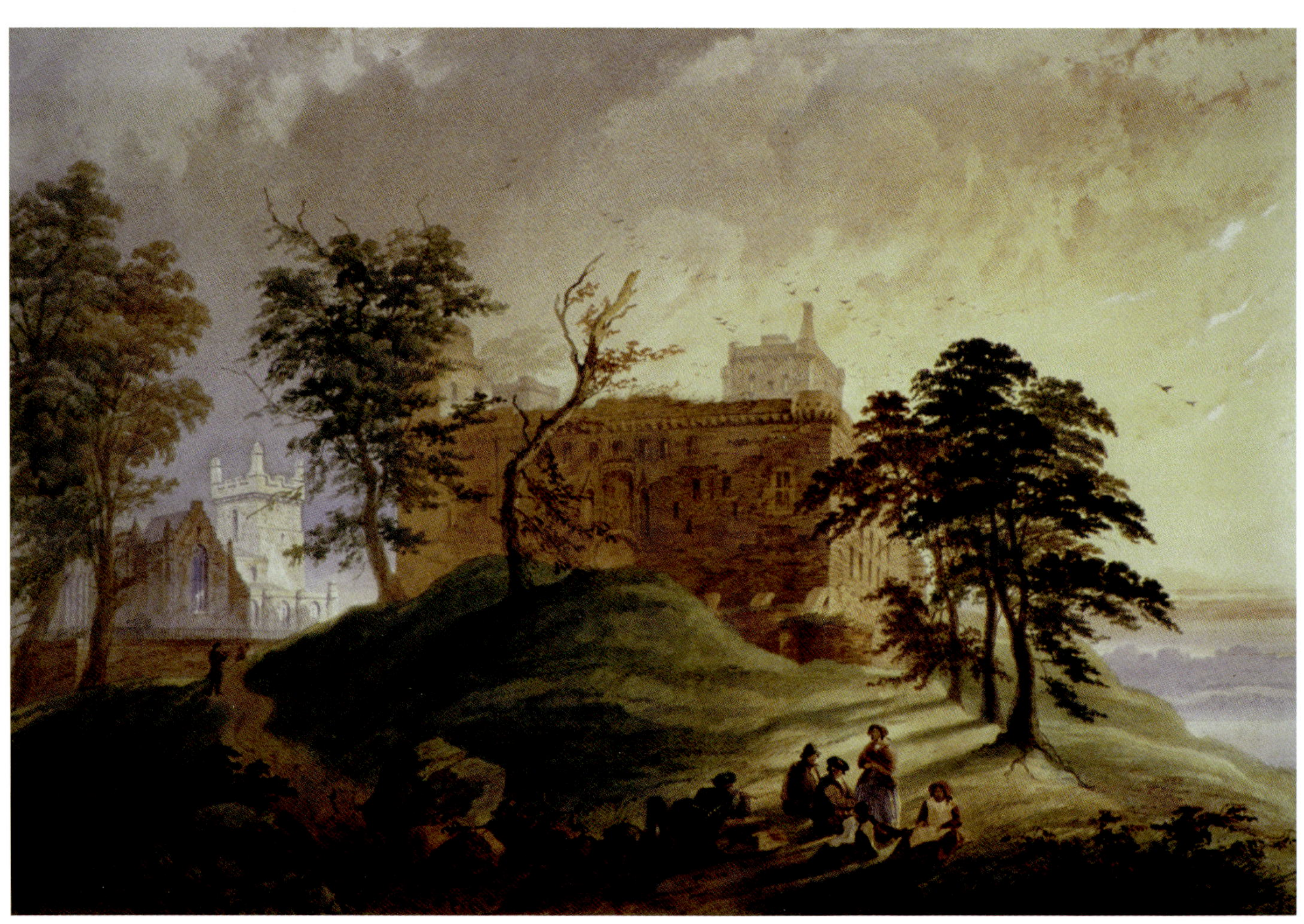

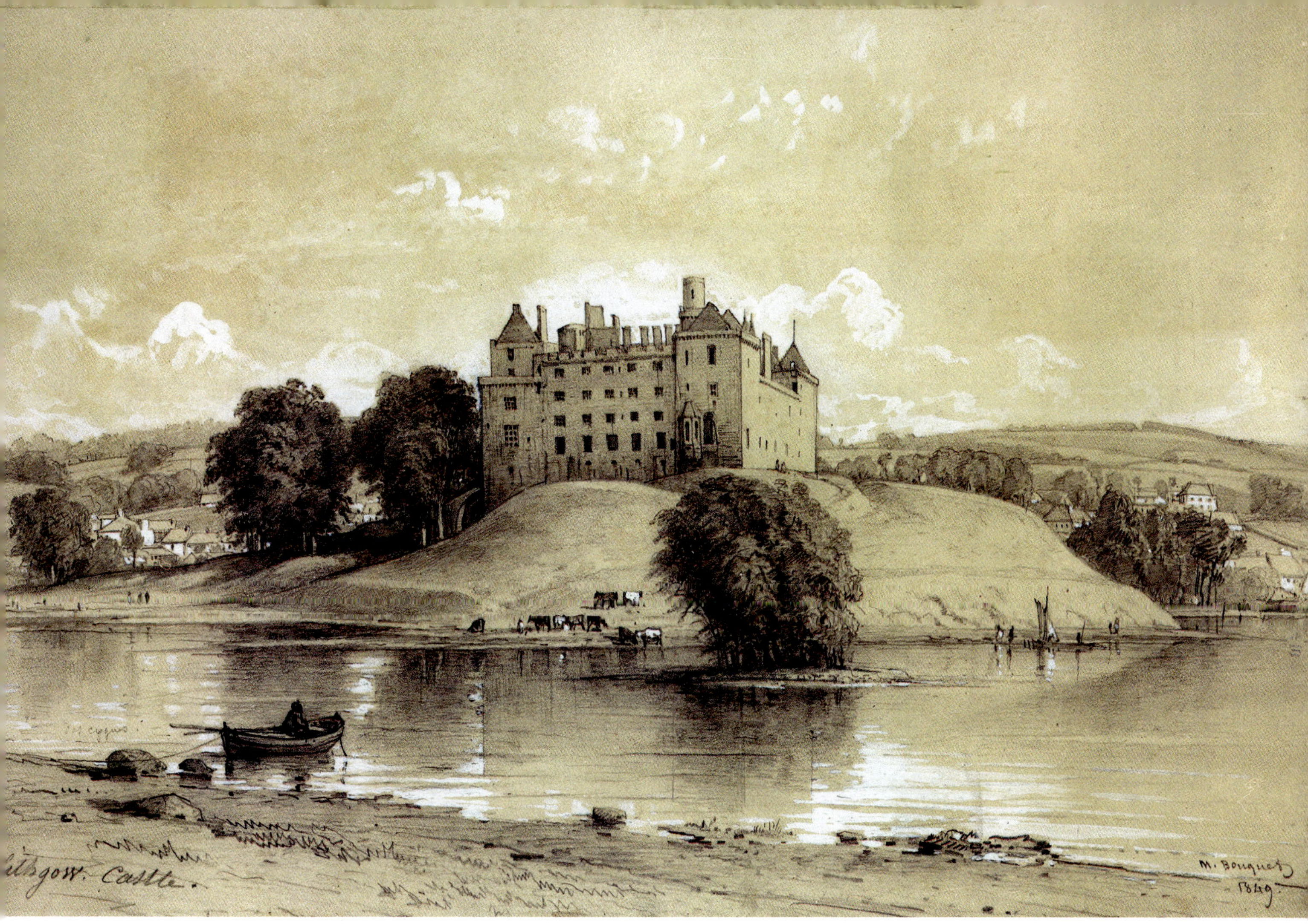

Linlithgow Castle by Michel Bouquet circa 1849
© Courtesy of HES
(Above)

Michel Bouquet was an accomplished French landscape painter and lithographic artist, who lived between 1807 and 1890. He was best known for his landscapes of the British Isles. The excellent pen and ink drawing is entitled 'Linlithgow Castle' and dates from about 1849. The north side of the ruined 'castle' is central to the picture, sitting on an exaggerated hill, obscuring views of the Parish Church and the Town House. The rural, lochside scene shows Rickle Island, cows grazing on the Peel and fishermen in action, as optimistic as today. Buildings in the burgh are drawn accurately on either side of the palace.

View of Linlithgow Palace by David Allan (attributed) Reproduced by the kind permission of the National Trust for Scotland Photo Library (Opposite)

This is a marvellous view of Linlithgow Palace. It is owned by the Earl of Mar and Kellie and is permanently displayed at the National Trust of Scotland property, Alloa Tower.

Morning light floods onto a fine Linlithgow scene showing two women laying out cloth on the ground. The location is beyond the town wall in the area which today is called Friars Brae. This view, in the Romantic style, shows the tower of St Michael's Parish Church, without its crown steeple, in the centre of the picture. The loch is clearly visible through the trees on the left; houses lead up Kirkgate with sheep grazing one side and tombstones leaning near the church. Rows of red pantiled roofs are shown along the High Street, as well as the Town House (today's Burgh Halls), the chapel in Dog Well Wynd and the smoke from numerous houses. The Spanish Ambassador's House, a prestigious building in its day, is visible. A man takes a dog for a walk.

It is possible that the women in the foreground were bleachers. Daniel Defoe in his Tour through the Whole Island of Great Britain, published 1724-27, mentions seeing linen laid out for bleaching and implies that the water was drawn from the loch: 'At Linlithgow there is a very great linen manufacture... and the water of the lough, or lake here, is esteemed with the best in Scotland for bleaching or whitening of linen cloth; so that a great deal of linen, made in other parts of the country, is brought either to be bleached or whitened.' There was a bleachfield in Linlithgow for much of the 18th century. An open grass area was needed where the linen, after repeated washings, was spread out to be bleached by the action of the sun and water - either by rain or by being sprinkled with water at regular intervals. Open bleachfields began to fall out of use after the discovery of chlorine in 1785. It is strange that the site depicted here was so distant from the loch.

The oil painting is attributed to the artist David Allan who was born in Alloa in 1744 and died in 1796. Allan was known as the 'Scottish Hogarth' after his depiction of satirical village life and at his death in 1796 he left a series of drawings illustrating the poems of Burns. The painting is, however, a puzzle because Allan had died long before some features of the scene were realised. It appears more likely that the picture was painted in the period circa 1821 to 1847, by a disciple of David Allan. A number of clues suggest a later artist, the chief being that the crown spire of the parish church was taken down in 1821 and the Town House spire was destroyed by fire in 1847, when David Allan would have been long dead.

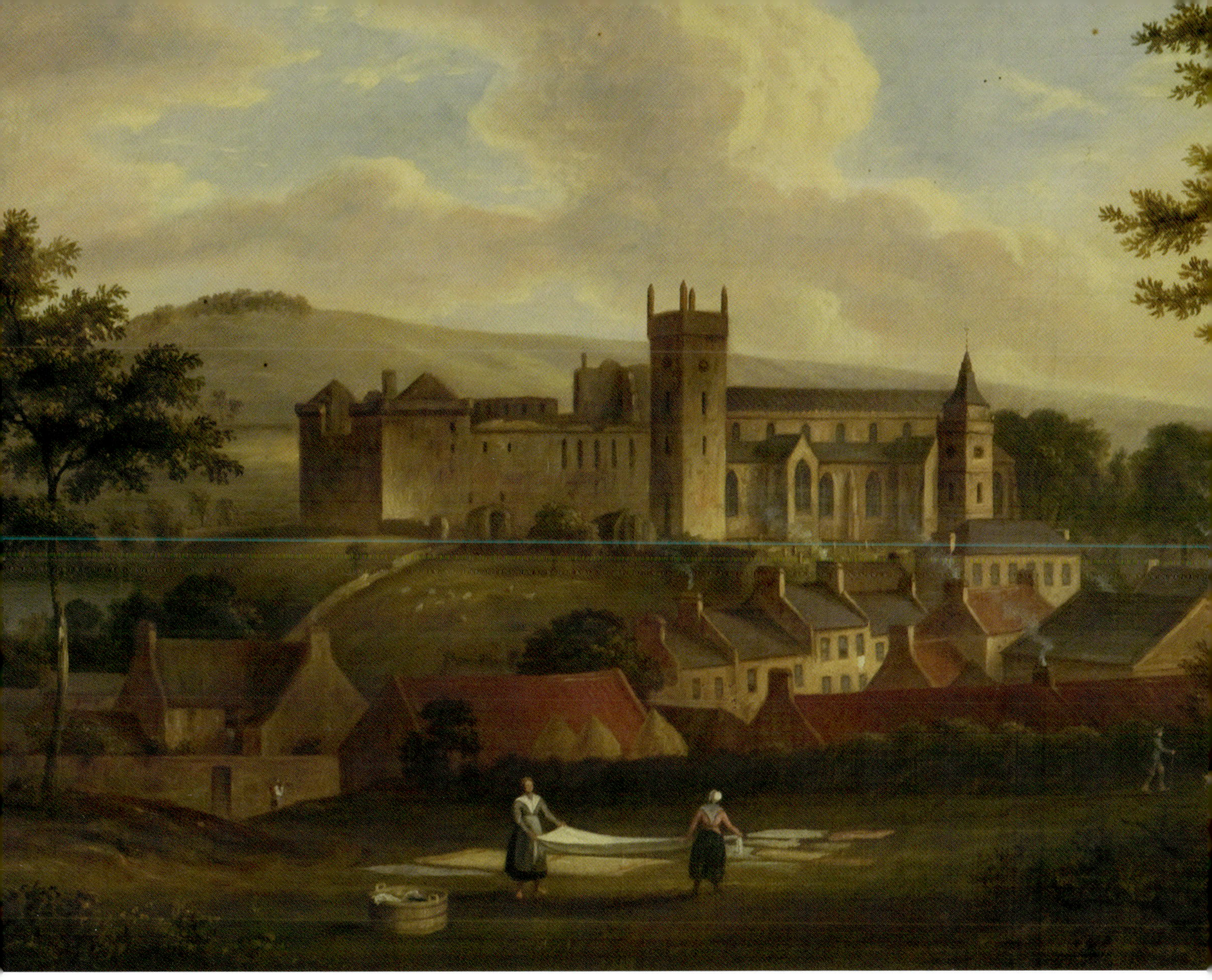

The peaceful painting by Scottish artist, Robert Macaulay Stevenson, entitled 'Linlithgow Palace', is the property of the Hunterian Art Gallery, University of Glasgow. It is not on public display. The Scottish artist was born in the middle of the 19th century and died in 1952. Stevenson initially studied engineering but later changed to study art at the Glasgow School of Design. He worked for some time in France and was influenced by contemporary French artists such as Jean-Baptiste-Camille Corot. This fine picture was painted when he was 44.

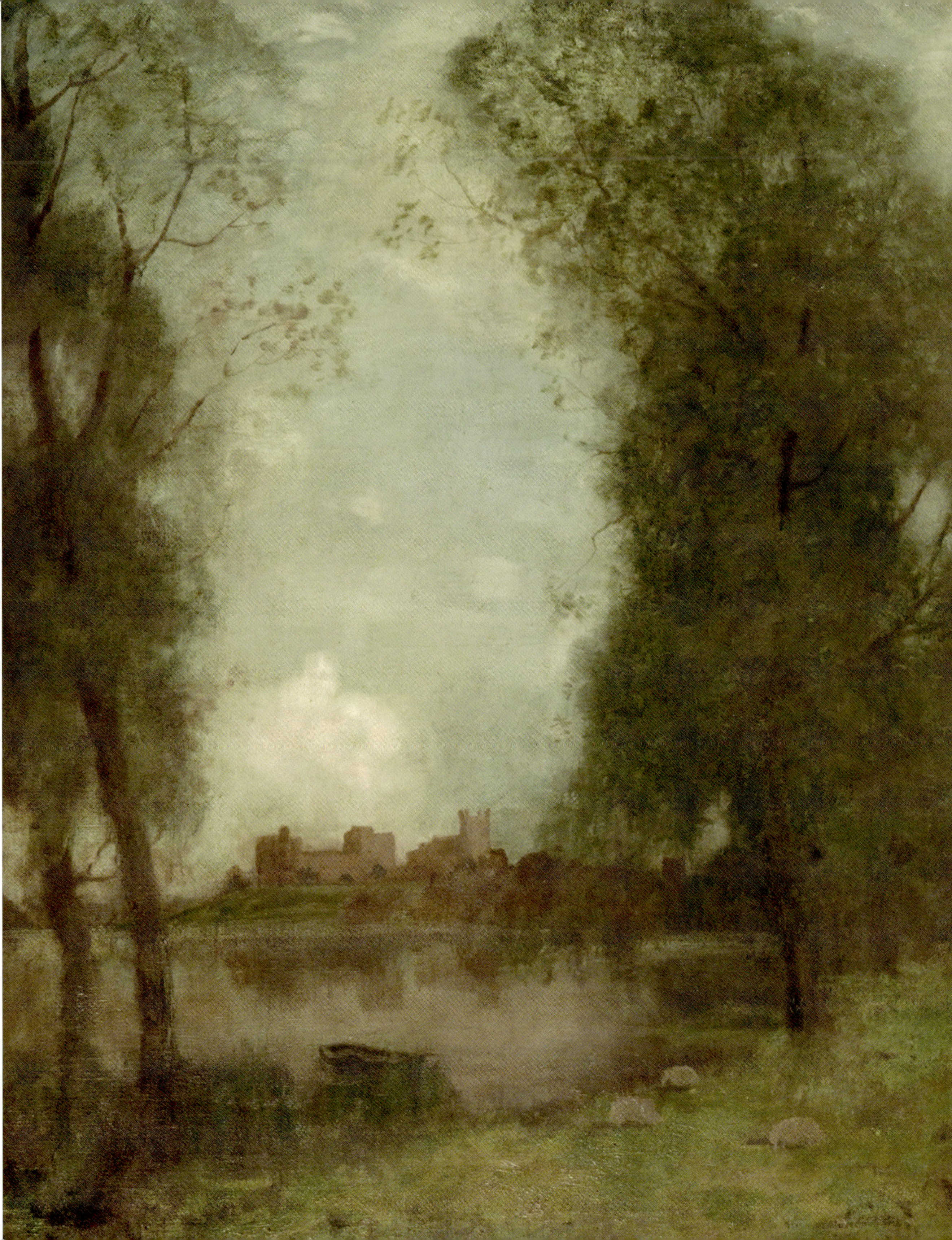

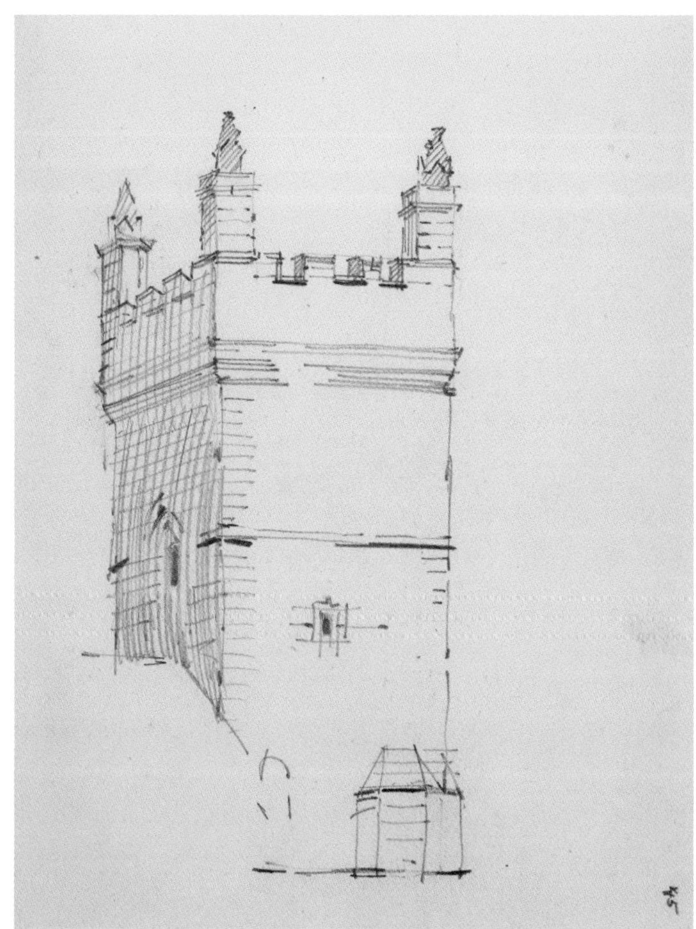

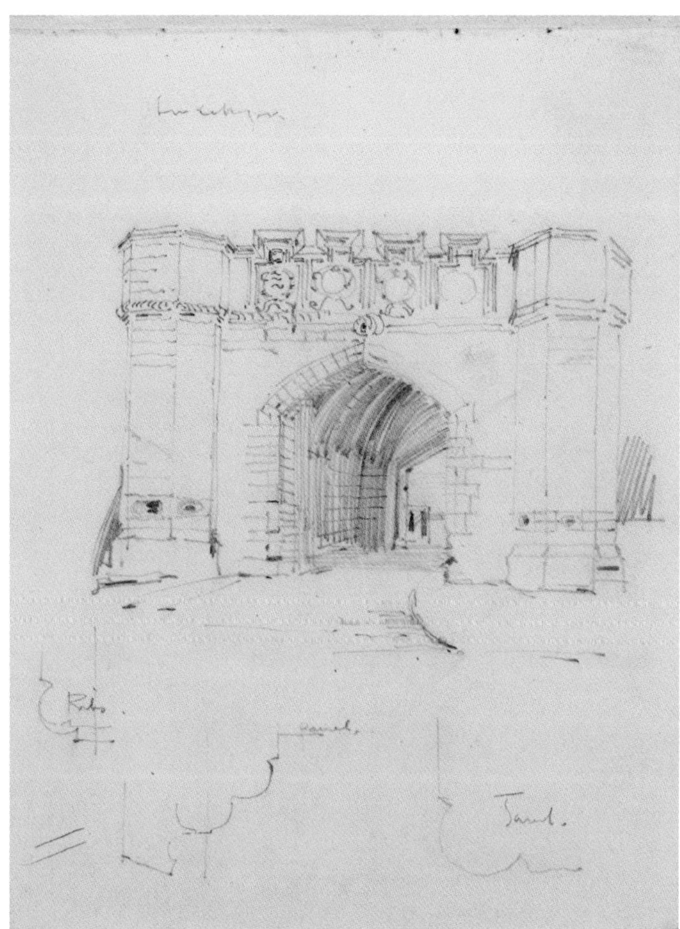

View of Linlithgow Palace by Robert Macaulay Stevenson, 1898 © The Hunterian, University of Glasgow 2018 (Opposite)

Drawings of the West Tower, St Michael's and the Palace Gateway by Charles Rennie Mackintosh
These images are reproduced courtesy of the National Library of Ireland
(PD 2009 TX 45 and PD 2009 TX 16)
(Above)

A century after Turner, a young architect and artist with sketchbook in hand looked at Linlithgow and drew sketches of what he saw. Charles Rennie Mackintosh, in the last decade of the 19th century, visited the burgh. He may well have had an involvement in the 1894-96 restoration work at St Michael's Parish Church as a junior member of the architectural practice of John Honeyman & Keppie. John Ferguson's history of St Michael's 'Ecclesia Antiqua' states: 'the pulpit and baptismal font are from designs by Mr John Honeyman, architect, Glasgow, under whose guidance the committee carried through the restoration.' Mackintosh made a number of undated pencil drawings of St Michael's Church in his sketch books which are now located in the National Library of Ireland in Dublin, but there is no documentary evidence that he worked on the church.

The illustrations shown here are the gateway to the palace with details of the stonework and the west tower of the church, after the removal of the stone spire. It is interesting to conjecture what he would have made of today's modern crown spire.

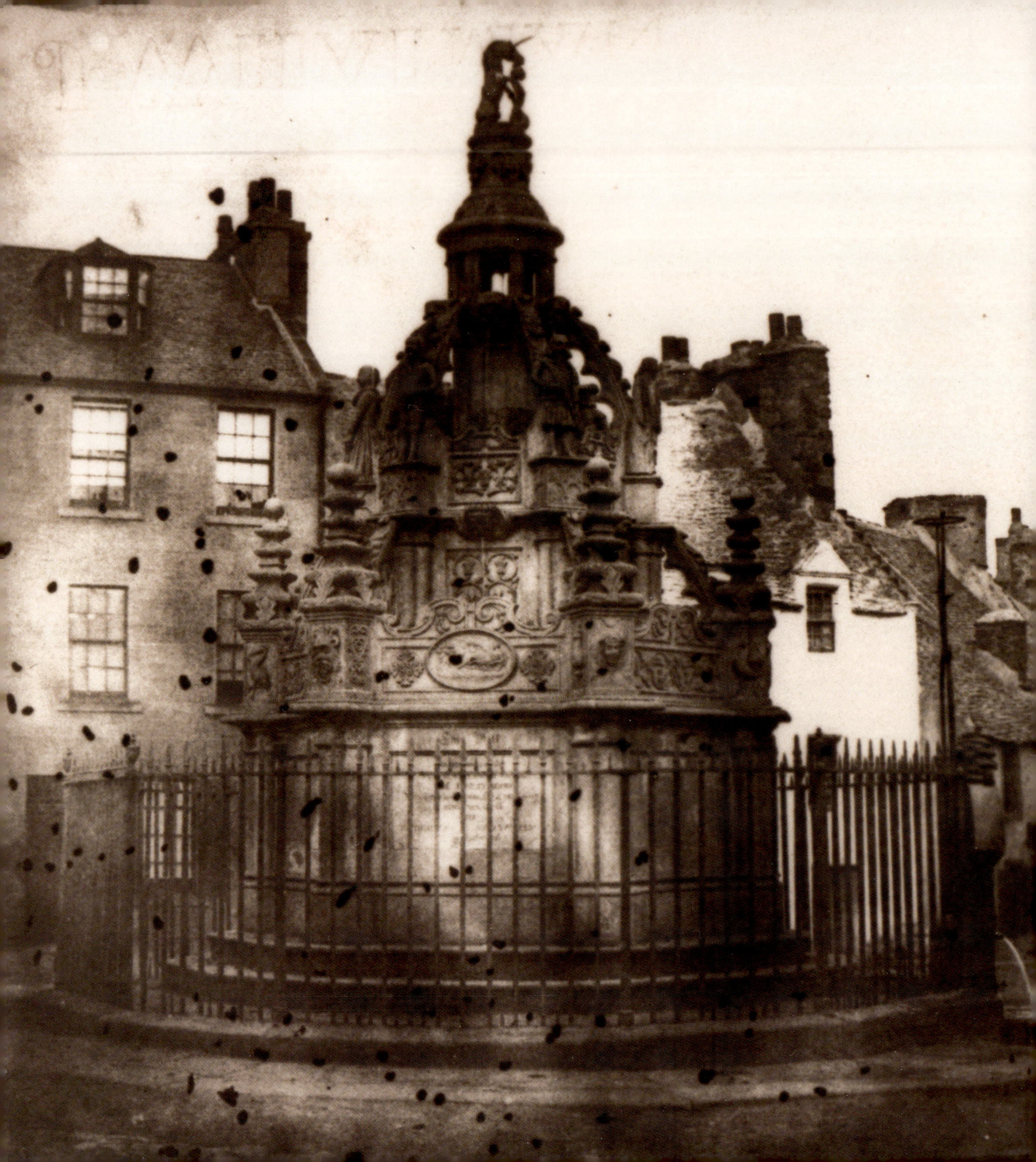

Water flowing from the Cross Well, photographed by Robert Adamson in July 1845
By permission of University of Glasgow Library, Special Collections
(Opposite)

Postcard depicting the Victoria Hall and High Street, Linlithgow
Private collection
(Below)

Linlithgow has played a role in the development of photography in Scotland. On Platform 1 of its railway station is a plaque recording how it is thought likely that it was the very first station to be photographed. It was the work of David Octavius Hill and Robert Adamson – two pioneers who were among the first in the world to realise the artistic possibilities of photography. Roddy Simpson in his book 'Hill and Adamson's Photographs of Linlithgow' records that they became partners to photograph the hundreds of individuals for Hill's painting recording the Disruption of the Church of Scotland in May 1843. David Octavius Hill was an accomplished painter and Robert Adamson a talented, pioneering photographer. The purpose of the Linlithgow Station photograph, taken in 1845, was probably to enable Hill to utilise it in a painting for John Miller, the engineer in the company of Grainger and Miller who built the Edinburgh and Glasgow Railway, which opened in 1842.

The depiction of the water flowing from the Cross Well, is thought to be the earliest photograph of Linlithgow and was taken by Robert Adamson on July 28th 1845. Most of the buildings have been replaced. Water can quite clearly be seen gushing from the well. The negative, now housed in Glasgow University Library Department of Special Collections, was made on paper watermarked 'J. Whatman'. It shows many defect spots as a result of the technical challenges of the process used at the time.

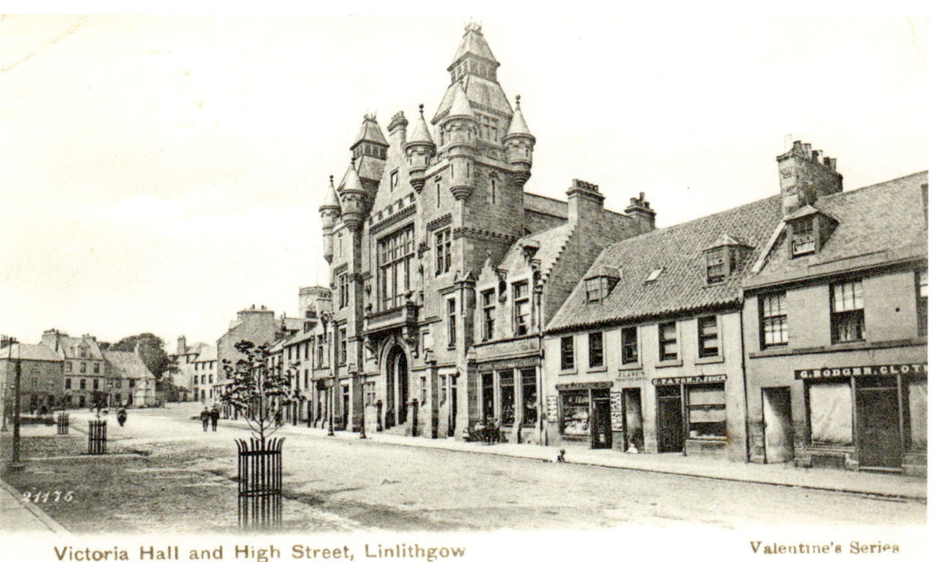

Linlithgow has long featured in published postcards. Other manufacturers included Francis Frith, J.B. White, John Mackay and J. Valentine and Co. of Dundee. One of the Valentine Series showed the Victoria Hall in all its original, baronial glory, standing in a quiet, car-free High Street.

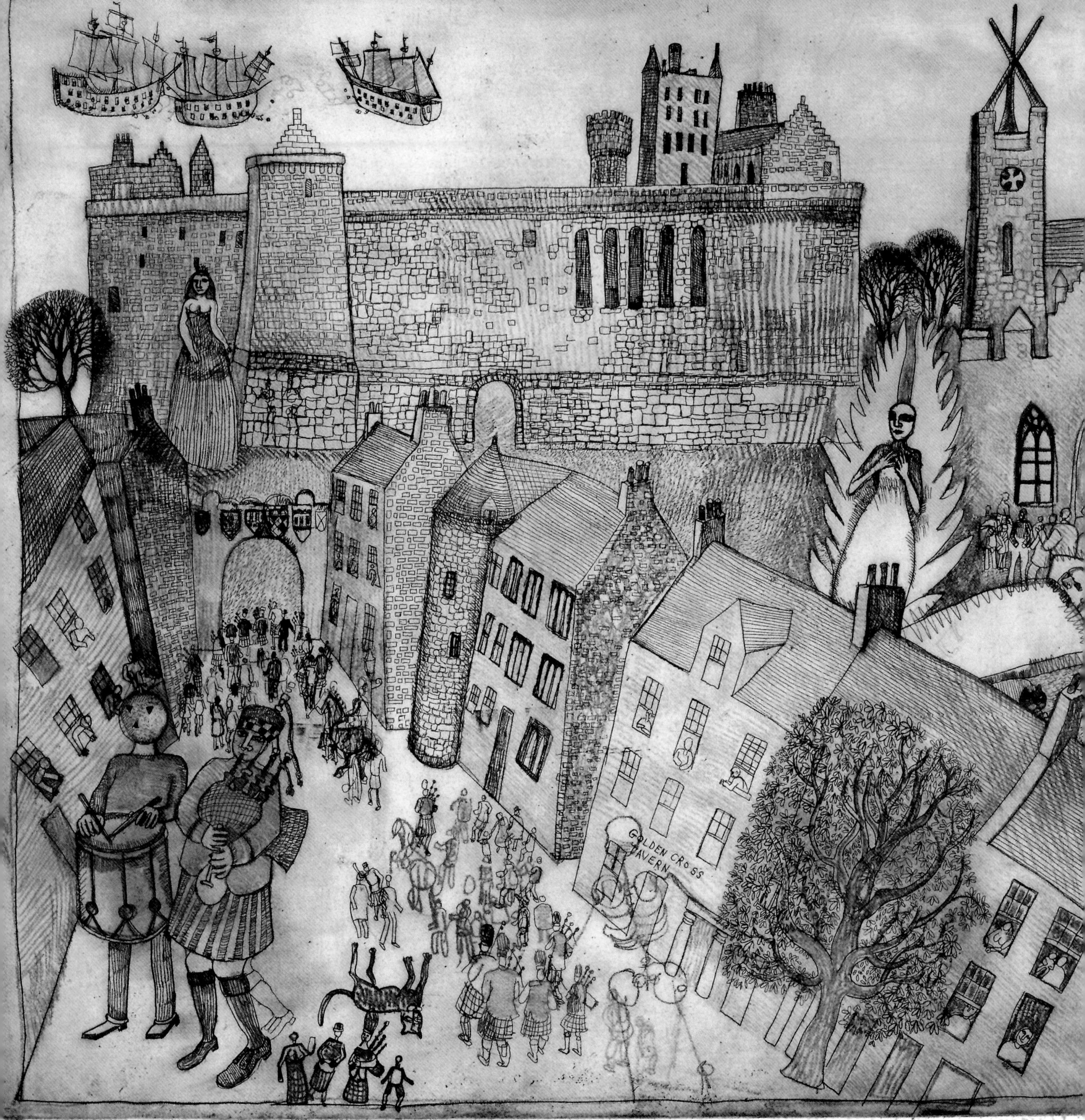

6/45 LinLithgow

THREE

Linlithgow and its Community

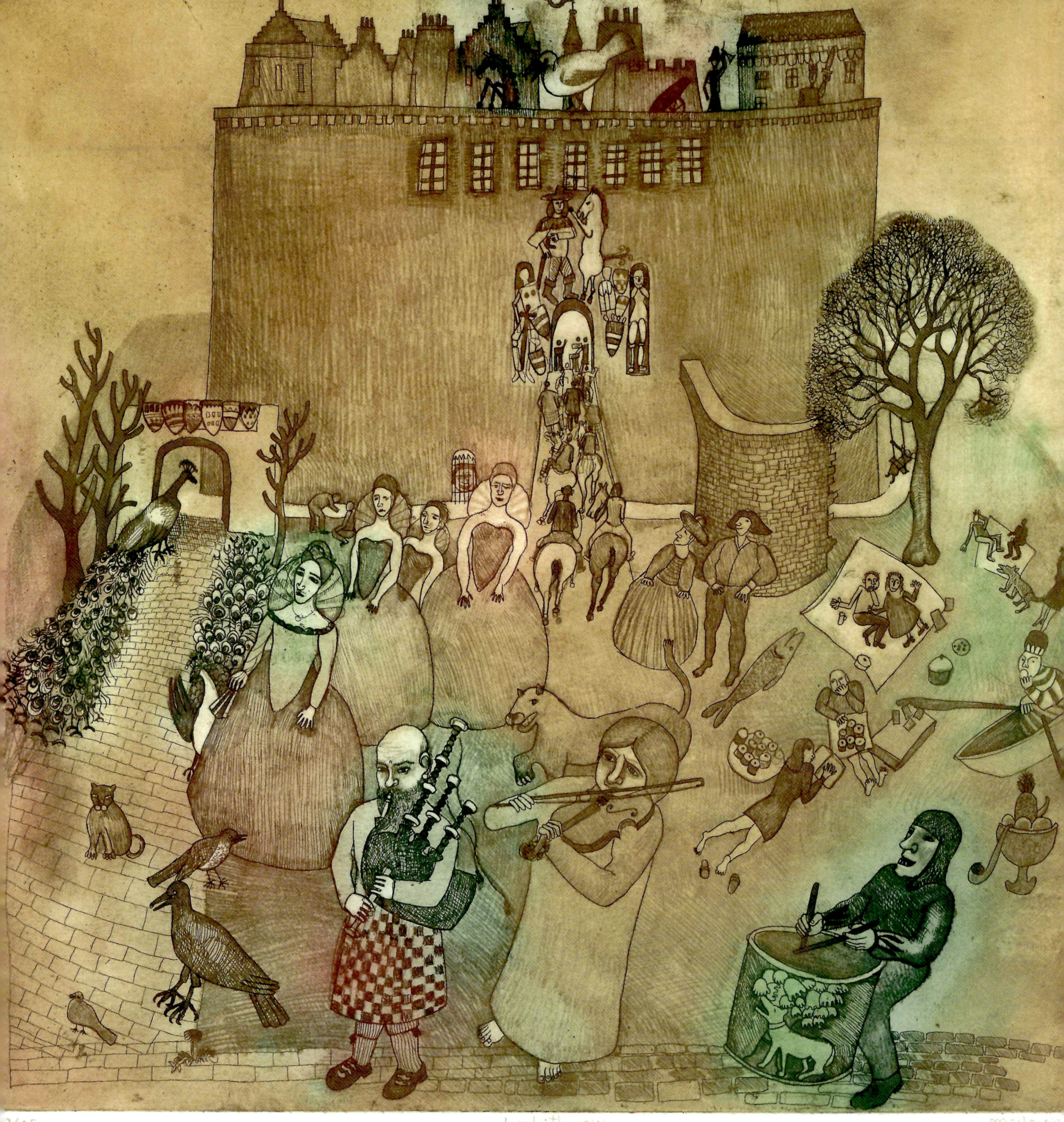

2/45 Linlithgow

Etching of Linlithgow (1) by Michael McVeigh
© Michael McVeigh
(On page 60)

Etching of Linlithgow (2) by Michael McVeigh
© Michael McVeigh
(Opposite)

Delft-type tiles illustrating the town trades
© Douglas Watson Studio. Commissioned by West Lothian Council
(Below)

Linlithgow has long celebrated its distinctive sense of community. The climax to the community calendar is the annual Marches Day which is held annually on the first Tuesday after the second Thursday in June. This retains an old reference to Holy Thursday and was fixed by the Burgh Council in 1767. The second Thursday was fixed as the date of the Whitsunday Fair. The day-long Marches celebration started with the Provost's Breakfast attended by the leading officials of the burgh. This was followed by a procession around the town's marches (boundaries) with representatives of the town's trades: hammermen, tailors, baxters, cordiners, weavers, wrights, coopers and fleshers. The office of Deacon Convenor or Lord Deacon was held exclusively by the Deacon of the Hammermen for many years but later by the other deacons in rotation. Today this honour is held by the deacon of the last remaining trade fraternity – the Dyers. In place of the old trades, representatives from the many town organisations now take part. In days past the honour of carrying the burgh standards, the craft pinzel (flag) and the merchant pinzel was much sought after. The trade flags were carried for many years by the Incorporation of Weavers whose flag-bearer bore them to and from the Burgh Halls. Today the honour of carrying the town flags and those of many organisations is still eagerly pursued. These days the organisation of the spectacular event is conducted by the Court of the Deacons of the Ancient and Royal Burgh of Linlithgow.

This section explores how artists have portrayed Linlithgow's community.

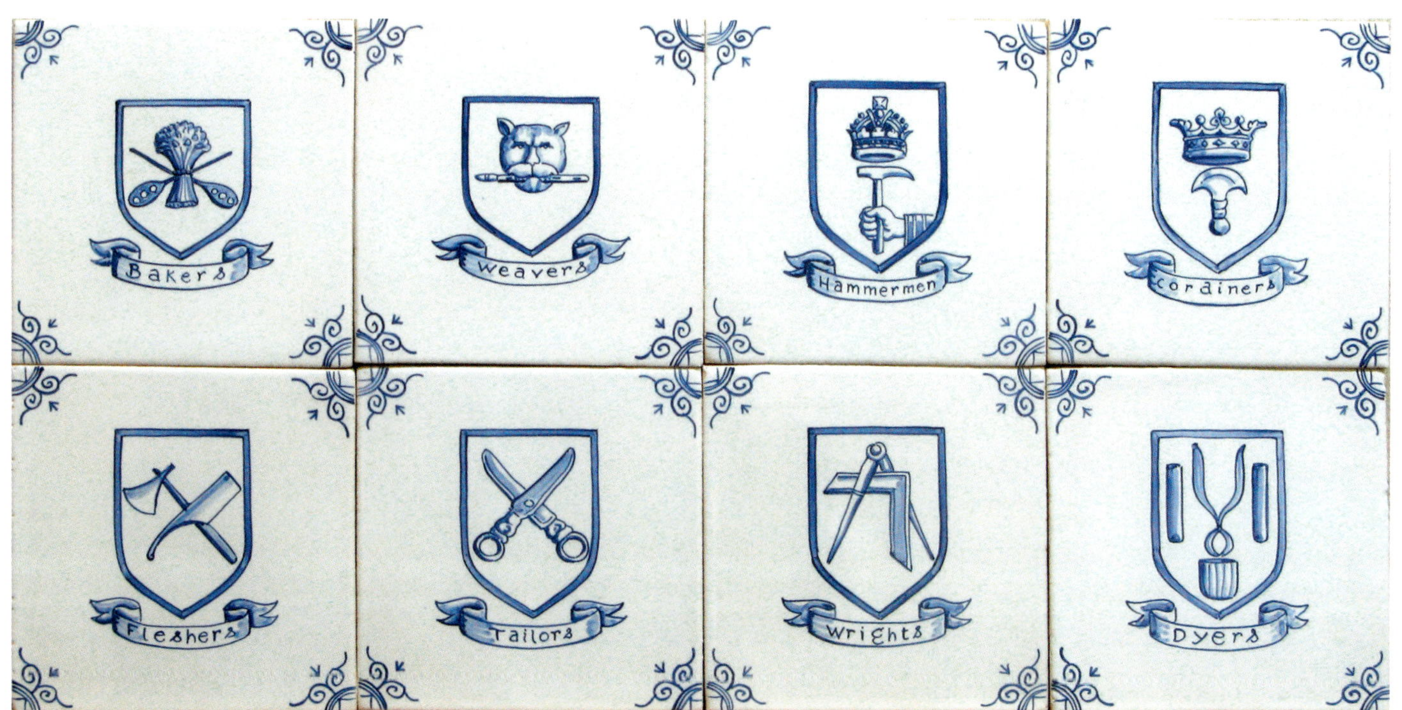

In a rarely viewed sketchbook held for safe keeping at Register House in Edinburgh is a small watercolour of Marches Day painted in 1914. Sybil Henderson was the daughter of John Henderson, of Nether Parkley, who was county clerk from 1901 to 1946. She recorded her impressions of the festivities between the statue of Lord Hope, known now as the 'Green Man,' on the left and the Cross Well to the right. Sybil Henderson paints the town festooned in bunting as spectators gather to watch the parade. In the foreground a musician holds his drum.

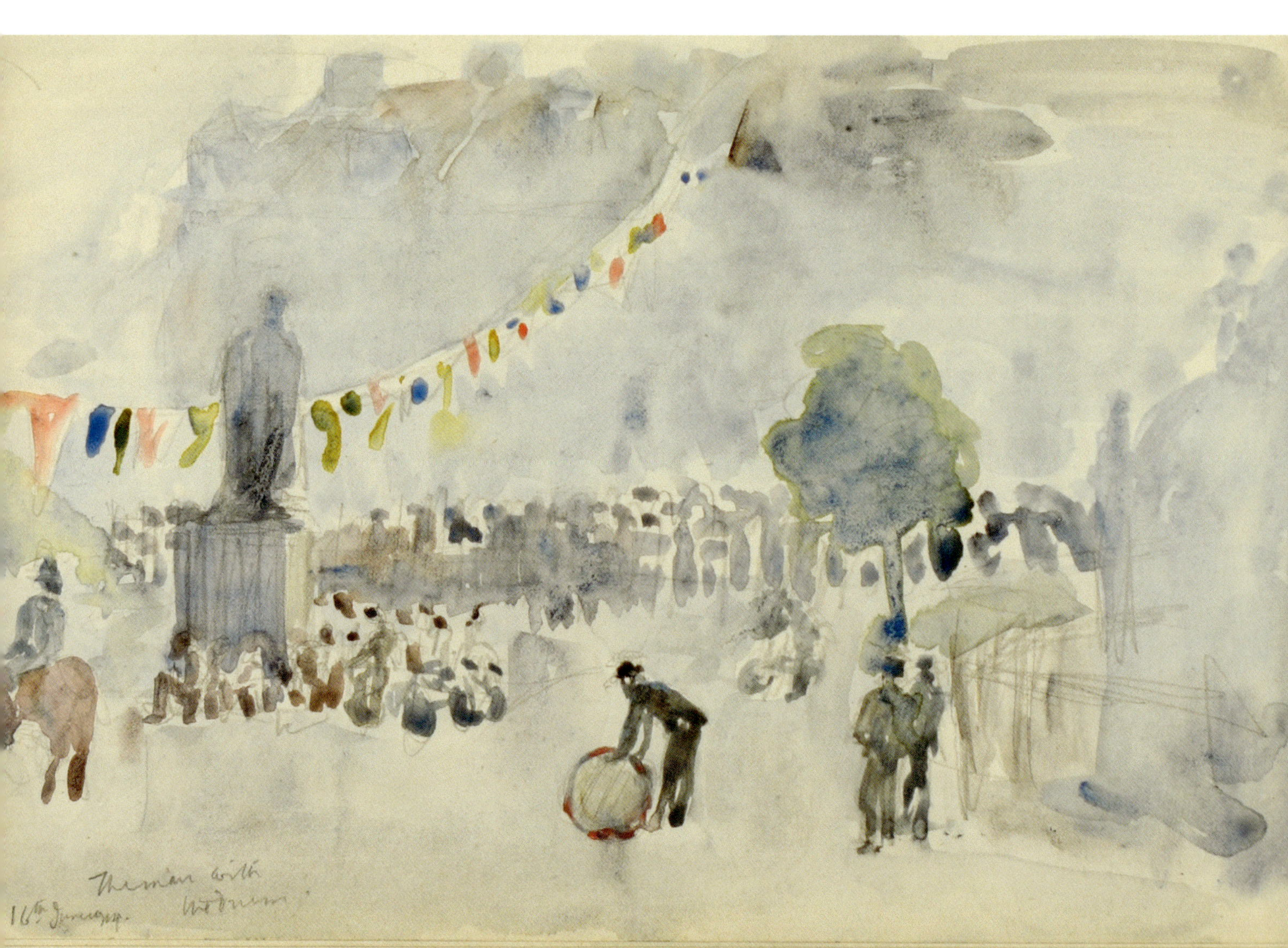

The Man with the Drum by
Sybil Henderson
National Records of Scotland
(GD76/527)
(Below)

Linlithgow Cross at the Marches by Chris Taylor

Flags and balloons festoon the same square over 100 years later captured in a painting by local artist Chris Taylor. He says, 'I always hope that my paintings speak for themselves - that way I know they work!' At the top of his watercolour is the contemporary spire of St Michael's Parish Church and to the left the well.

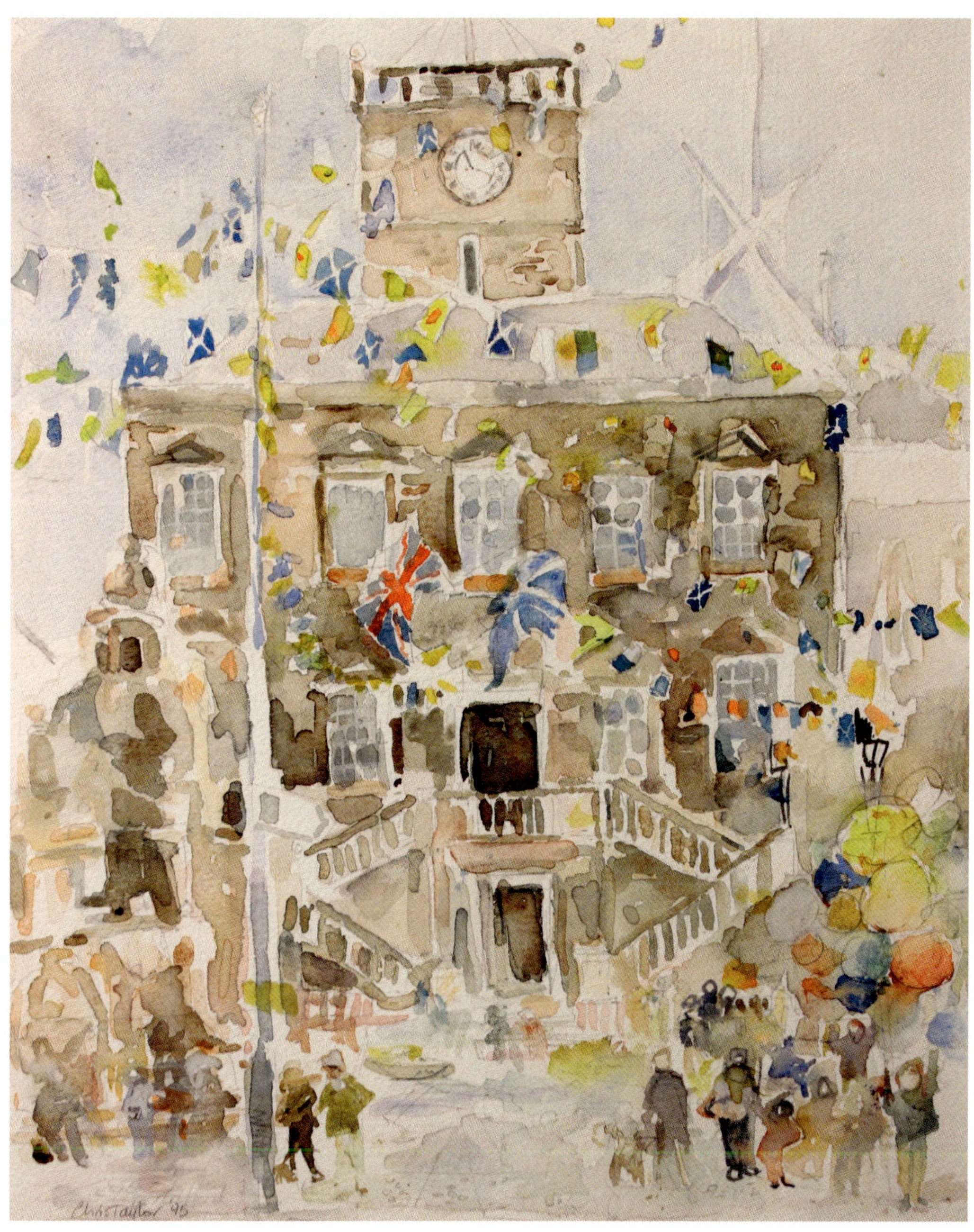

Figure playing the fife at the Cross Well
© Calum Smith photographer
(Lower left)

Sashed bailie of the town
© Calum Smith photographer
(Lower right)

Town drummer
© Calum Smith photographer
(Opposite)

Linlithgow Cross, one of the finest civic stage-sets of any Scottish town, features a magnificent well or fountain which shows off the prestige of the former royal burgh. The original well, one of many in the town, was probably what was known as a 'dipping well,' erected about 1535. The well was repaired in 1756-60 by a stonemason named James Thomson. By 1774, the well needed to be renovated once more and yet again at the start of the 19th century, when the mason, Robert Gray, was commissioned to rebuild it to the original design.

The well was a source of water for the use of the inhabitants and was, and is, also an ornamental fountain. It is hexagonal in shape with three descending basins into which the water is fed from the unicorn at the top. From here it flows to the basin immediately below through grotesque gargoyles. The outlet at the front, immediately under the burgh coats of arms, carries the motto: 'My Fruit is Fidelity to God and the King.' At each of the six angles stand: St Michael, patron saint of the burgh, overlooking the High Street; a bailie of the burgh, with the words 'God Save the King' inscribed on a sash; a jolly deacon holding a drum, a monk in a cloak, a figure of a man playing the fife and a town drummer.

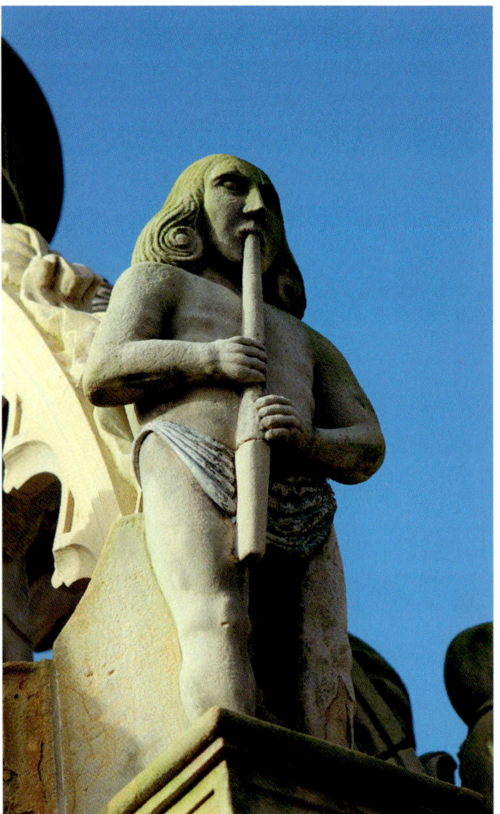

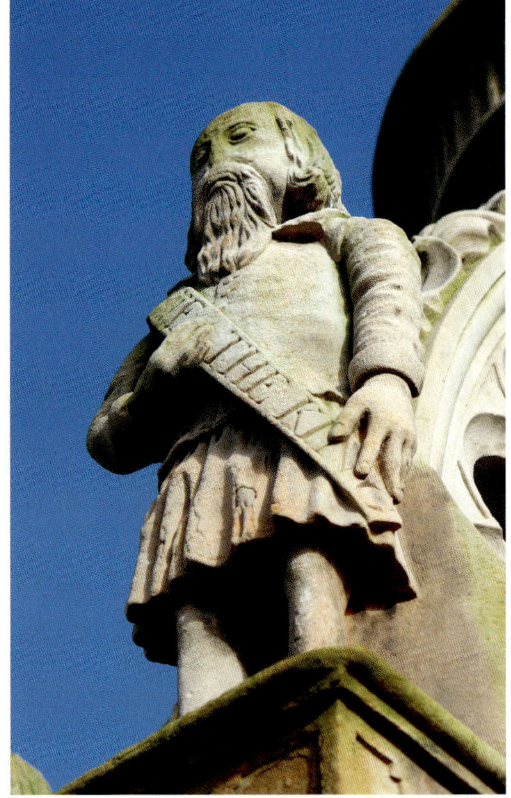

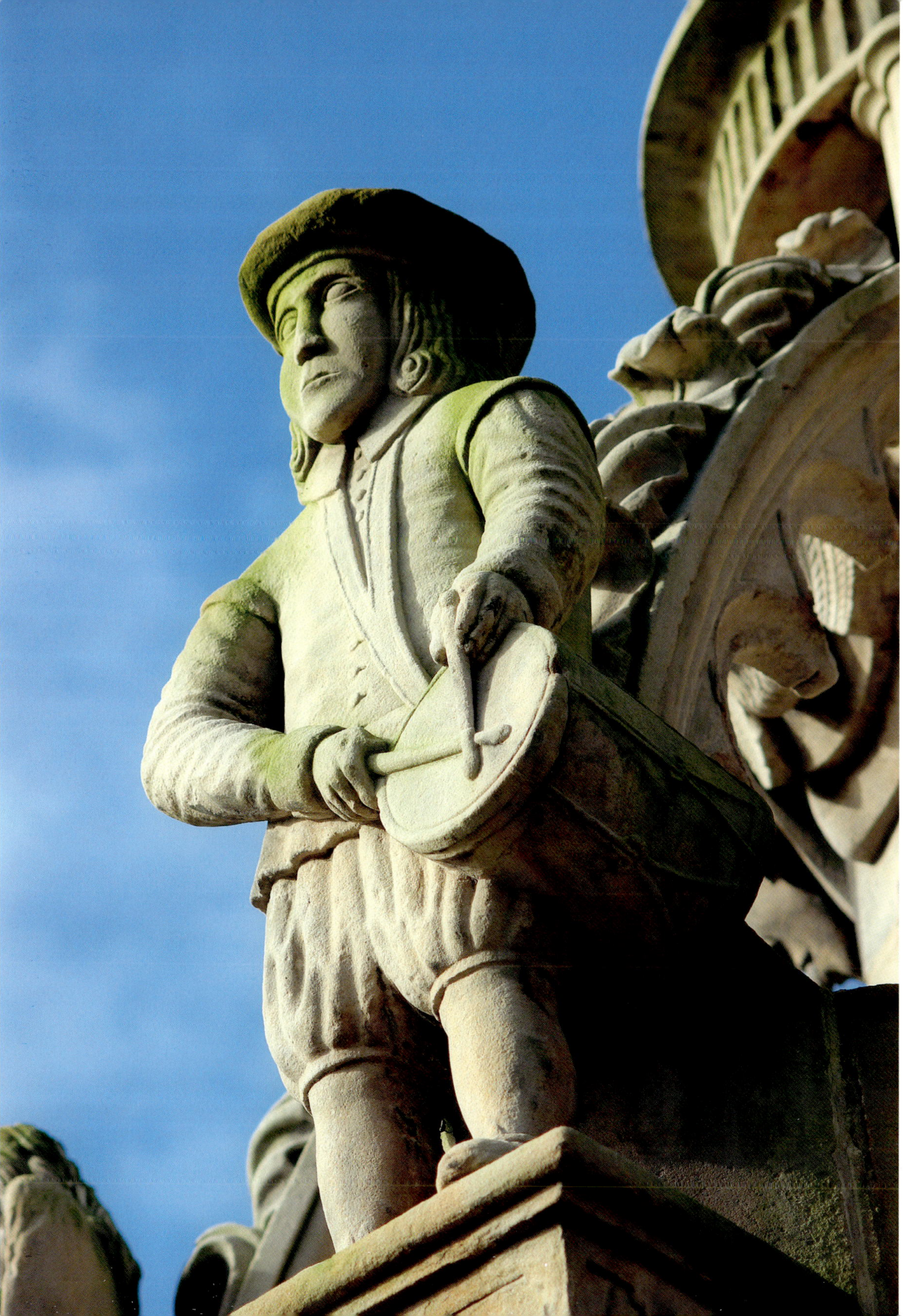

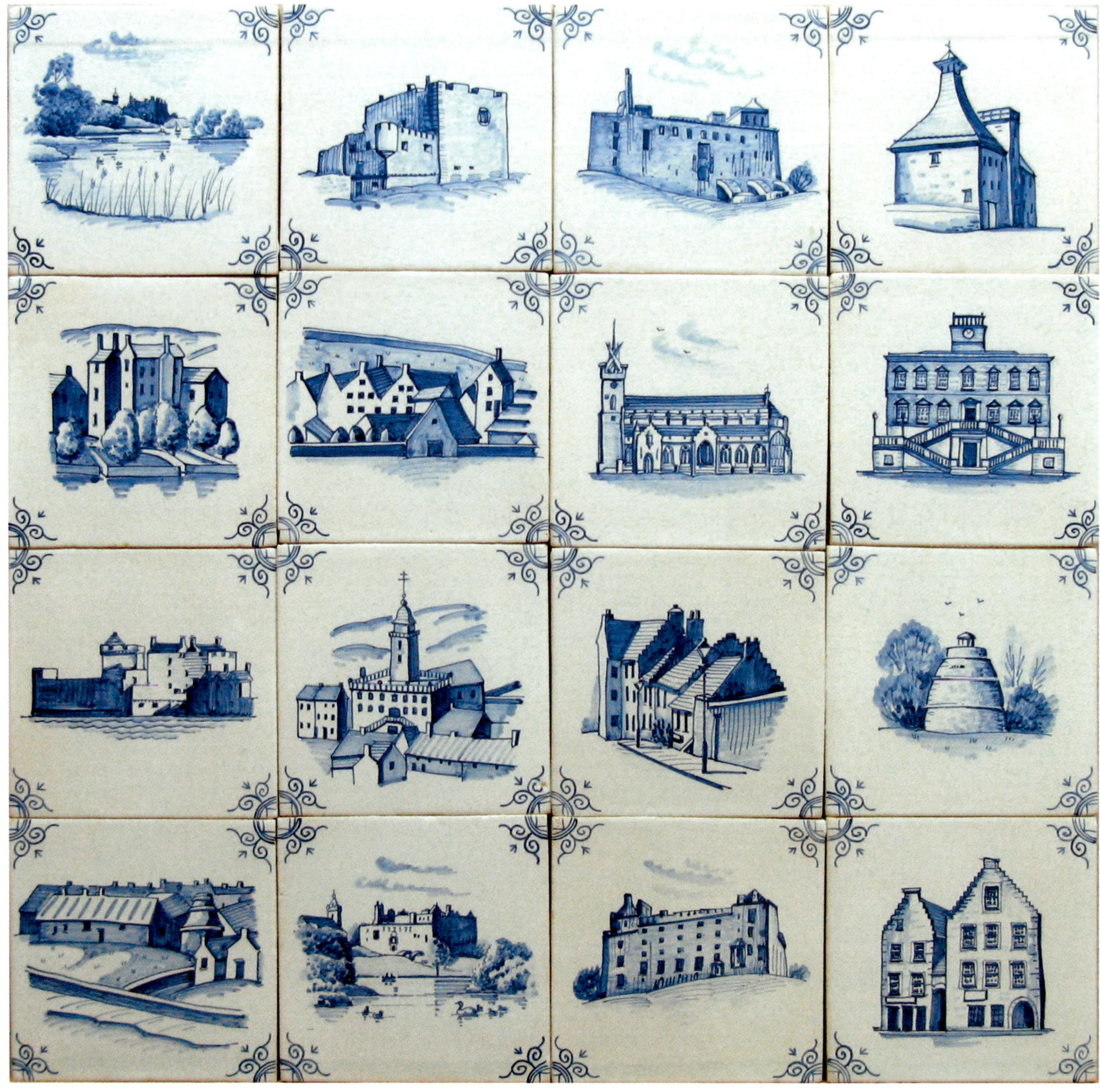

Delft-type tiles illustrating historic buildings of Linlithgow and Blackness
© Douglas Watson Studio
Commissioned by West Lothian Council
(Opposite)

Behind the fountain are located the Burgh Halls, the former Town House, now owned by West Lothian Council. It was recently converted by the Edinburgh architect, Malcolm Fraser, and now provides outstanding public spaces as well as a visual arts centre. During the renovations the council commissioned art installations of merit, led by Camille Archer, Visual and Public Art Officer with the Community Arts service. These included gates to the rear garden, Delft-inspired tiles and two pictures by the contemporary Edinburgh artist, Michael McVeigh – three examples of modern art in a very old building.

In my opinion, the south, or Bailie Hardie Hall, in the Burgh Halls, is the finest space in Linlithgow, where ancient, carved, stone fireplaces on the two end walls were brought back to life during the renovations. Community Arts, within West Lothian Council, commissioned public art, funded by Creative Scotland.

The Douglas Watson Studio, from Henley-on-Thames in Oxfordshire, won the commission to design and manufacture Delft-inspired tiles for the three fireplaces, in 2010. They are a contemporary interpretation of original Delft tiles. Thus they explore the Delft tradition, and bring character to the rooms but they also refer to the history of the building, the Royal Burgh, the town today and the future. Many of the tiles are a representation of those once participating in the Marches Day, hammermen, fleshers, dyers, and pipers, some still central to the Marches Day.

The frames above the two fireplaces in the Bailie Hardie Hall lay empty for many years. There was no evidence of what may have filled the spaces. In 2009 artists were invited by West Lothian Council to tender for the commission to create an original work of Linlithgow. The aim was to create two significant and permanent works of art that would be specific to the site, using local cultural references.

Michael McVeigh was selected by the Community Arts Service of West Lothian Council and Malcolm Fraser Architects. Michael was born in Dundee in 1957 and he studied drawing and painting at the Duncan of Jordanstone College of Art from 1977-82. His paintings and prints are figurative pieces based on everyday Scottish life with a dreamlike quality that reflects a vibrant personal imagination.

The artist set about a personal and imaginative journey into the historic as well as the contemporary life of Linlithgow. His observations, talks with local people, walks through the town, sketches, etchings and dreams resulted in the two artworks, 'East' and 'West'. They are a wonderful introduction of contemporary art into these historic over-mantels in the Bailie Hardie Hall.

East, below and West opposite by Michael McVeigh © Michael McVeigh Commissioned by and © West Lothian Council

A dominant foreground image in the 'East' painting is a bare footed figure of a man in a white gown lying beneath a flowering tree. When asked about this character, Michael replied, 'Well, he is a shoemaker, so naturally he is not wearing any shoes.' One very powerful image in the 'West' painting shows Shakespeare and Robert Burns having a duel. Michael says that the writers are duelling with words to express the power of literature. Books strapped to their bodies form their protection.

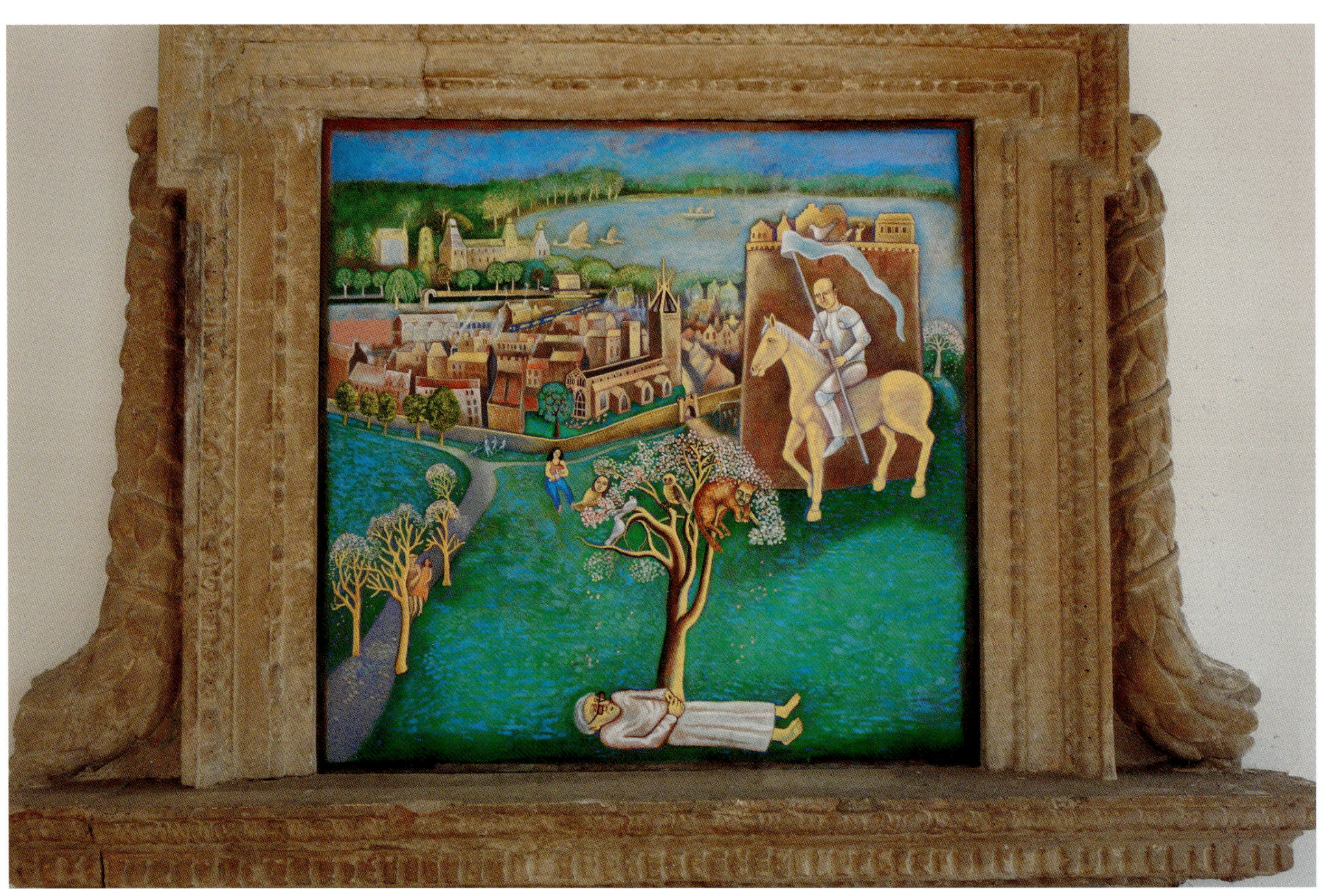

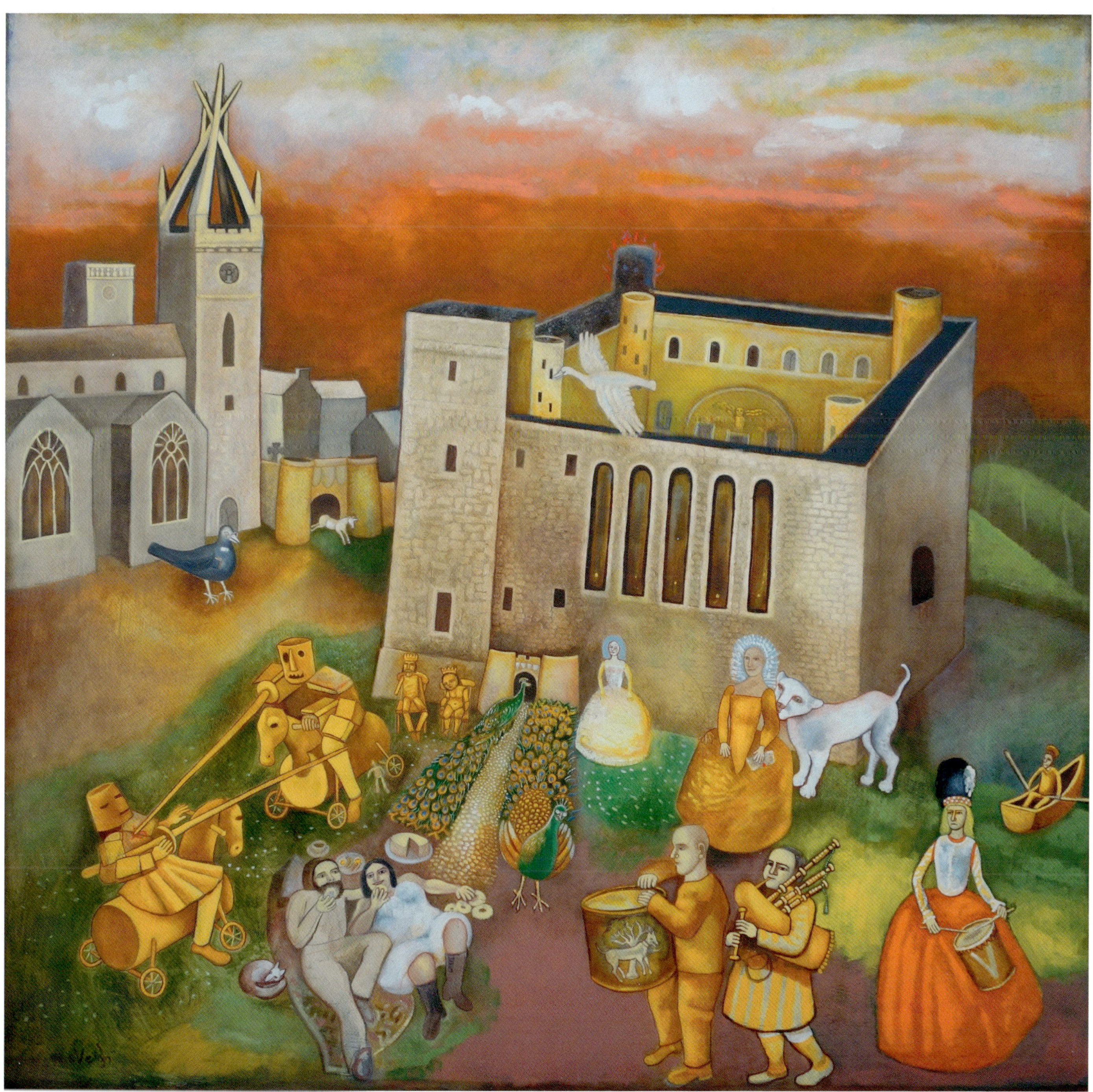

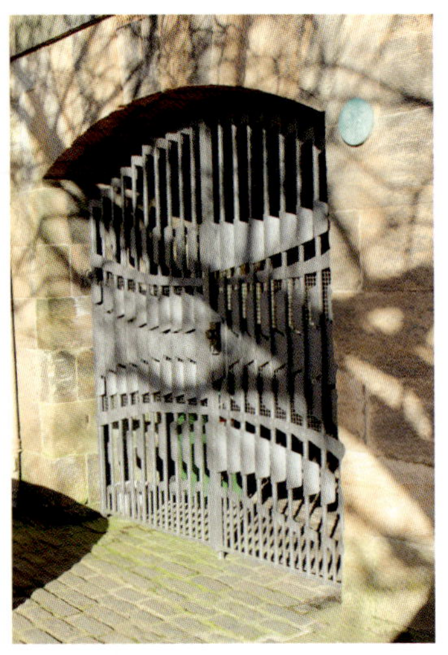

Pend gates at the Burgh Halls, Linlithgow by Byres Forge, Ratho
© Byres Forge, Ratho
© Calum Smith photographer
(Above)
Commissioned by West Lothian Council

New gates to the pend at the side of the Burgh Halls were commissioned as part of the refurbishment works by the architect Malcolm Fraser. These gates close off the side entrance to the halls and they represent a modern interpretation of traditional Scottish defensive portals. The works were designed and created by the artists of Byres Forge, at Ratho. This company has recently installed a second gate in the same style to the rear of the hall as well as preparing decorative, protective gates to the south porch of the nearby St Michael's Parish Church.

In 1995 the citizens of West Lothian were invited by the council to sew the story of their communities. The result was a series of seven colourful wall-hung banners depicting the stories and local people from the council area. The project entitled 'Sew to Speak', was led by the textile artist Kim Patterson.

In her project statement the textile artist said: 'Many of the workshops for this panel were held in an unused shop unit in Linlithgow High Street. We had great fun trying to settle into the space and organise some home comforts like tea and coffee. We soon organised these things into a very productive workspace. Members of the public were invited to drop in and contribute to the making of this panel. Many craft traditions are practised expertly in the Linlithgow area and, with such a wealth of talented artisans, we could not fail to produce a beautiful panel. The virtuoso cross stitch was created by the tapestry group at Cross House (St Michael's church hall) and the intricate woven panels were executed by the women's weaving group. The detail captured here is an amazing representation of 'The Riggs.' Notice the tiny little hens for which real feathers were used and the sweet little hedgehog patiently created with tiny brush bristles.'

The Linlithgow banner depicts a fantastic scene of harlequins dancing in front of the palace gateway, with the palace and the parish church behind, the Cross Well, the Learmonth dovecot and the palace outlined in the distance. Swans fly overhead and also swim in the loch, while an angler casts his line and a dinghy sailor catches the wind. St Magdalene, the passenger canal boat, features at the top with monarchs and armorial arms.

Sew to Speak by Kim Patterson
© Kim Patterson
Commissioned by West Lothian Council
(Below and opposite)

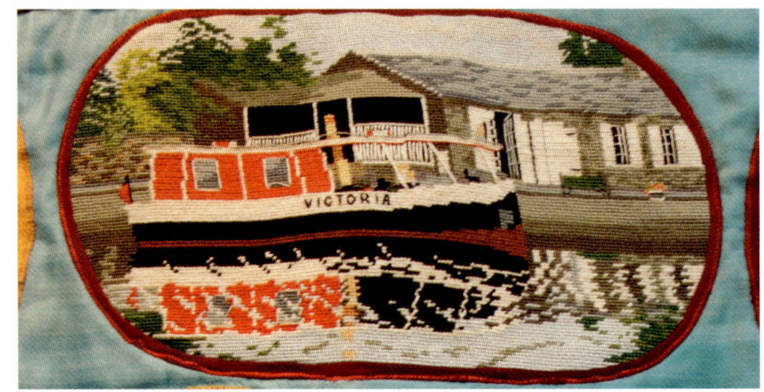

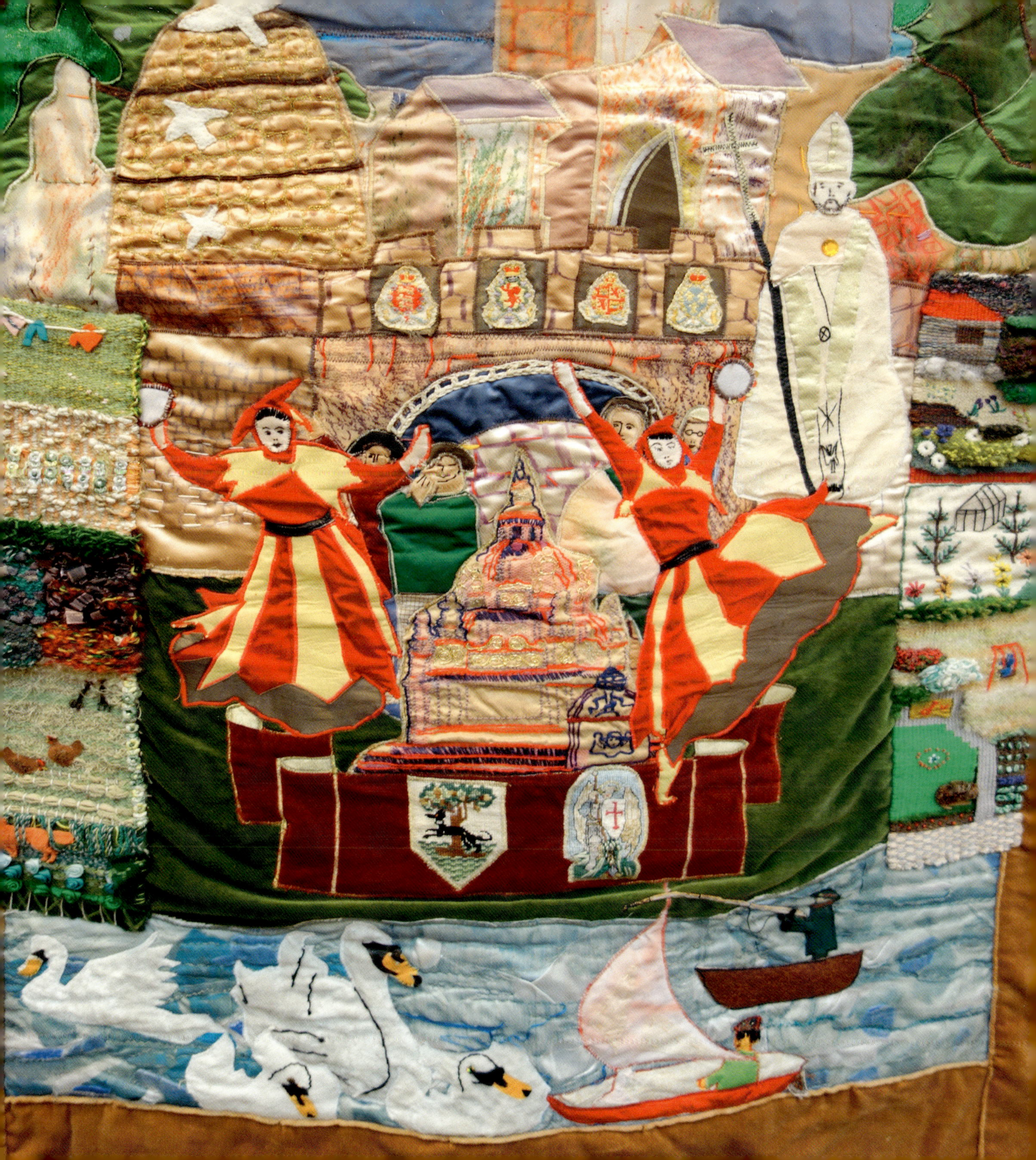

Mary Louise Coulouris catches the sense of Marches Day
© Mary Louise Coulouris
Permission by Gordon Wallace
(Below)

Mary Louise Coulouris captures the Reed Band at the Cross
© Mary Louise Coulouris
Permission Gordon Wallace
(Opposite)

In 'Singing Softly to the Light: The Biography of Mary Louise Coulouris,' Gordon Wallace recalls how 'through the passenger seat window I saw a small town sitting by the side of a loch with what I took as a ruined castle by its banks and an old church with a modern spire towering above it. I took the next slip-road exit and doubled back on a pleasant tree-lined road running between fields of grazing cattle. Shortly, a sign told me I was entering the Royal Burgh of Linlithgow. It was news to me: even as a Scot I hadn't heard of the town before.' This was how Mary Louise Coulouris, Gordon's wife, first came to Linlithgow.

Mary Louise Coulouris caught the sense of a vibrant community in her exuberant Marches Day mural painted in the upstairs waiting room of Linlithgow station. Her commission was part of the improvements to the station carried out in 1985. Floats, bands and spectators are captured in vivid colours. She said, 'Art should be the place where people can slow down, indulge their senses with a static image that can take being looked at for more than twelve seconds.'

Gordon recalls: 'The wall given to her for the mural measured around 20 feet long and 12 feet tall at its highest point. It was a large area to fill and it faced passengers as they climbed the stairs to the eastbound platform and took their seats in a newly-appointed waiting area. The main question though was the content. People in the town had plenty of suggestions. Railway enthusiasts suggested commemorative scenes of the steam era;

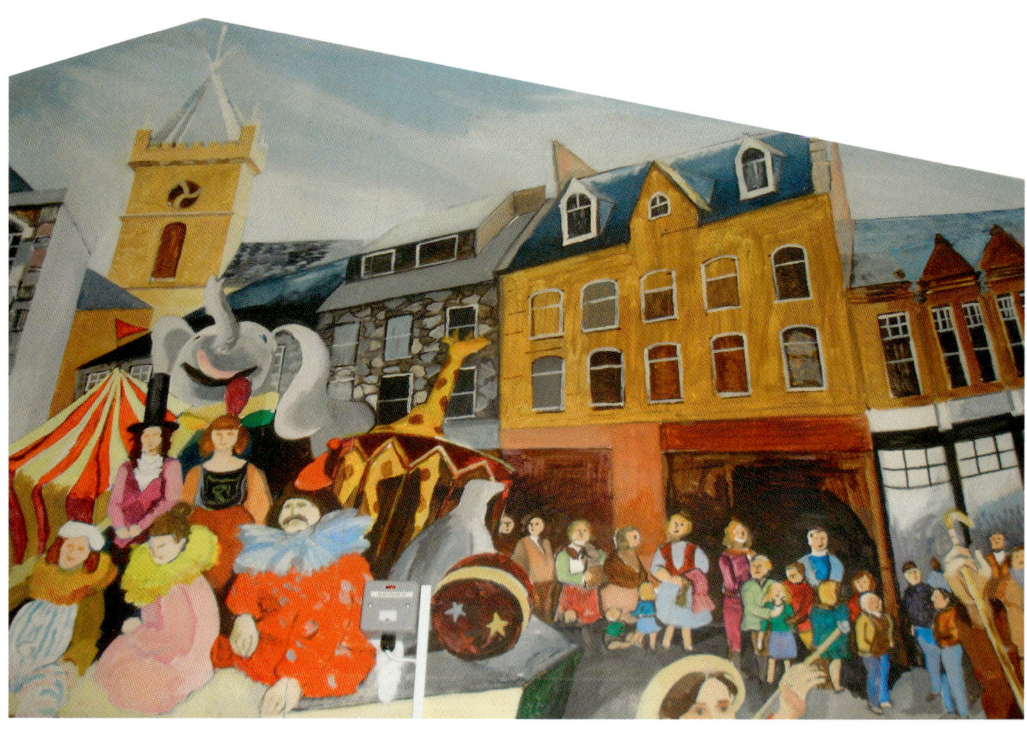

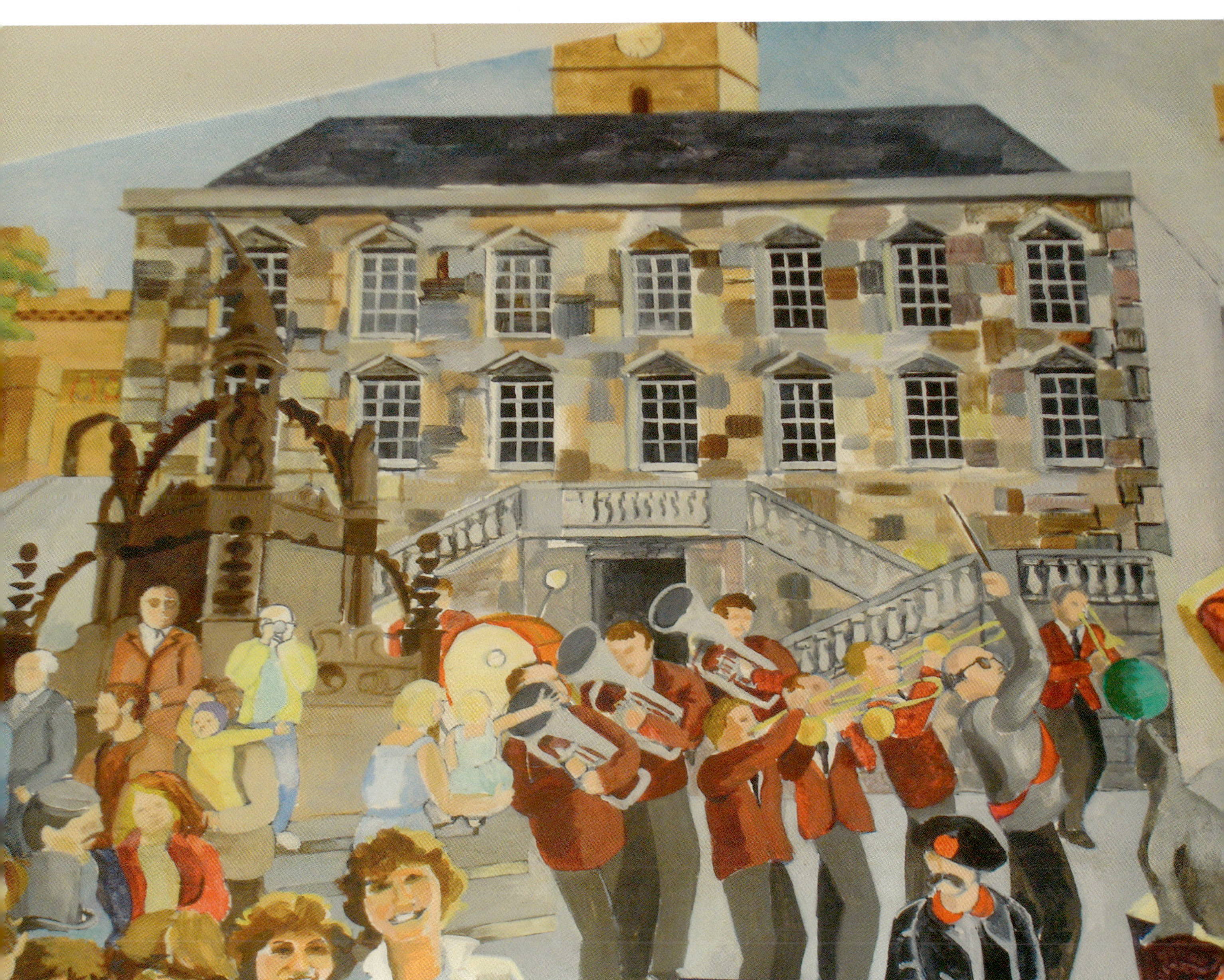

Linlithgow in Bloom by local primary school children, a Burgh Beautiful project
© Calum Smith photographer
(Below)

Union Canal Linlithgow by Mary Louise Coulouris
© Parliamentary Art Collection
www.parliament.uk/art
(Opposite)

others proposed an amalgam of the town's history marked by its many buildings dating back to medieval times. Yet others recommended a simple landscape scene based on the rolling farmland and low hills surrounding Linlithgow. Mary Louise listened, but it is doubtful if she ever considered anything other than the idea which had sprung immediately to mind as soon as she heard she had been given the commission. The mural would contain many of the suggestions people made: at heart, however, would be the whole idea of people in the community.'

Born in the USA, Mary worked from her Strawberry Bank studio, in Linlithgow, and was experienced in the creation of public art in health facilities as well as in play areas. An award-winning mural inspired by her at the Springfield Community Wing in Linlithgow has, unfortunately, been painted over.

Three paintings by Mary Louise Coulouris hang in the Palace of Westminster in London, including a lively watercolour entitled 'Union Canal Linlithgow.' It looks across the Linlithgow Canal Basin, from the towpath towards the four moored canal boats. The doors of the canal tearooms are flung wide open indicating that the Linlithgow Union Canal Society is ready for business.

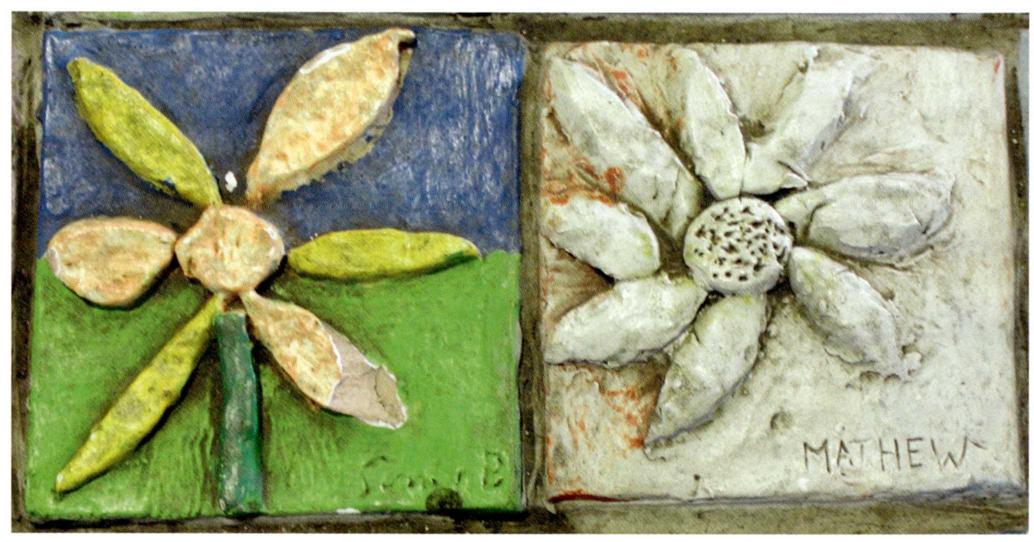

Also at Linlithgow Station, in the same space as the Mary Louise Coulouris mural, is a display of ceramic tiles entitled 'Linlithgow in Bloom'. In 2006, the artist Colin Parker, commissioned by First ScotRail, taught local primary school children to design ceramic tiles with a floral theme and to sign their pieces, thus leaving their mark.

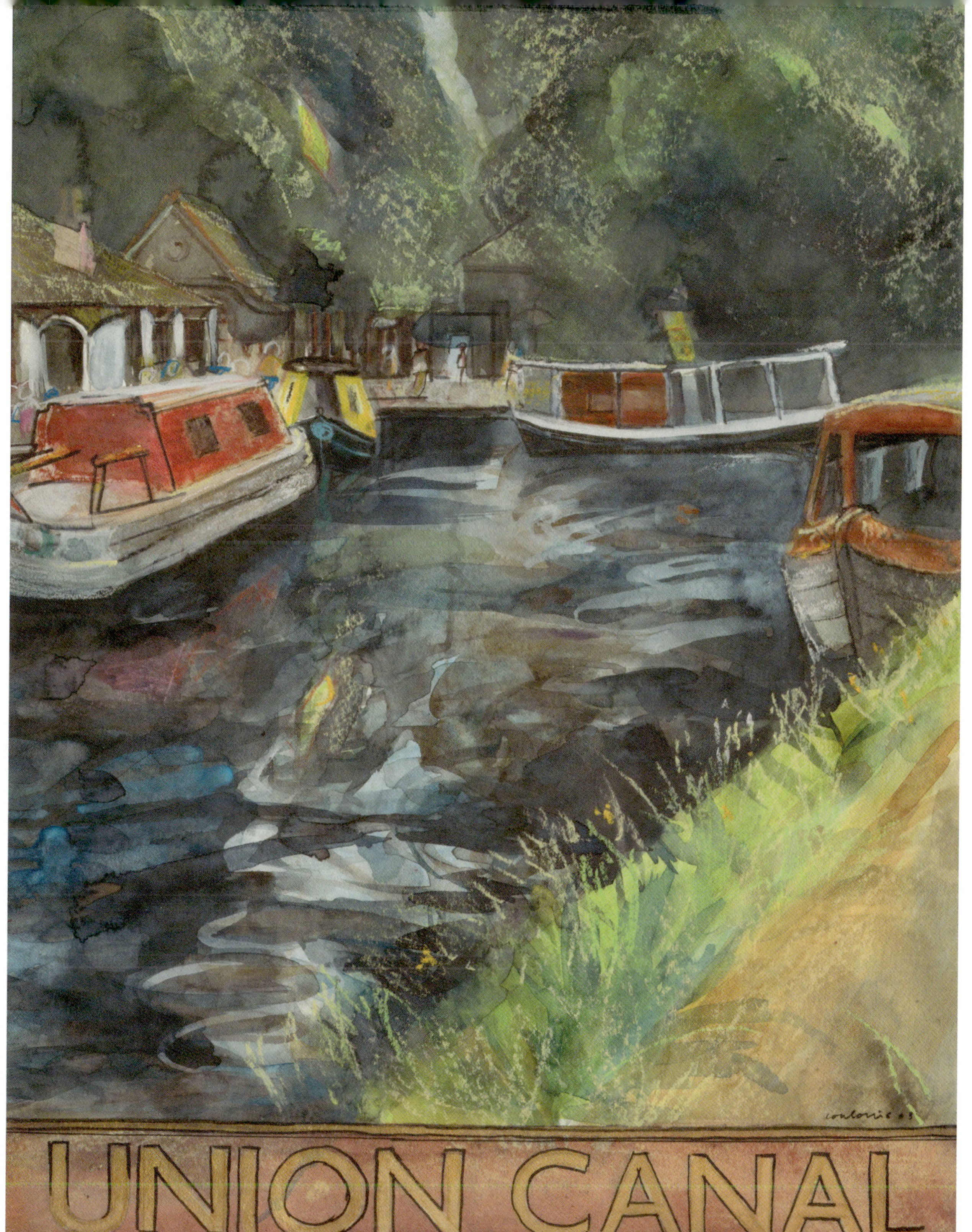
UNION CANAL
LINLITHGOW

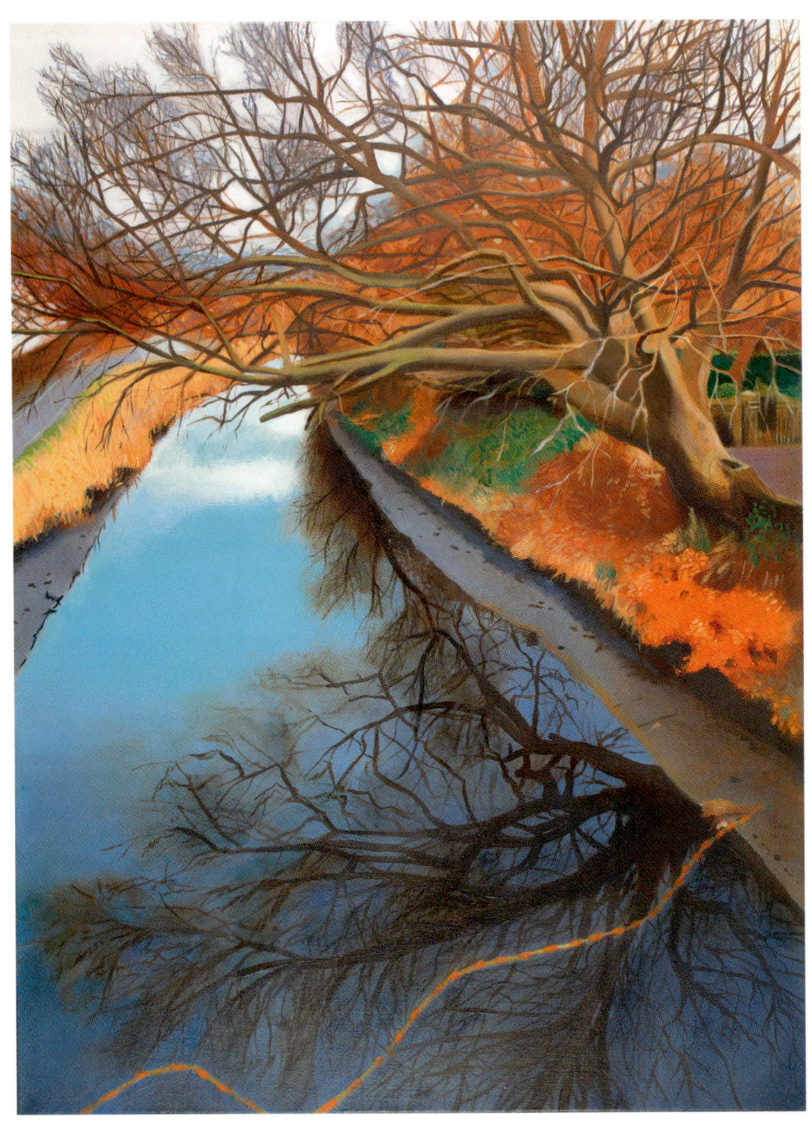

The day they drained the canal at Linlithgow, by Lesley Banks © Lesley Banks (Right)

Winter Pinks and the Giant Beech by Kate Downie © Kate Downie (Opposite)

The water of the canal has long exerted an interest for painters. At bridge no 44, two contemporary artists have looked from the same viewpoint: Lesley Banks and Kate Downie. Kate's colours are subdued in her painting, 'Winter Pinks and the Giant Beech,' capturing the reflection of the mature tree on the south bank as well as two canal-side houses and the spire of St Michael's Parish Church in the distance. It featured in the 2011 'Dialogue with the Land' exhibition in the town. Work periodically is required to be carried out to the Union Canal. In her oil painting, Lesley Banks captures the canal-side mud exposed by the dropping of the water level. The reflection in the water of the same tree is beautifully captured.

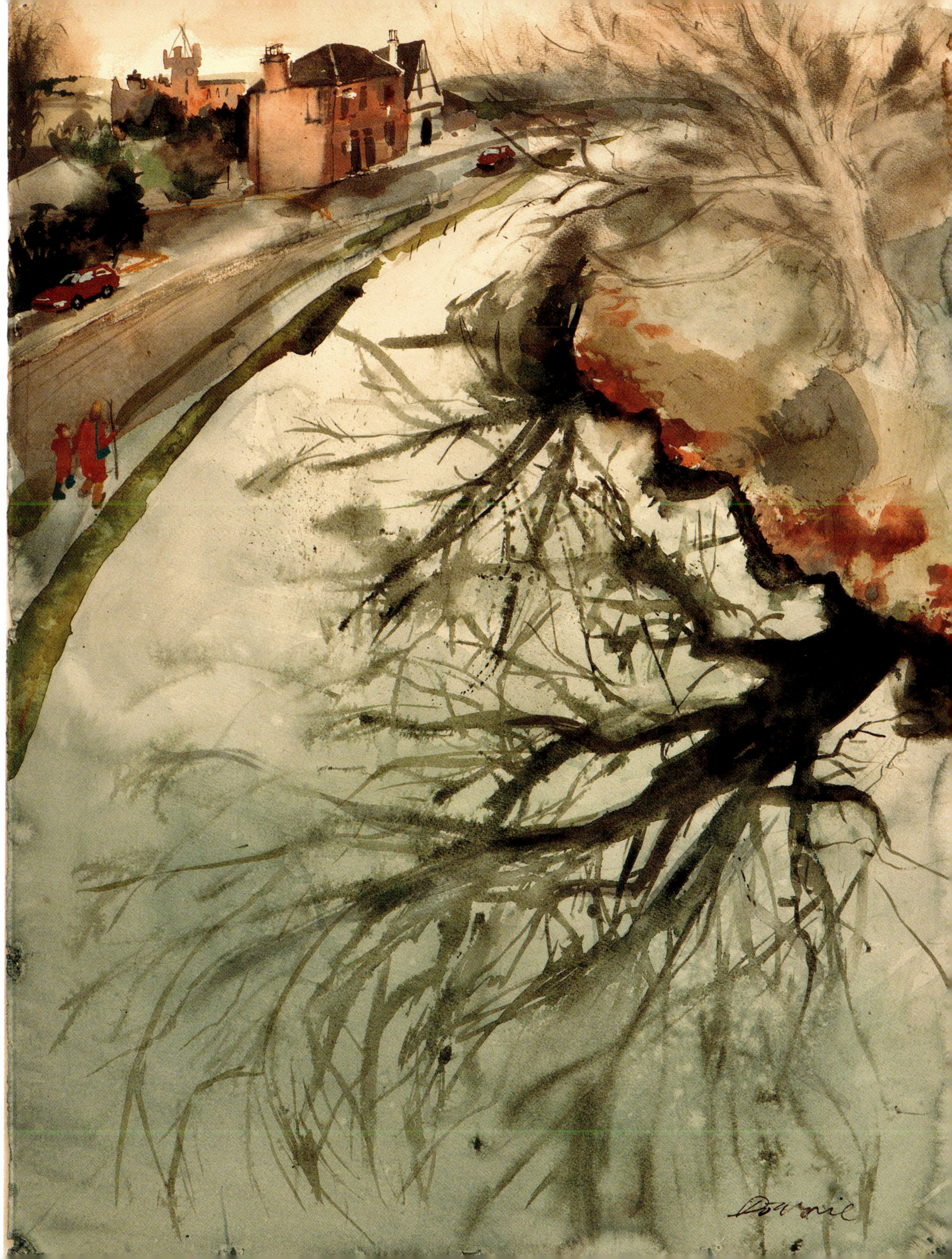

Once again textile art is on display at Linlithgow. Three banners depicting aspects of Linlithgow hang at the mezzanine level of Linlithgow Station in full view of all who pass. They feature aspects of Linlithgow including a collage of some of its notable buildings, among them the church spire with a base of flowers and the town's iconic heraldic dog.

These exquisite wall hangings were commissioned by Burgh Beautiful Linlithgow, hence the floral emphasis, and were designed and sewn by Linlithgow and District Embroiderers' Guild and funded by ScotRail.

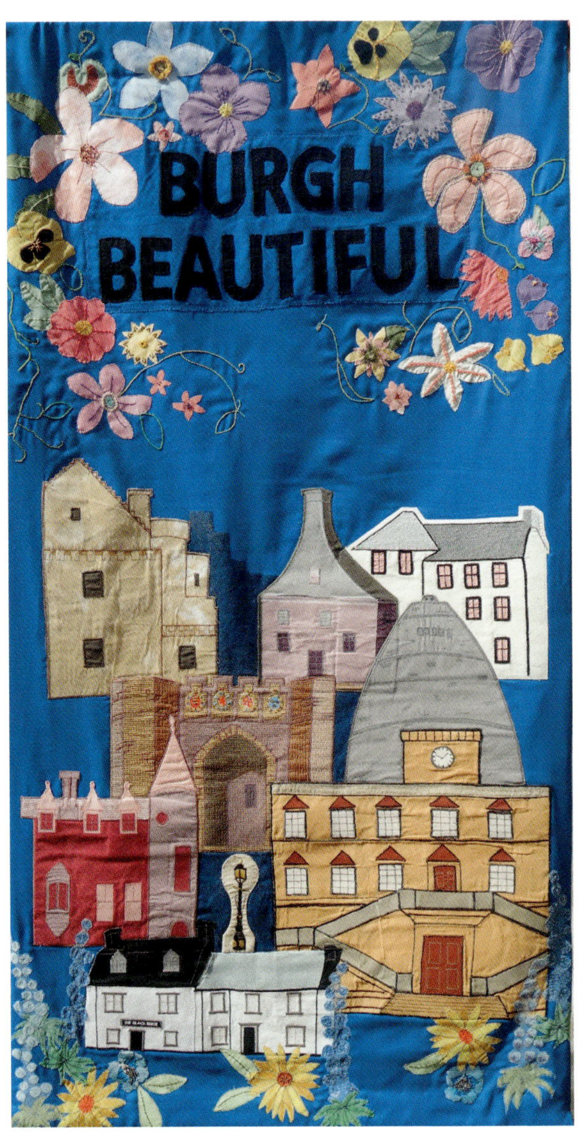

Linlithgow in stitches featuring Burgh Beautiful and the town of Linlithgow
© Linlithgow and District Embroiderers' Guild
(Right)

Linlithgow in stitches featuring the spire of St Michael's Parish Church
© Linlithgow and District Embroiderers' Guild
(Opposite, left)

Linlithgow in stitches featuring the Black Bitch
© Linlithgow and District Embroiderers' Guild
(Opposite, right)

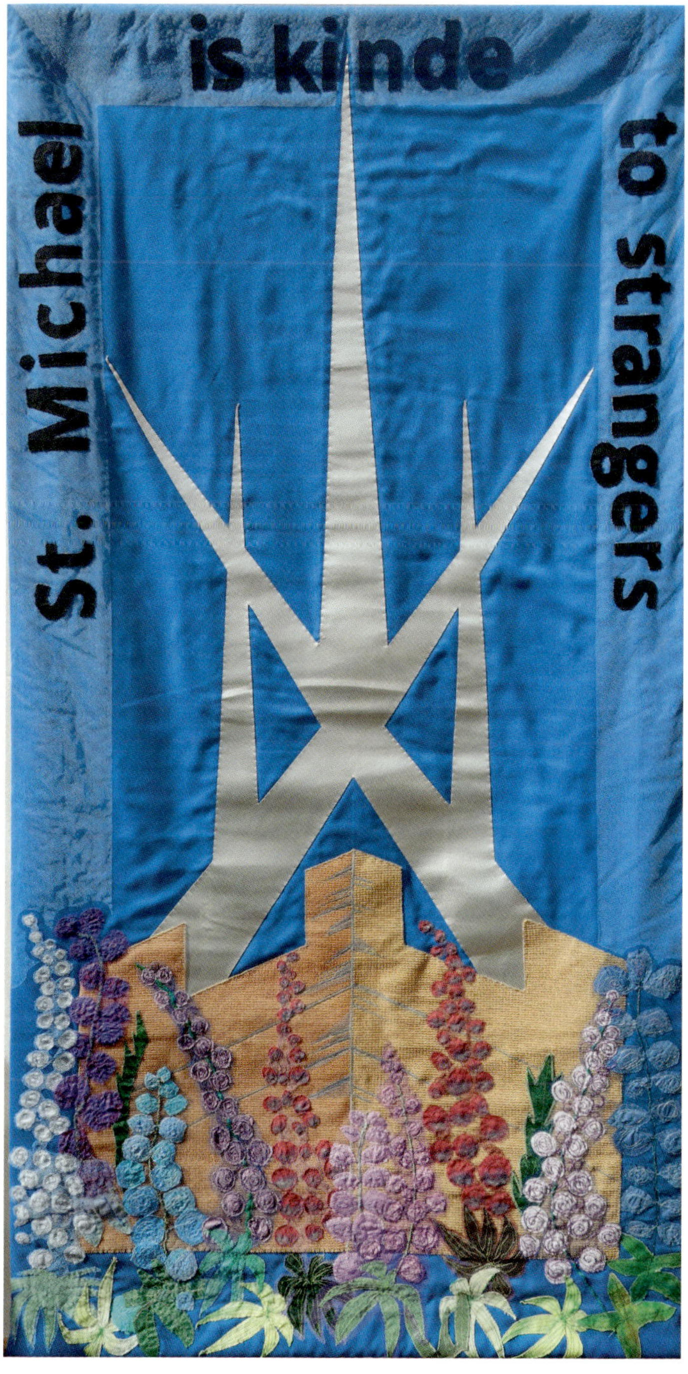

St. Michael is kinde to strangers

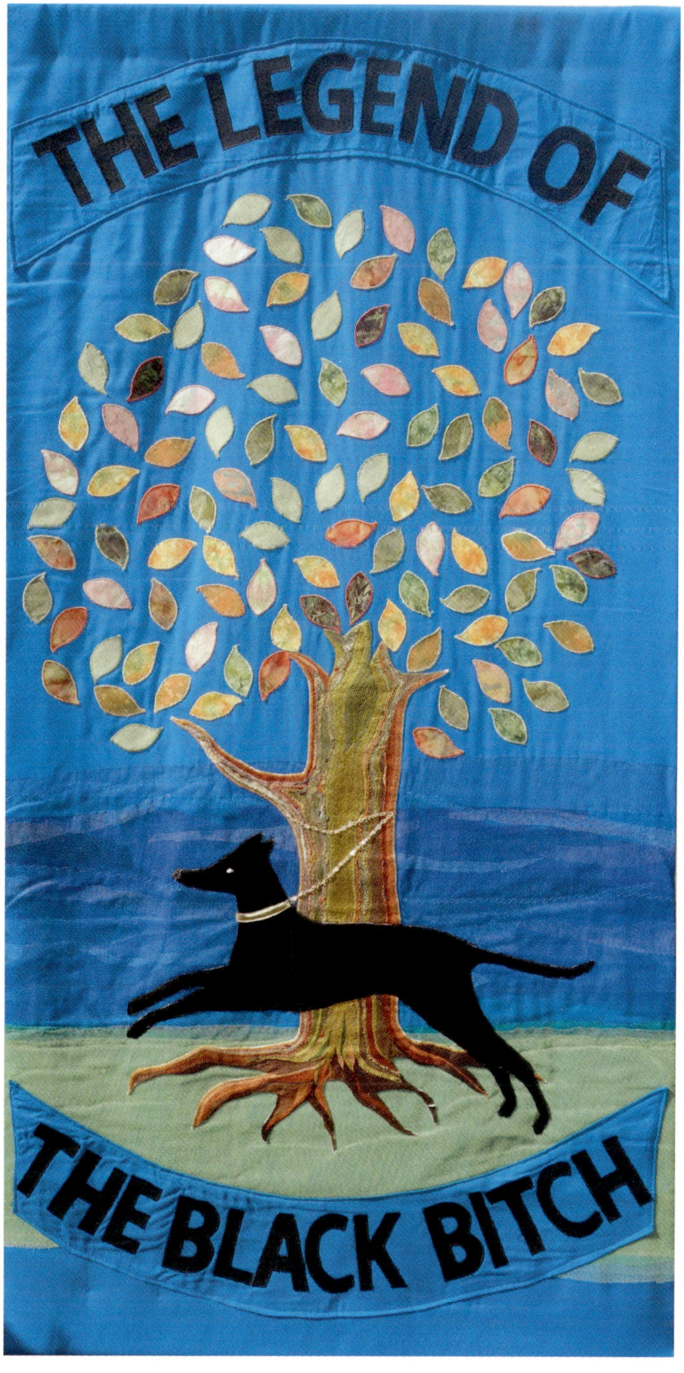

THE LEGEND OF
THE BLACK BITCH

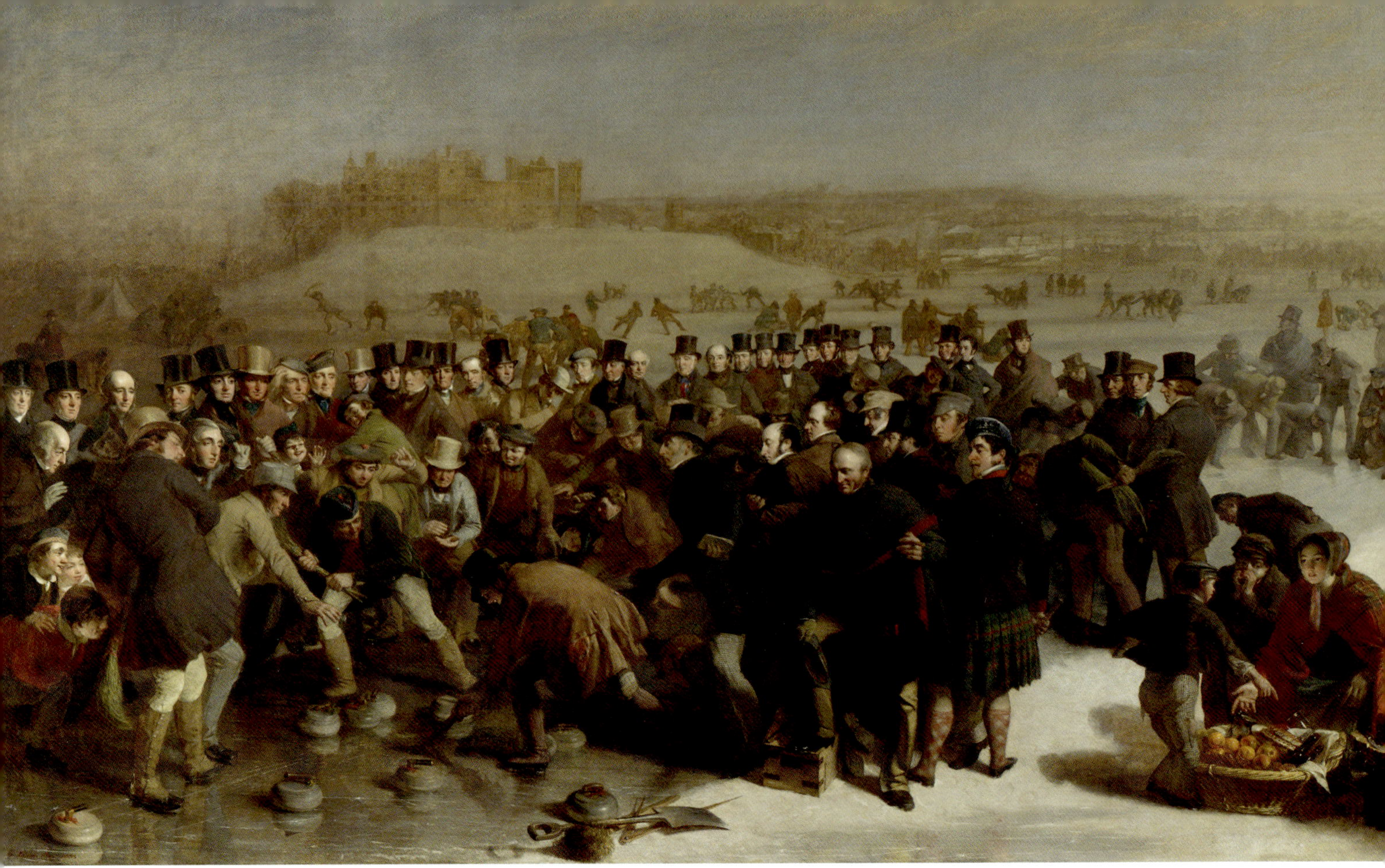

'The Grand Match of the Royal Caledonian Club at Linlithgow, 1848' by Charles Lees
© Charles Lees. 'The Grand Match of the Royal Caledonian Club at Linlithgow, 1848' National Galleries of Scotland Long Loan in 2014
(Above)

Linlithgow Curling Club, founded in 1820, is one of the oldest curling clubs in the world. Its logo features Linlithgow's Black Bitch image. Over many centuries, curling has been played in icy weather on ponds and lochs across Scotland.

'The Grand Match of the Royal Caledonian Club at Linlithgow, 1848' is a painting of curling on Linlithgow Loch which can be viewed at the Scottish Portrait Gallery in Edinburgh. It is a large oil painting and was painted between 1848 and 1849 when the sport was very popular. It is among the best known images of curling and belongs to the Royal Caledonian Curling Club.

The painter, Charles Lees (1800-80), was born in Cupar, Fife, and trained as a painter in Edinburgh with the artist Sir Henry Raeburn. Lees was elected a Royal Scottish Academician in 1830 and specialised in depicting sporting scenes. 'The Golfers' was his first major sporting picture. A subsequent painting is the 'Grand Match' which took place on January 25, 1848.

There is evidence to suggest that Lees travelled to the homes of curlers to sketch them, so that their likenesses could be accurately included in the large painting which was completed in 1849. The painting shows clearly the curlers' clothing and the single-soled shoes which were in use at the time.

With global warming, future generations may not be able to participate in curling and skating on the ice at Linlithgow Loch. But there has always been the danger of falling through the ice. The presence of underwater springs in the loch is said to have made the practice of curling at Linlithgow dangerous – as Jane Ferguson, the daughter of the Rev. John Ferguson of St Michael's, found out to her cost when she fell through the ice and drowned in 1899. Eleven years earlier, her sister, Esther Struthers Ferguson, was killed when her nightdress caught fire in her home at the top of Manse Road. She is commemorated in the window, entitled 'The Infant Samuel', in the north transept of St Michael's Church – in a position where her father could see it from the pulpit which was then positioned on the north side of the chancel.

The Infant Samuel window in the north transept, St Michael's Parish Church
© Gordon Young photographer
(Below)

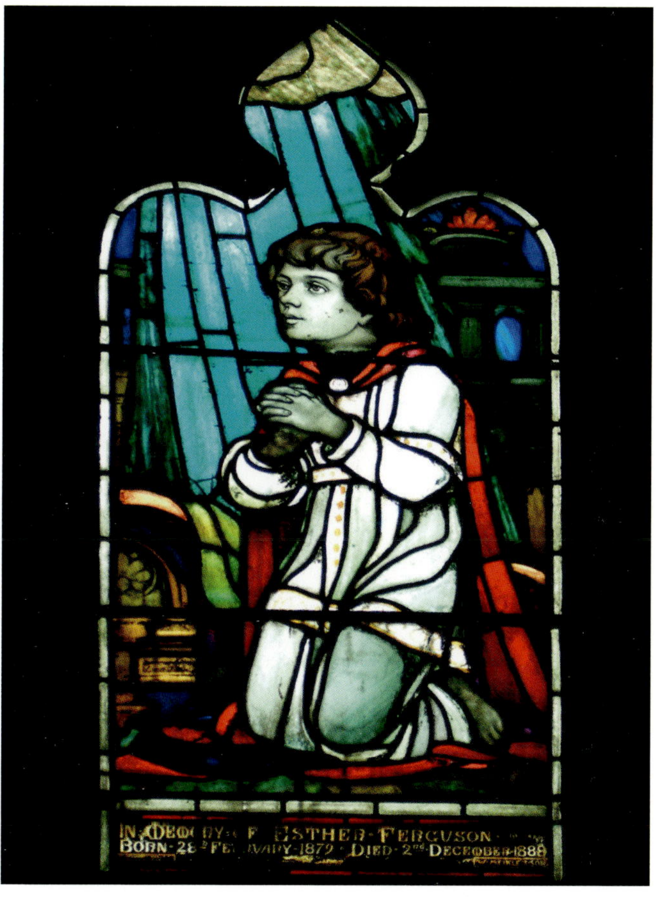

Linlithgow Palace by Chris Taylor
© Chris Taylor
(Below)

Linlithgow Palace by John Lowrie Morrison
© Linlithgow Young People's Project
(Opposite)

The loch takes on another dimension in freezing weather as captured in the oil painting entitled 'Linlithgow Palace' by Chris Taylor. Ice forms a mirror, broken in front where the ice has shattered and is melting. This picture hangs in the Star and Garter Hotel in the High Street, Linlithgow.

Alex Salmond, Scotland's then First Minister, commissioned John Lowrie Morrison (Jolomo) in 2006 to paint the First Minister's Christmas card. Jolomo said: 'Alex phoned the Studio to ask me to do an image for his first card... to which I gaily said yes… however when I put the phone down it dawned on me what I had agreed to, what the heck will I do, I thought?' He said that he quickly thought of a snow scene of Linlithgow Palace. This was the start of many Scottish artists painting a Christmas card and raising a great deal of money for various charities. Jolomo's original painting was sold at auction for £10,000 and the copyright was given to the Linlithgow Young People's Project. Sales of the reproduction continue to go to this worthy cause.

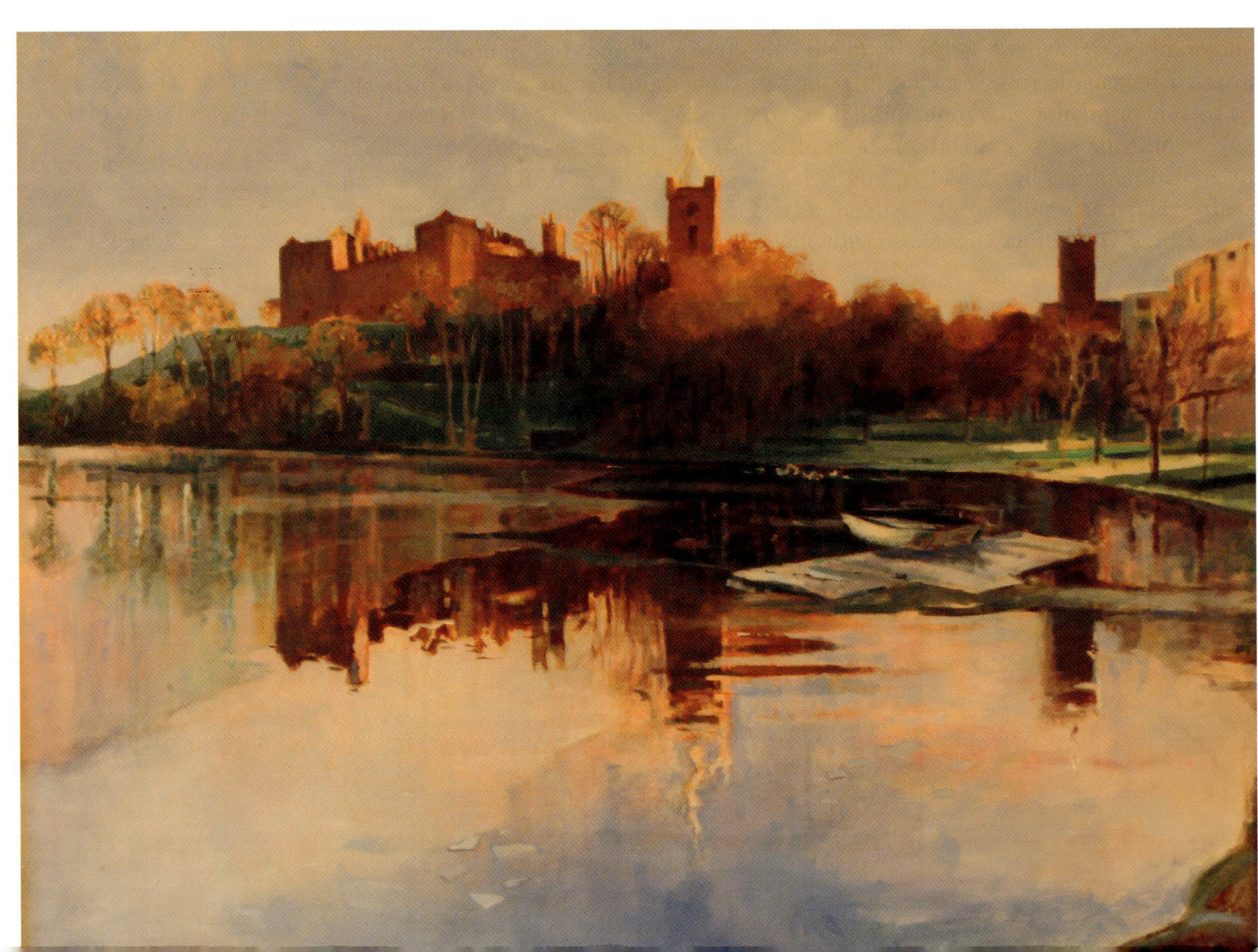

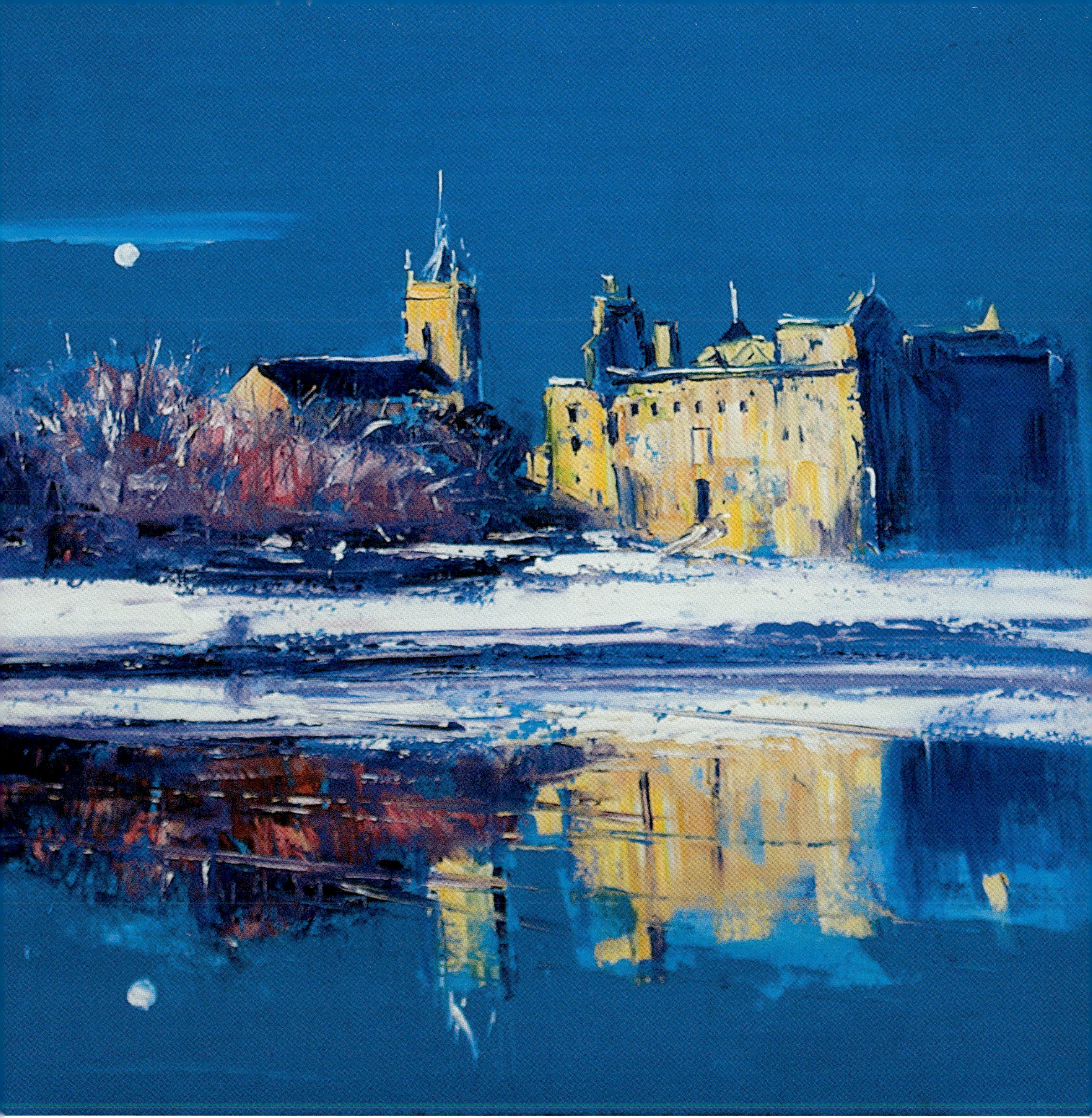

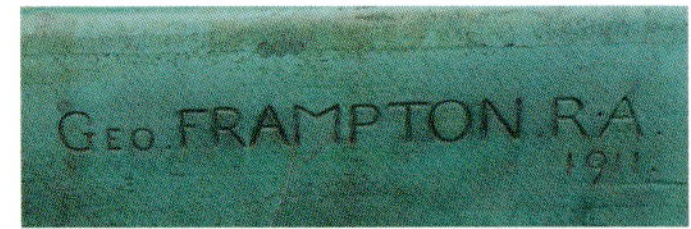

Name of the sculptor, George Frampton RA and detail of John Hope, 1st Marquess of Linlithgow
© Christopher Long photographer
(Above)

The Green Man sculpture by George Frampton
© Christopher Long photographer
(Opposite)

The Green Man sculpture by George Frampton
© Calum Smith photographer
(Below)

Located behind the Burgh Halls and hidden from the High Street is the statue of the right honourable John Adrian Louis Hope, seventh Earl of Hopetoun and first Marquess of Linlithgow. This dignified bronze statue, commissioned by private subscribers, was sculpted by the English artist Sir George Frampton (1860-1928) and was unveiled with great ceremony in front of the Burgh Halls in 1911. Frampton was also the sculptor of the famous statue of Peter Pan in Kensington Gardens in London.

The Times, of 6th October 1911, described the ceremony in detail, saying: 'The memorial, which is the work of Sir George Frampton R.A., takes the form of a bronze statue, the figure, 8ft. 6in. high, resting on a granite pedestal, 9½ ft. high. The figure is shown in a pensive attitude. A scroll is held in the left hand and the robes are of those of the order of the Thistle, with the Star. The figure is considered an excellent likeness.' However, he appears to be holding a hat, not a scroll in his left hand.

He is shown in his official robes as first Governor-General of Australia. John Hope was created first Marquess of Linlithgow in 1902. Over time oxidisation of the metal has turned the bronze green and a misguided cleaning process made the situation worse. Originally located at the Cross, by 1970 the statue and its pedestal had become an obstacle to traffic and were moved to the garden behind the Burgh Halls. He stands there still, forgotten, and with broken sword, affectionately known locally as the 'Green Man'. As Wendy Ball writes in 'Out in the Open, Public Art' in West Lothian: 'He now stands quiet and pensive amongst the trees, but he retains his dignity and brings interest into the gardens.'

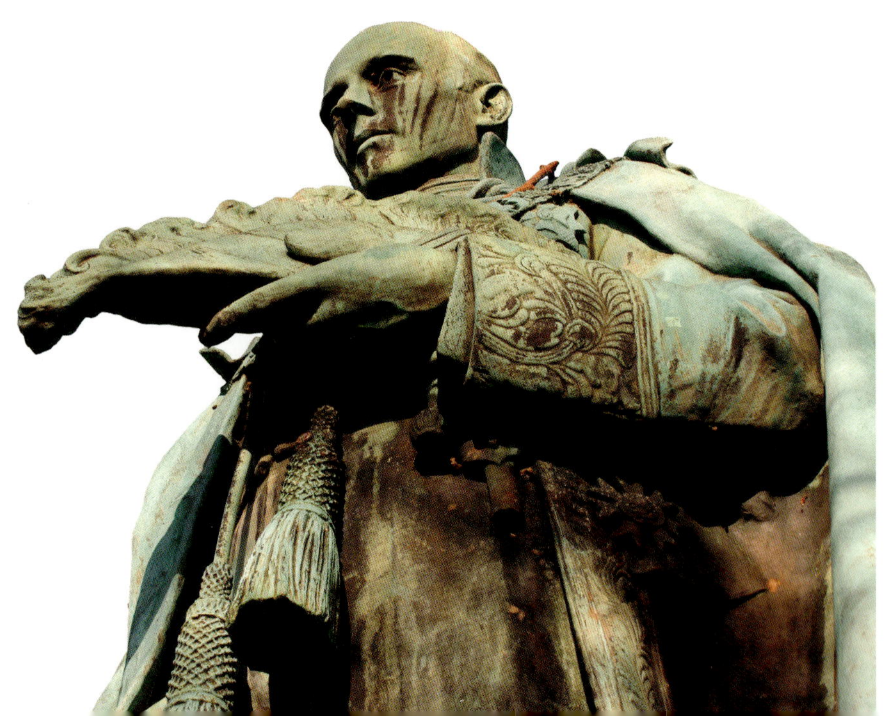

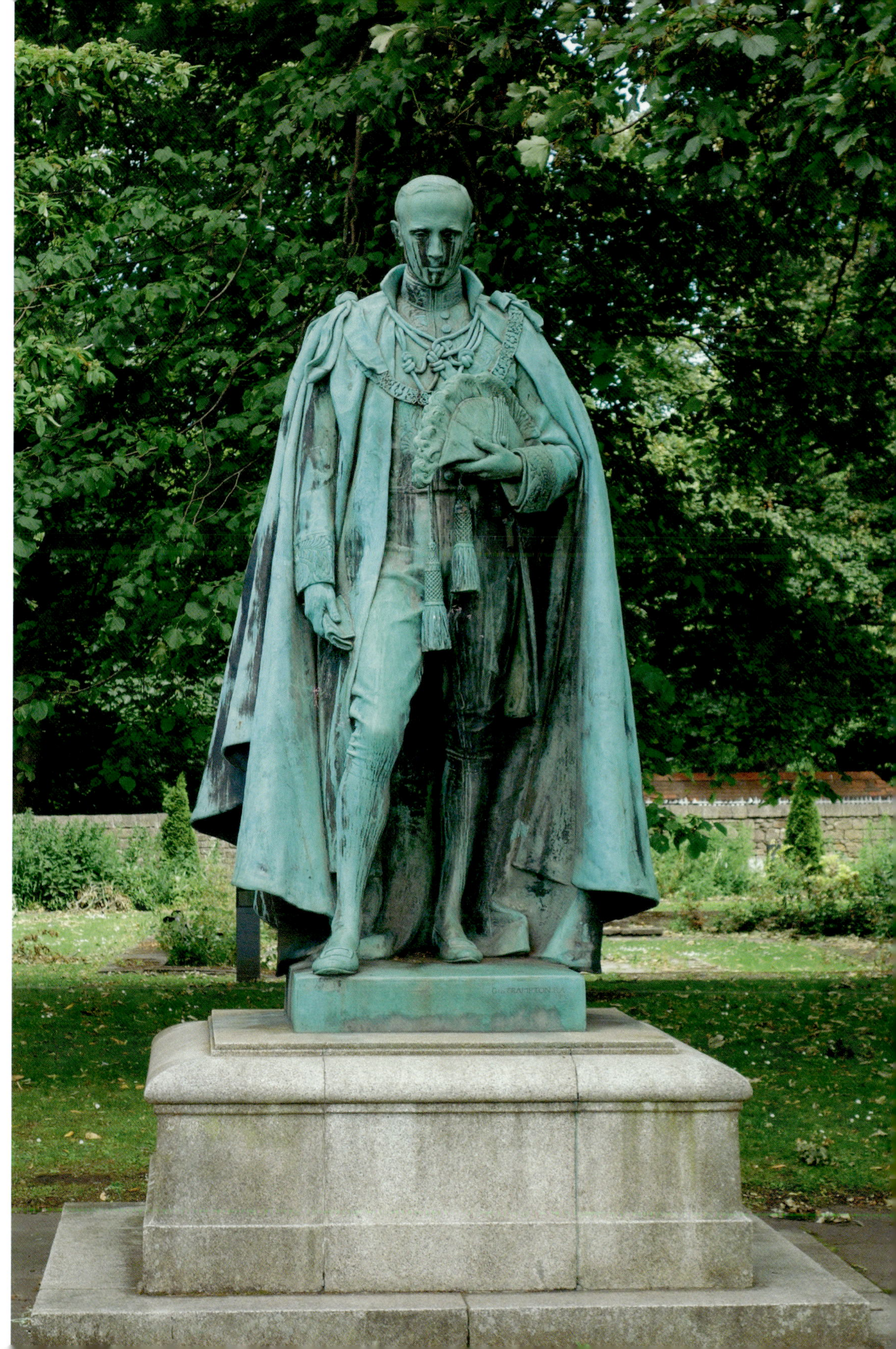

Plan of the Estate of West Port, by John Lauder, 1814
© Heriot-Watt University
(Lower left)

'Katie Wearie's hours' by Tim Chalk
© Tim Chalk
© Mark Donaldson photographer
(Lower right)

Sitting under a tree at the west end of Linlithgow is a sculpture of Katie Wearie. Local legend has it that she was a cattle drover who would stop for her cattle to drink the water at a pond at the west end of the town. She looks exhausted.

The bronze was commissioned by West Lothian Council and Town Management Group in 2011 and was executed by the Edinburgh-based artist Tim Chalk. At the base of the statue are the following words by Paul Streater: 'Katie kens the burns and braes and where the kine can drink, which gies oor Katie plenty time to sit awhile and think.' The sculpture is designed to act as a large sundial with the shadow cast from the sculpted tree above her head.

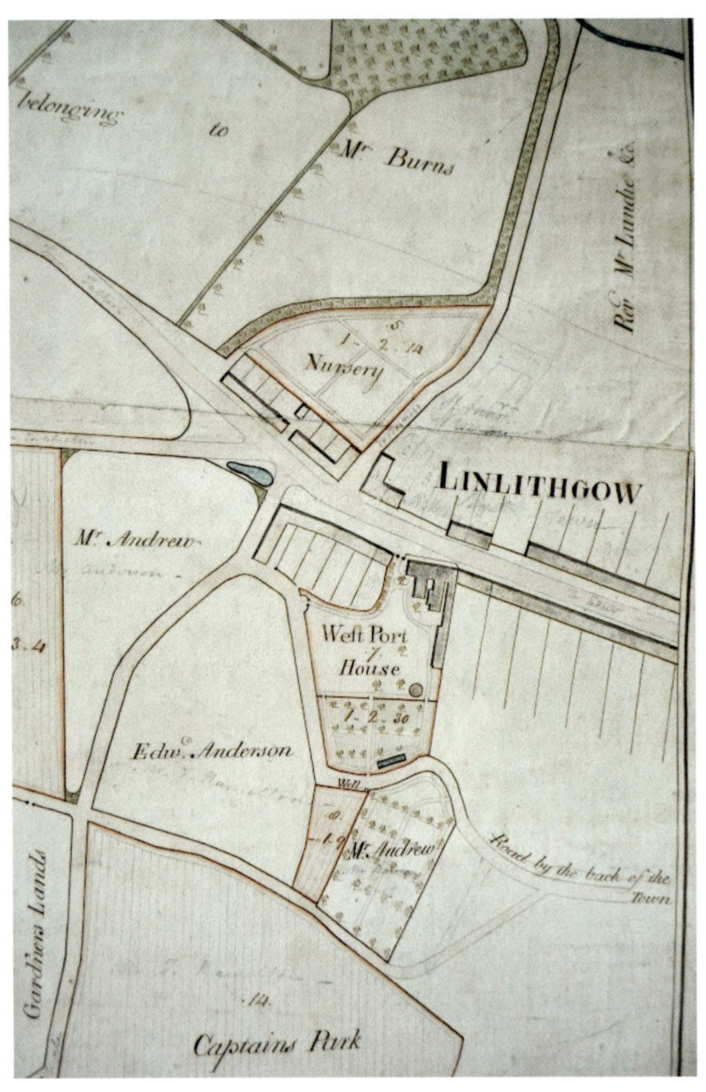

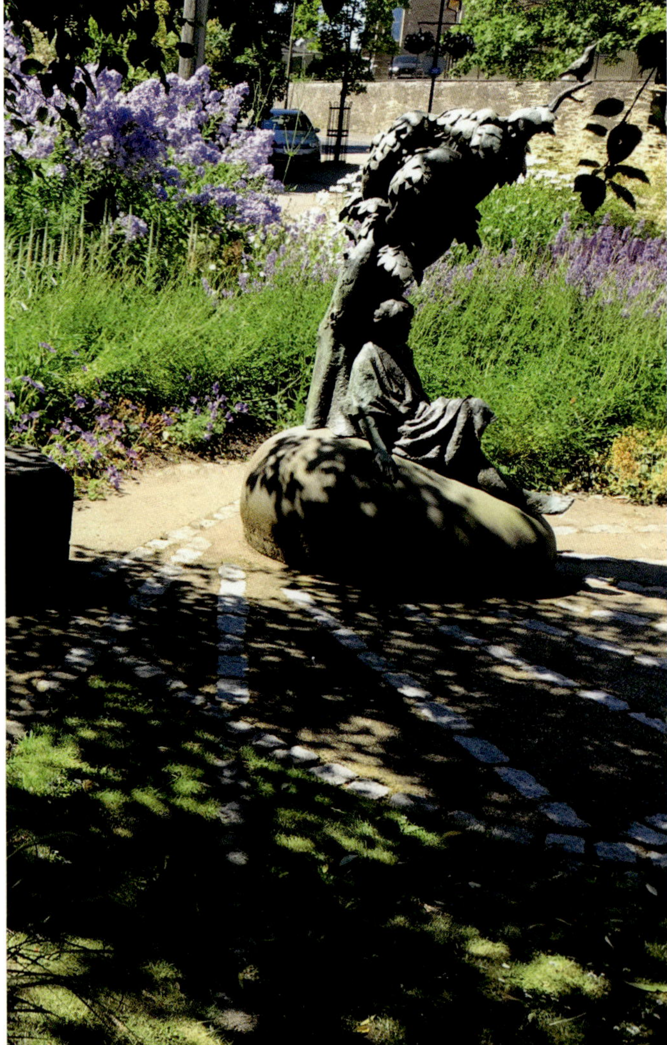

Unrecognised by the majority of Linlithgow townsfolk and visitors there exists in the town a large wall painting that deserves wider recognition. As author Jack Firth, describes in his appreciation entitled 'James Cumming':

> 'Day out, day in, many pass it on the stairs of the Low Port Centre and it does not assault them with self-importance. As he made it, children came and watched James Cumming and he stopped, talked to them, won their confidence and was even ready to take their advice. At a glance it looked like a fairy tale, which meant an open door for understanding to the children, but not necessarily for the adults. There was something distinctly odd about every one of the figures which appeared on the wall, all absorbed in their business, something even dream-like about the gentle colours, the rounded hills in the background.
>
> 'Cumming created spaces for everyone, never separating one from another but linking them with curves which often derive from the occupations of the people. This is their town, their place and they are possessed by it.
>
> 'In the town, the greens and browns express the good earth under their feet: not just Linlithgow, but any small town could be as human as this one. At the top of the mural is the church, another reminder that these people live within the frame of mortality, yet each has the spring of life to them, the running boy, the cat, the dog, the marching drummer. The bustle of life is here, and life with a purpose.'

The mural was painted by the artist, James Cumming, and is entitled 'The Community: A Festival of Time'. In 1987 he was awarded a commission for the Low Port Centre, Linlithgow, by the Edwin Austin Abbey Memorial Trust Fund for Mural Painting in Great Britain. The fund was administered by the Royal Academy of Arts in London and the artist was recommended by Anthony Wheeler, who was the architect of the Low Port Centre.

Cumming was born in Fife in 1922 and pursued what might be called an individual style, separate from the contemporary mainstream of the time. He spent a formative period in Lewis, never stopped working and studied in great detail everything he came across, from the paints he should use to the intricacies of cell structure to space travel. He filled sketchbooks with prodigious drawings, now preserved at the Royal Scottish Academy of Art & Architecture in Edinburgh. In 1994, Edward Gage wrote in the foreword of 'James Cumming,' (published by Mercat Press): 'Sometimes appearing so irascible that sparks seemed literally to emit from his bristling moustache, the artist hummed with latent energy, pzazz and humour – profound and witty enough to encapsulate the highways, byways and personalities of Scottish art in a masterpiece of stand-up comic invention.'

The Community: A Festival of Time by James Cumming
© James Cumming; the artist's estate
(Opposite)

Detail of the mural: Senior Citizen from The Community: A Festival of Time
© James Cumming; the artist's estate
(Below)

James Cumming lived at the Low Port Centre for the three months of painting and became part of the community, known to users of the building. It was a demanding job applying acrylic paint to a hard plaster surface. James thoroughly planned the painting and worked to a definite grid. He died not long after the completion of the mural.

James painted the people found in a small community like Linlithgow. He had decided to paint a mural which transcended any sense of period but depicted people who were part of the continuum. Close examination from the stairway of the Low Port Centre reveals the layers of meaning represented in the mural through people and buildings. Organisations such as the church, the market place, space travel symbolised by the moon, stages of life from childhood through youth, graduation, marriage, widowhood and old age and figures representing professions such as the engineer, teacher, nurse and postman are all there. The artist was keen to explain his thinking behind the images and prepared a key diagram which is framed nearby, in the Low Port Centre. Look out for the figure of the Senior Citizen (number 34 on the diagram) – not a self-portrait as Cumming was too modest for that but a reference to himself through the bushy moustache such as he sported.

This fine mural is an under-appreciated jewel that should be treasured by the townsfolk of Linlithgow.

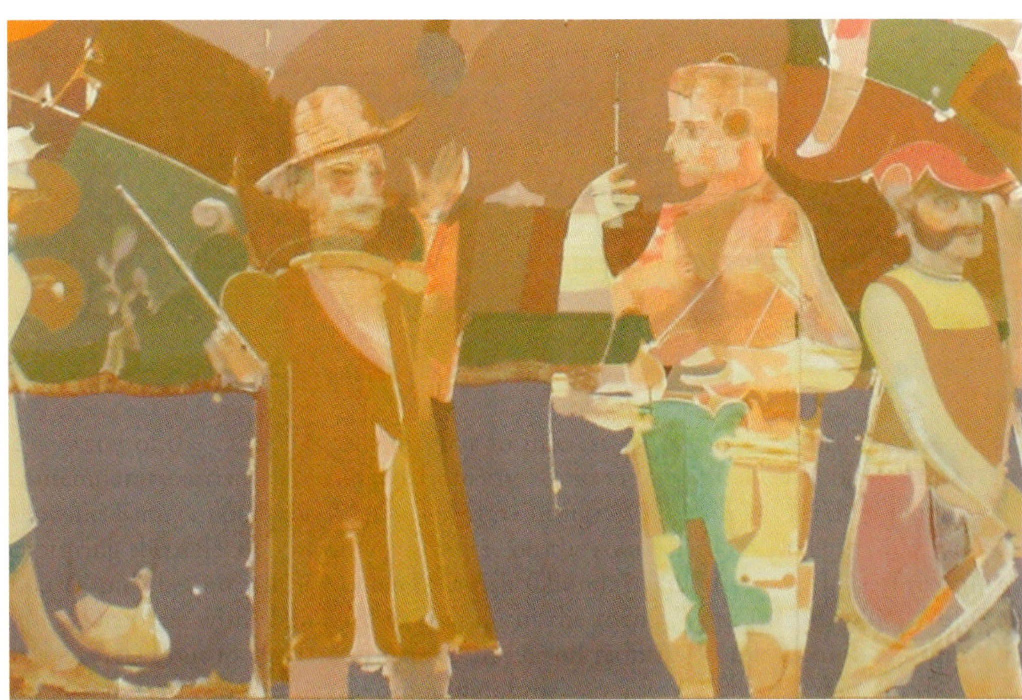

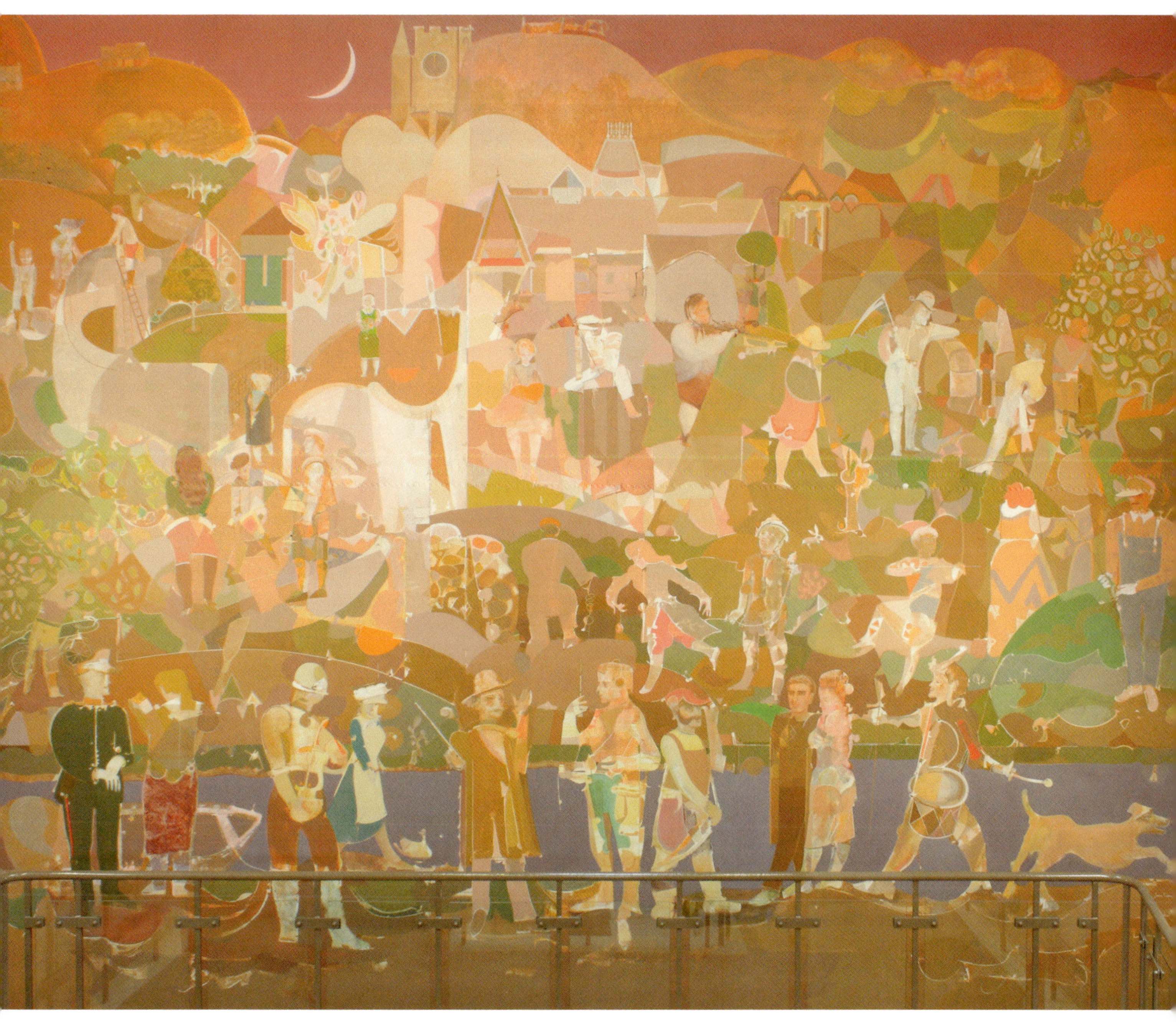

Right Honourable John Hope, Fourth Earl of Hopetoun by Henry Raeburn, 1820

(Opposite)

Also of national importance and equally little known is the treasure house in Linlithgow's unrecognised art gallery – the County Buildings, now known as Tam Dalyell House, opposite the Cross. The buildings demonstrated the burgh's status as county town of West Lothian. This position was lost to Bathgate with local government reorganisation in 1975, and later to Livingston.

Richard Jaques and Charles McKean, writing in 'West Lothian, An Illustrated Architectural Guide', were succinct in dismissing the County Buildings, designed by J. Walker Todd and opened in 1935 as lacking 'fizz' and correct in observing a 'smart interior with good Raeburns.' The building externally displays a provost's lamp decorated with halberds and the Linlithgow coats of arms with coloured glass to the lamp. Handles to the external doors of the building feature lion heads. The principal staircase includes metal balustrades with thistle motifs fabricated by McDonald and Creswick, Edinburgh bronze founders and metal workers. The main stairs in the building were, undoubtedly, designed to accommodate several large pictures moved from the old County Hall (the part of the Burgh Halls on the Kirkgate) and were effectively built into the structure.

Art UK (www.artuk.org) is a website that works with UK public art collections to make them available online. Art UK's mission is to open up public art collections for enjoyment, learning and research and its website has recorded over 200,000 oil paintings of merit throughout the United Kingdom. It comments that 'much of the Council's art collection consists of commissioned portraits of important Linlithgowshire landowners and politicians.'

Several of these paintings, worthy of examination, say something about society of the time. Two are illustrated here. First is the massive painting of John Hope (1765–1823), Earl of Hopetoun, by the artist Henry Raeburn (1756–1823). A plaque below the painting gives details of the sitter's life and career. It reads:

> 'Right Honourable John, Earl of Hopetoun, Viscount Aithrie, Lord Hope Baron Hopetoun, Baron Niddry, Lord Lieutenant of the County of Linlithgow. Knight Grand Cross of the Most Honourable Military Order of the Bath. Lieutenant General. Colonel of the Ninety Second Regiment of Highland Infantry. As a Soldier his name will be classed with those of Abercromby, Moore and Wellington, under the two former of those illustrious Generals, he distinguished himself in high and important Commands in the West Indies, Holland, Egypt, Spain and Portugal. With the latter he was associated in the Gallo-Spanish Campaign, 1813–1814, which shed so much Glory on the British Arms, and gave to Europe the Earnest of its deliverance from the Gigantic Ambition and Tyranny of France. To his Country the value of his Achievements was known, and he received from Parliament and from his Sovereign the highest testimonies and the most honorable rewards of Military Skill and Valour.

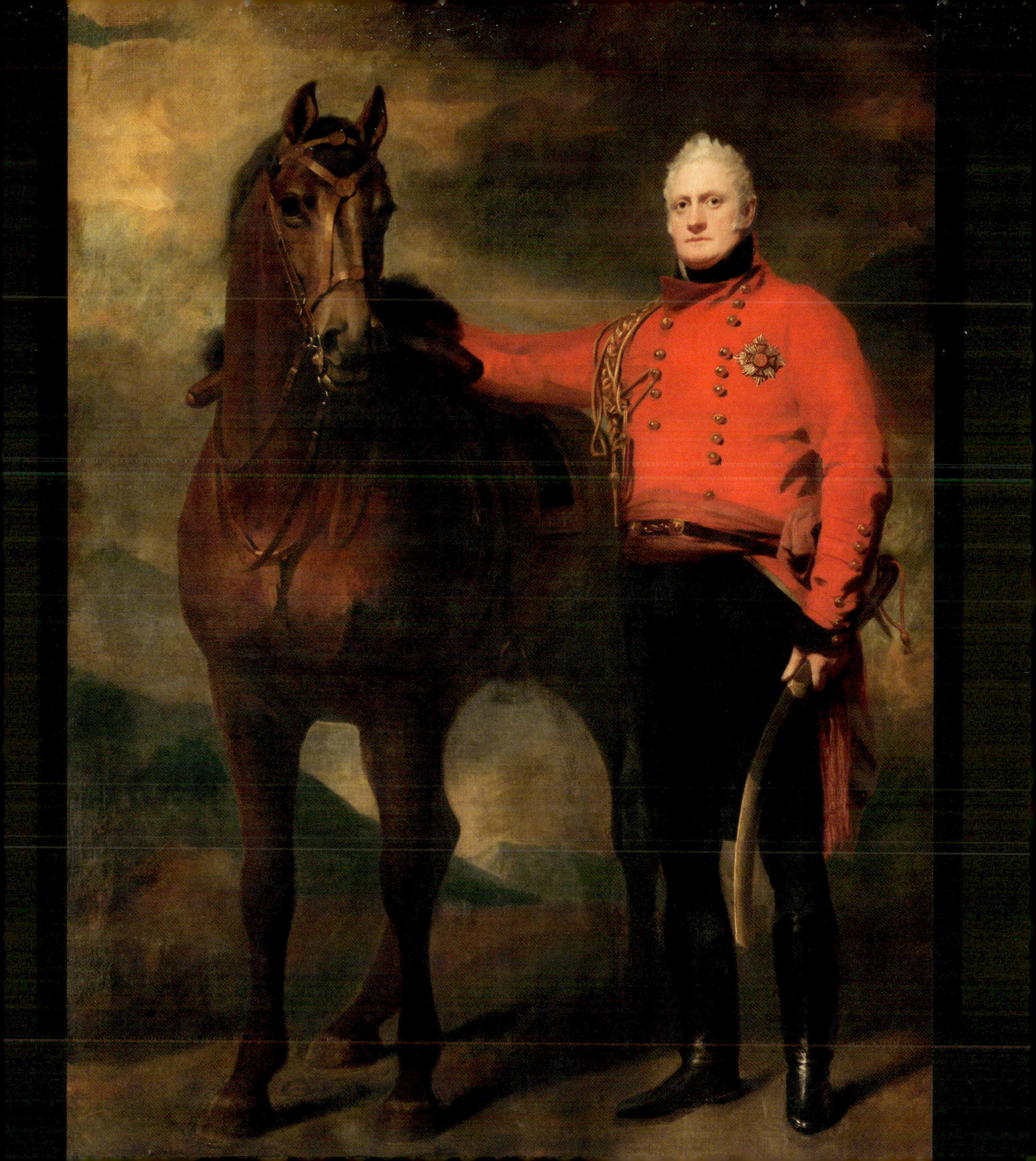

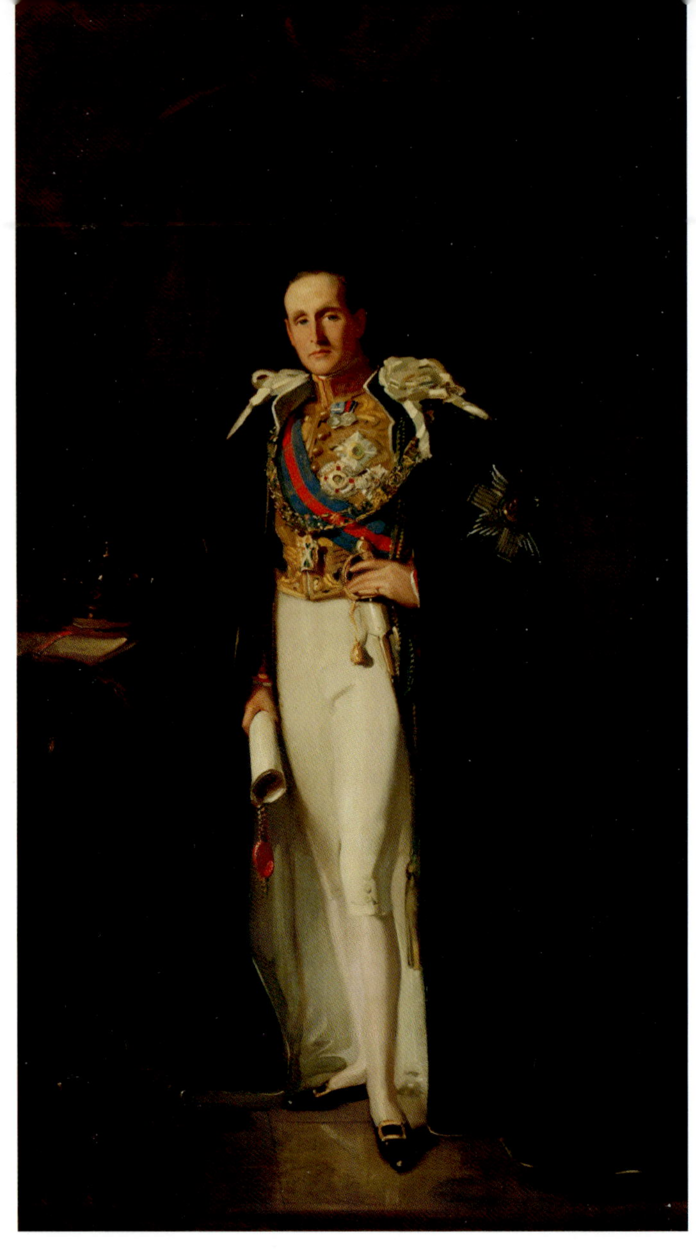

John Adrian Louis, Seventh Earl of Hopetoun and 1st Marquess of Linlithgow, by Robert Brough, 1904
© West Lothian Council
(Above)

In contrast is the fine large oil painting of John Adrian Louis Hope, the 7th Earl of Hopetoun and 1st Marquess of Linlithgow (1860-1908) painted, in court dress, by artist Robert Brough (1872–1905). The artist grew up in Aberdeen and worked in London. He died early as a result of a train accident. The inscription describes how the painting was presented by tenants, friends and neighbours when he retired as the first Governor-General of Australia 'in recognition of his great public services to his country and the respect and esteem in which he was held by all classes.' The sculpture of him behind the Burgh Halls now known as the 'Green Man' has been described previously.

A fine oil painting of Tam Dalyell, local member of parliament between 1962 and 2005, greets visitors to the new partnership centre in Linlithgow High Street which carries his name. The portrait which was painted by Victoria Crowe in 1987 to celebrate his 25th anniversary as the MP for West Lothian, incorporates references to his life, his home at the House of the Binns, including peacocks, and his interest in scientific publications. Peacocks strut in the garden of the House of the Binns, near Linlithgow.

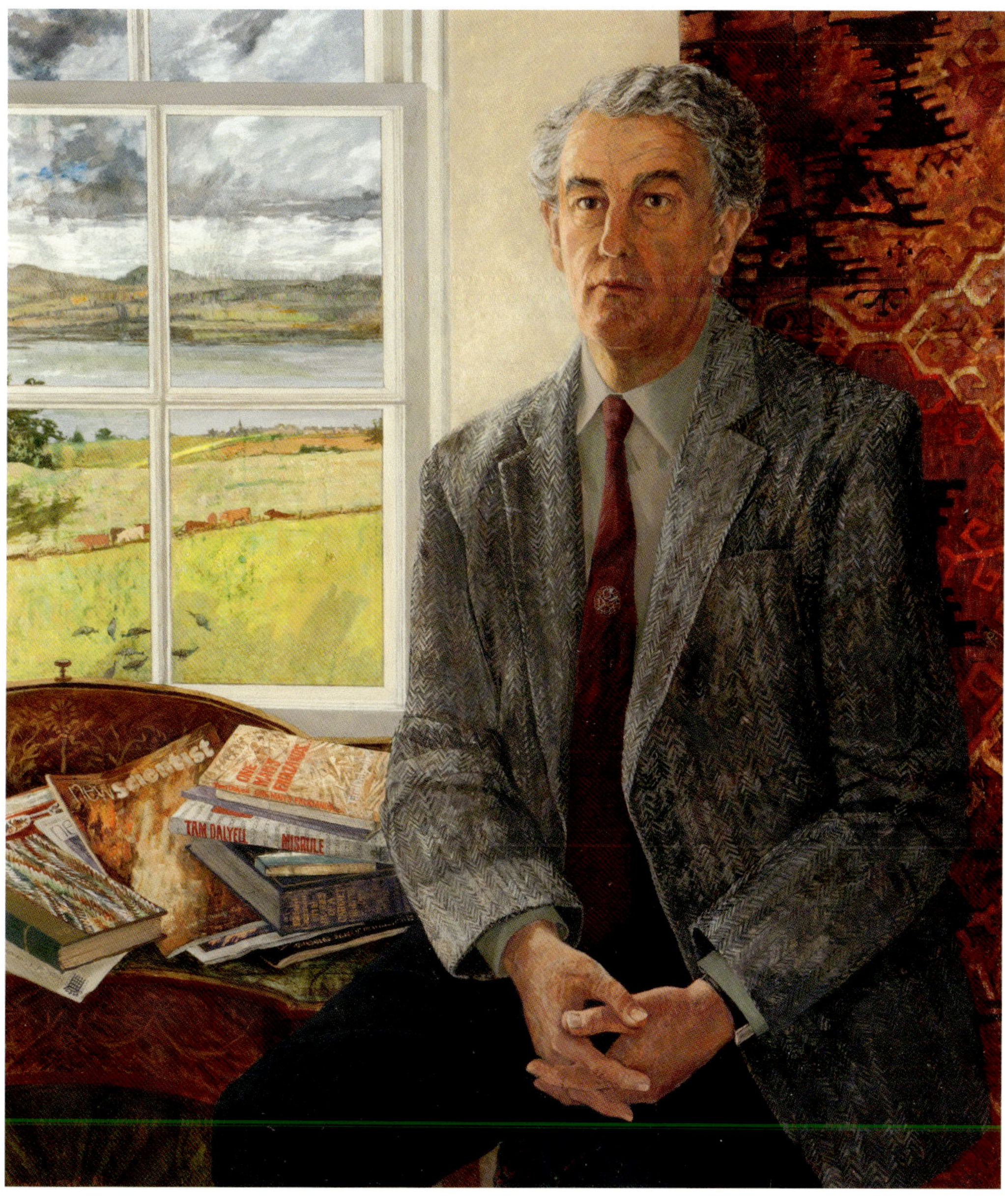

Tam Dalyell by Victoria Crowe, 1987
© Victoria Crowe
© West Lothian Council
(Below)

Bronze plaque of David Waldie by R. Hope Pinker, 1913
© Christopher Long photographer
Detail below and overall opposite

Victoria Crowe studied at Kingston School of Art and the Royal College of Art, London, before being invited to join Edinburgh College of Art in 1968, where she taught drawing and painting until 1998. She is one of Scotland's leading painters and has established herself as one whose work is instantly recognisable. The range of her painting covers landscape, still life and portraits. Her work features in many public and private collections. She lives and works in the Scottish Borders and Venice.

A first floor bronze plaque, now part of the façade of the Four Marys Tavern, 67 High Street, marks the home of a pioneer pharmacist, David Waldie. He was born in Linlithgow in 1813 and was educated in Linlithgow before going on to Edinburgh to study medicine. He practised as a surgeon and apothecary in Linlithgow for a few years before giving up medicine and moving to Liverpool, where he took the post of chemist to the Liverpool Apothecaries' Hall. While in Liverpool Waldie first encountered chloroform, which he managed to produce in an improved, purer form. In 1847 he suggested to James Young Simpson that chloroform might be suitable for use as an anaesthetic. In 1853 Waldie emigrated to India, where he established a chemical works, eventually dying there.

The bronze, by artist, R. Hope Pinker, dates to 1913. Waldie is shown holding a conical flask. The plaque shows a balance on the left and a retort flask on the right sitting on a Bunsen burner. Retorts were used for distillation, so it is possible he is looking at what he has collected in the conical flask from a distillation. The inscription reads:

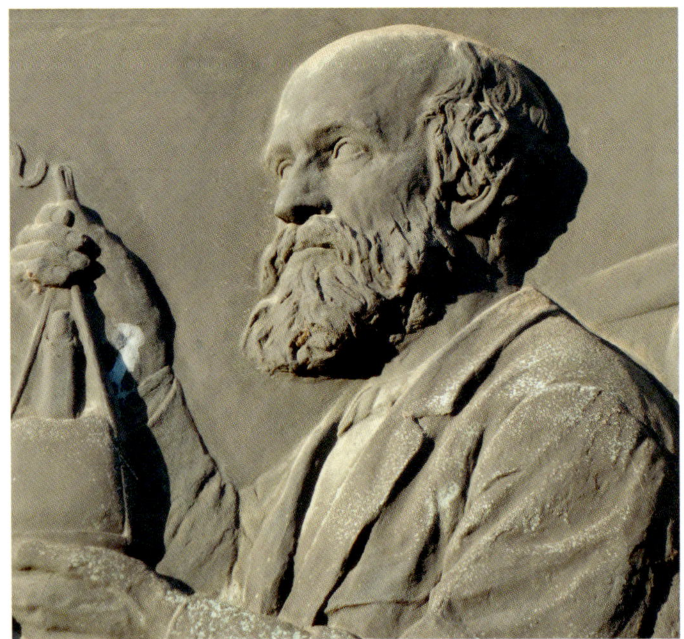

DAVID WALDIE

SURGEON L·R·G·S·E· AND CHEMIST

MEMBER OF ASIATIC SOC · BENGAL

B· LINLITHGOW 1813 D· CALCUTTA 1889·

A PIONEER IN ANAESTHETIC RESEARCH

TO HIM BELONGS THE DISTINCTION

OF HAVING BEEN THE FIRST TO

RECOMMEND AND MAKE PRACTICABLE

THE USE OF CHLOROFORM IN THE

ALLEVATION OF HUMAN SUFFERING

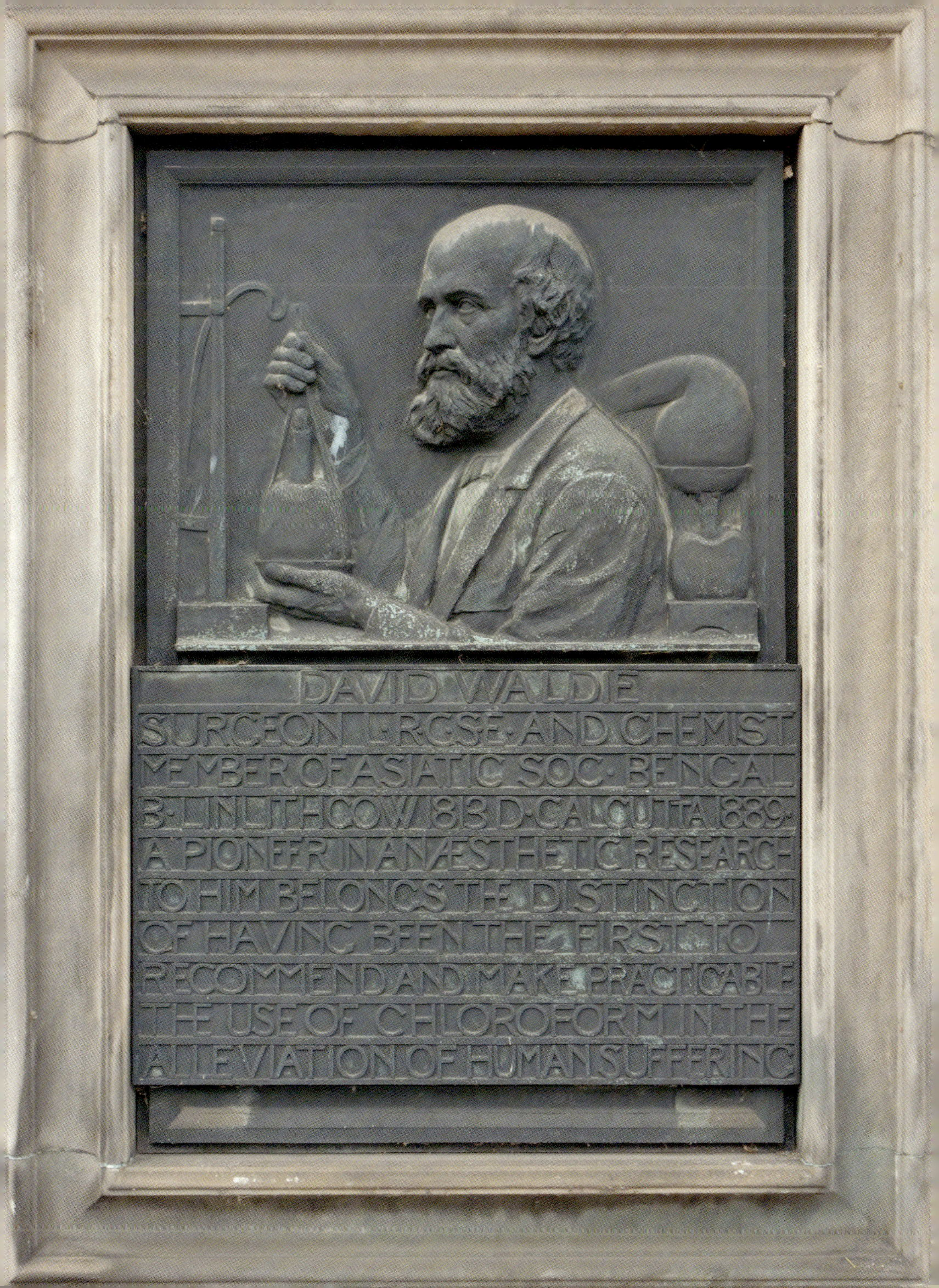
DAVID WALDIE
SURGEON L·R·C·S·E· AND CHEMIST
MEMBER OF ASIATIC SOC· BENGAL
B· LINLITHGOW 1813 D· CALCUTTA 1889·
A PIONEER IN ANÆSTHETIC RESEARCH
TO HIM BELONGS THE DISTINCTION
OF HAVING BEEN THE FIRST TO
RECOMMEND AND MAKE PRACTICABLE
THE USE OF CHLOROFORM IN THE
ALLEVIATION OF HUMAN SUFFERING

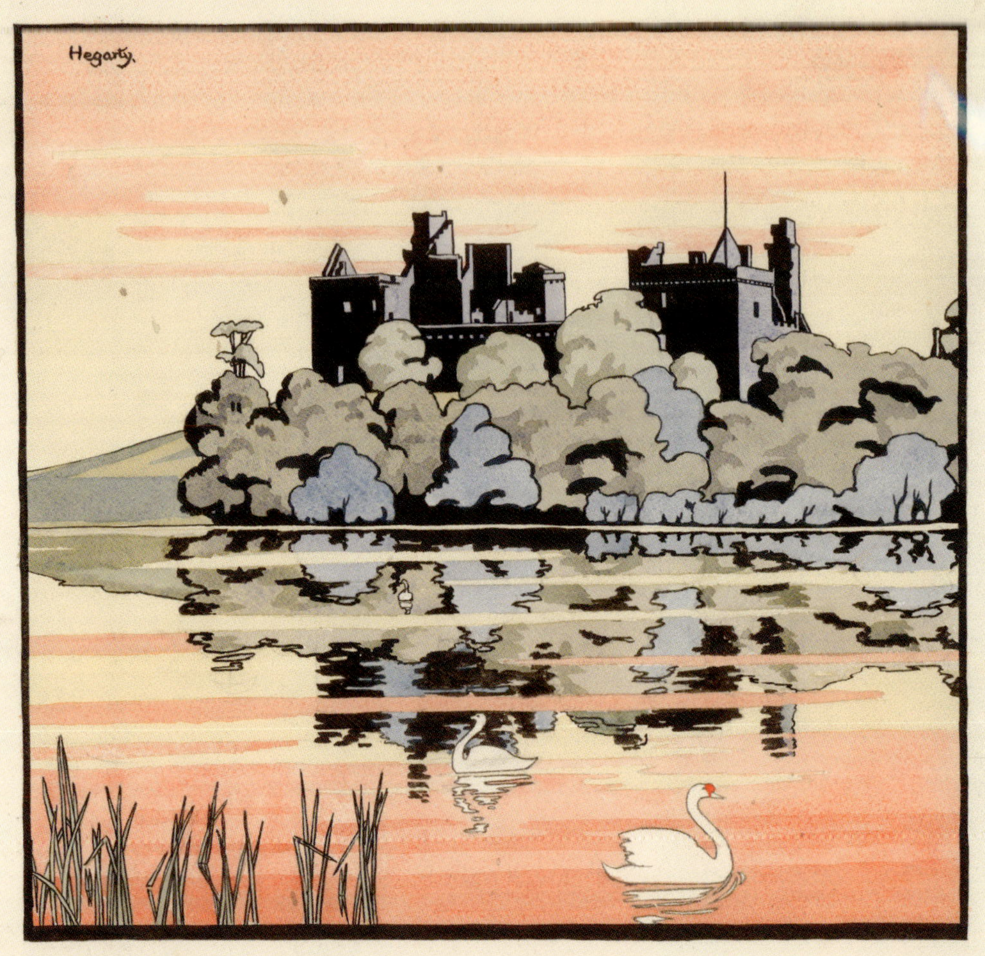

LINLITHGOW
PALACE.

SCOTTISH GENERAL OMNIBUS Coy. LTD.

FOUR

Imagery of Linlithgow

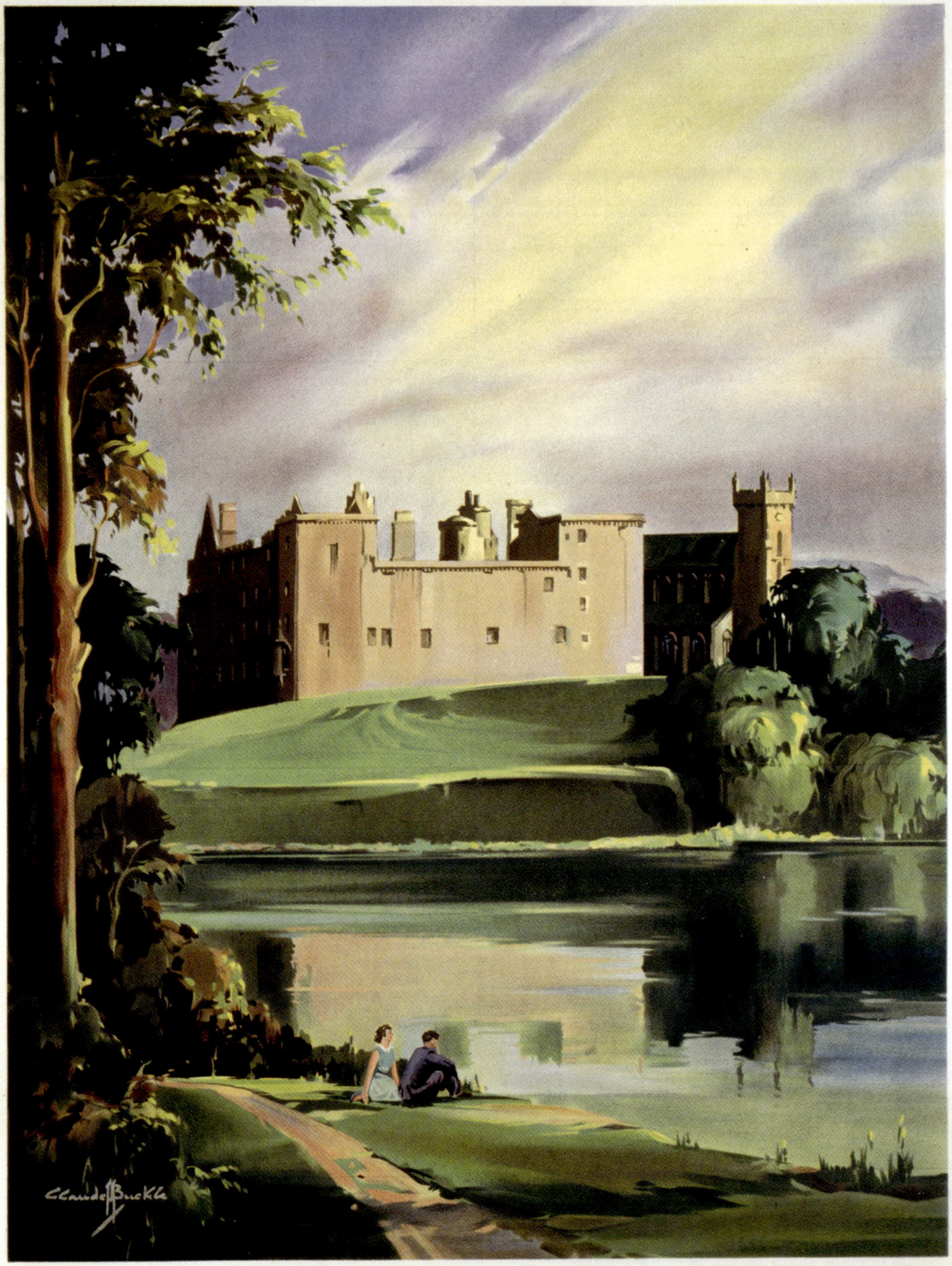

Linlithgow station — 17 miles west of Edinburgh

LINLITHGOW PALACE

Royal Palace of the Stuart Kings and birthplace of Mary Queen of Scots
Open to visitors

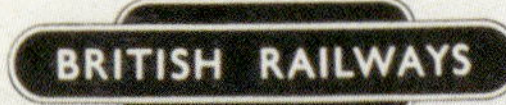

SEE BRITAIN BY TRAIN

PUBLISHED BY BRITISH RAILWAYS (SCOTTISH REGION) B 25762

PRINTED IN GREAT BRITAIN BY STAFFORD & CO. LTD., NETHERFIELD, NOTTINGHAM

Linlithgow Palace by John Hegarty
© The Glasgow School of Art
(On page 98)

Linlithgow Palace by Claude Buckle
© NRM/Pictorial Collections/ Science & Society Picture Library
(Opposite)

Tradesfolk and manufacturers have taken advantage of the opportunities to exploit Linlithgow's notable features. Examples include local butchers, shoe and boot makers, a clock maker, bakers and grocers. Artists have responded to this challenge.

There is a tradition of transport companies commissioning artists to portray attractive scenes to promote their business. Linlithgow was well served in this regard.

The artist, John Hegarty, trained at the Glasgow School of Art. In 1927 he painted a series of screen prints of Scottish scenes for the Scottish General Omnibus Company Ltd. The series included Castle Campbell near Dollar, the Wallace Monument outside Stirling as well as a fine poster titled 'Linlithgow Palace.' The picture at Linlithgow focuses on the dramatic ruins rising out of the trees, looking almost like an island in the loch. Swans glide in opposite directions past the reeds. The title panel illustrates the emblems of Scotland, England and France. The original is located in the archives of Glasgow School of Art.

Claude Henry Buckle (1905-1973) was an Englishman and known as a prolific painter of railway scenes. He produced over 80 images of attractive tourist destinations across the United Kingdom. Starting in the 1930s and continuing up to the 1960s, with a short pause for the war, he produced a steady stream of large, detailed railway posters to promote travel by rail. Originals are today collectable and of value.

His picture of Linlithgow Palace was commissioned by British Railways and is subtitled 'Royal Palace of the Stuart Kings and birthplace of Mary, Queen of Scots'. A couple relax sitting beside the placid water of the loch in the afternoon sun. The water of the loch reflects the bulk of the palace as well as the adjoining parish church of St Michael's.

Today there is a thriving market for attractive 'vintage' and other scenes on the internet using websites such as www.etsy.com. Missy Ames is American with Scottish roots. She portrays a similar view of the palace across the loch, capturing its scale with a matching reflection. Her business is to sell images of attractive locations throughout the world.

Linlithgow Palace by Missy Ames
© Courtesy of Missy Ames
(Overleaf)

W. L. Morrison was a long-established Linlithgow manufacturer of boots and shoes. The unknown artist used the east view of Linlithgow Palace to market the company's 'Hillman Boot'. There is no footwear in view only an attractive scene featuring the company name 'W. L. Morrison' written in the water.

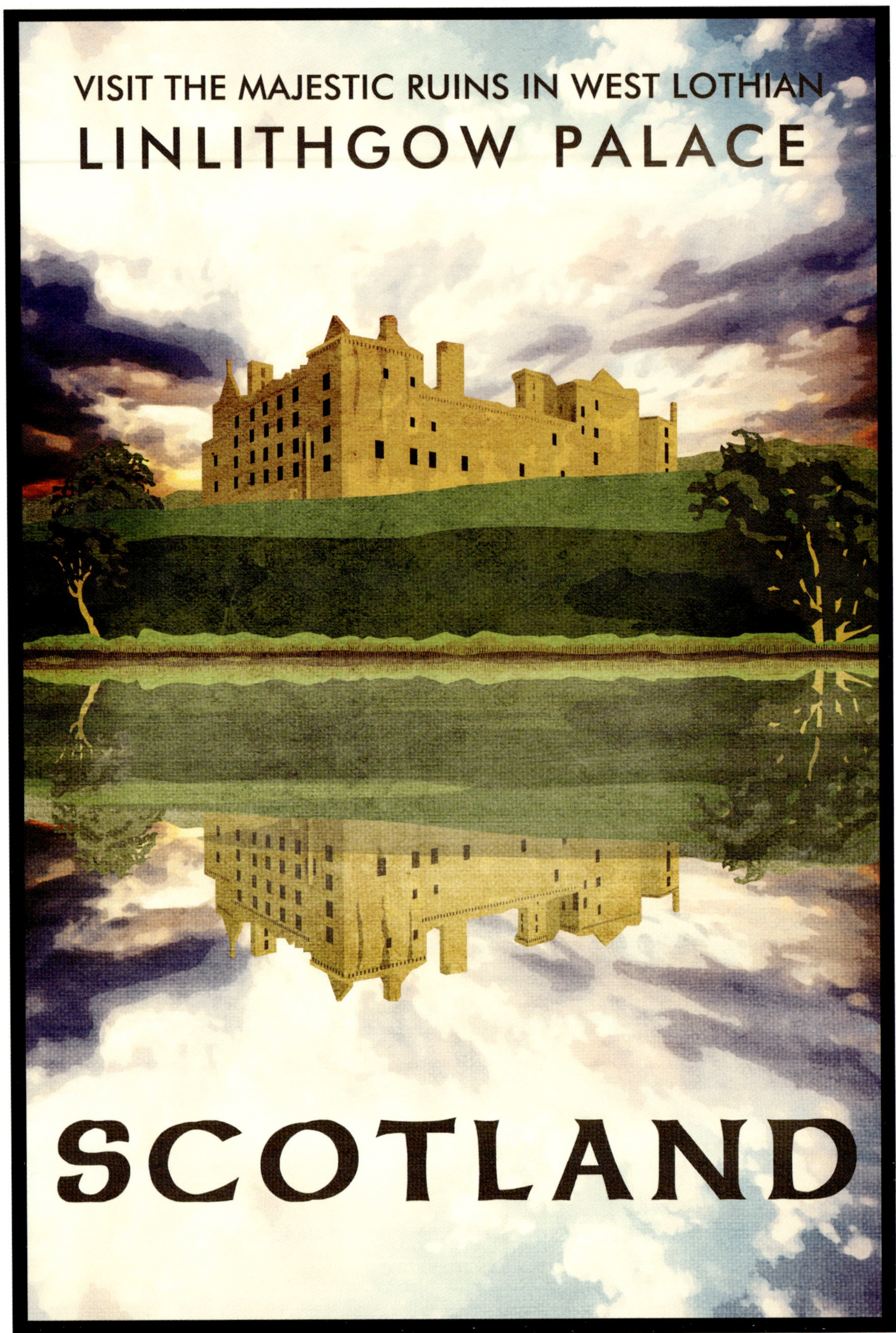
VISIT THE MAJESTIC RUINS IN WEST LOTHIAN
LINLITHGOW PALACE
SCOTLAND

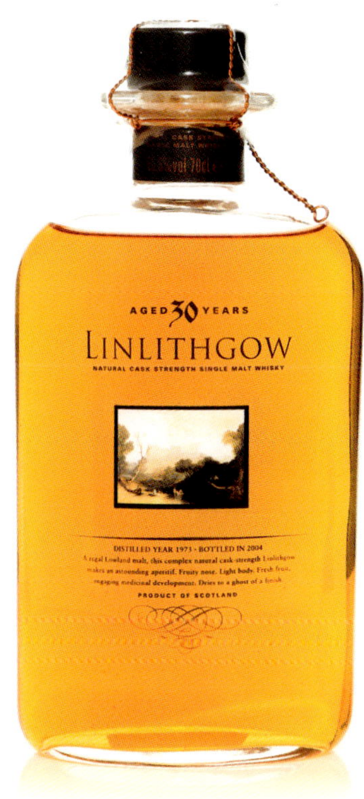

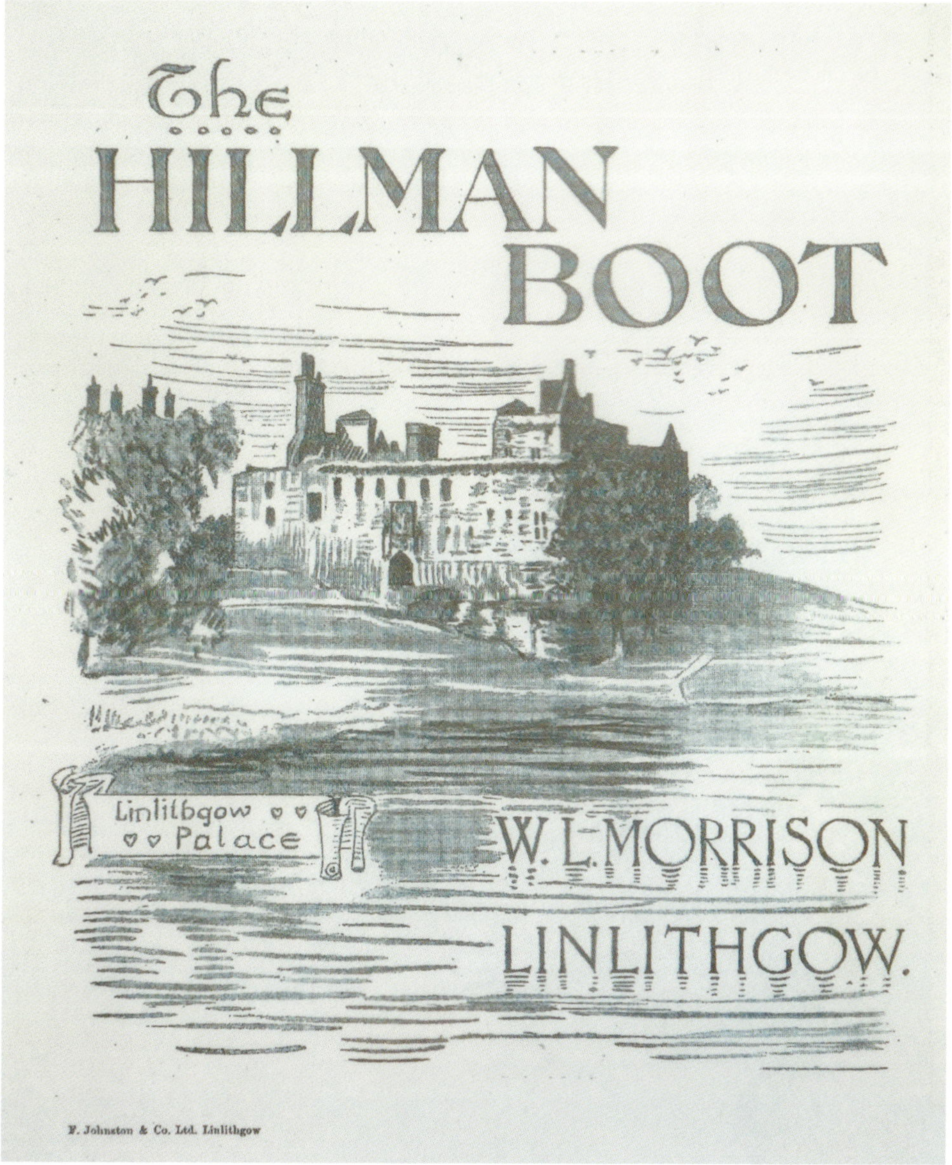

Linlithgow malt whisky with J.M.W. Turner image © Diaego (Above left)

The Hillman Boot for W. L. Morrison © Linlithgow Heritage Trust (Above right)

St Magdalene was the town distillery, founded by Adam Dawson, which produced whisky from the 18th century. A thirty-year malt whisky has been marketed using Turner's early 19th century picture, the original of which now hangs in the Walker Gallery, Liverpool. The label reads: 'Distilled year 1973. Bottled in 2004. A regal Lowland malt, this complex natural cask strength Linlithgow makes an astounding aperitif. Fruity nose. Fresh fruit, engaging, medicinal development. Dries to a ghost of a finish.' This St Magdalene malt is sought after and commands high prices today.

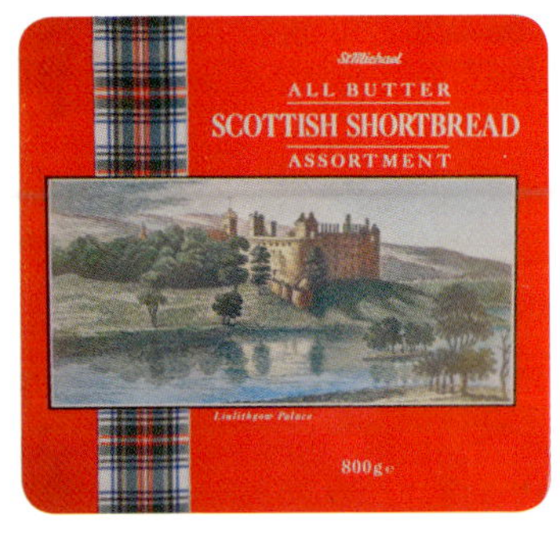

All Butter Scottish Shortbread by Marks and Spencer © Marks and Spencer (Above)

The label for Katie Wearie's Lithca' Pale Ale © Kinneil Brew Hoose (Lower right)

James Keiller preserve top Private collection (Lower left)

Kinneil Brew Hoose, in nearby Bo'ness, brews traditional real ales. One of their choice local brews is called 'Katie Wearie's and Corbieha' Pale Ale'. The bottle label states that the beer is 'a pale refreshing beer using German perle hops for a great lasting hop taste. Katie was a 19th century cattle drover who rested under a tree in Linlithgow. To this day, the tree is known as Katie Wearie's tree and a small memorial has been erected to her memory.'

Food purveyors, too, have used Linlithgow imagery. Two examples are the jam makers, James Keiller of Dundee, who sold their preserves with the familiar scene of 'Linlithgow Palace, West Lothian, Scotland' on the lid. There is an apocryphal story that Mary, Queen of Scots, ate this preserve when she had a headache and that the name is derived from the comment 'Marie est malade.'

Marks and Spencer, under its brand 'St Michael', has sold 800 gram tins of all butter Scottish shortbread using an image of the north-east view of the palace and St Michael's church with the original spire and cockerel.

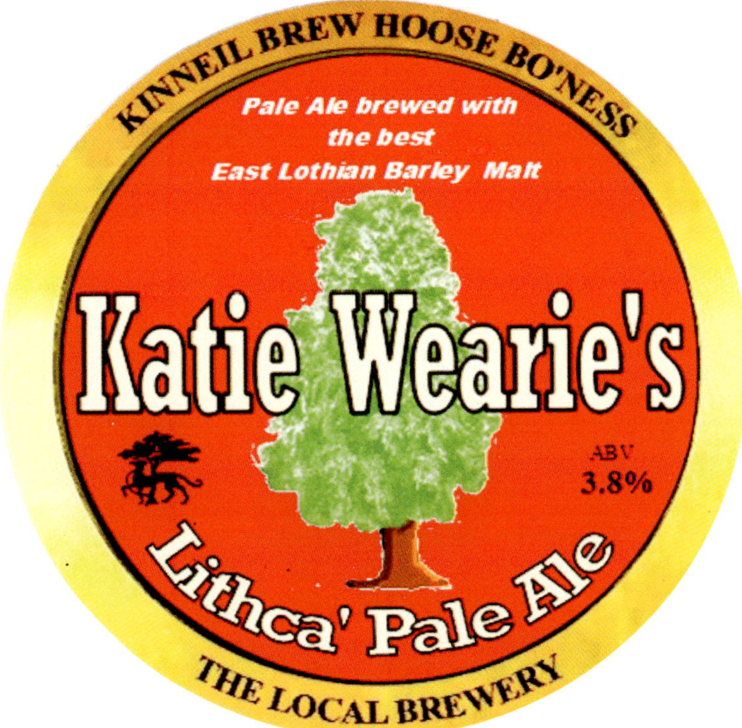

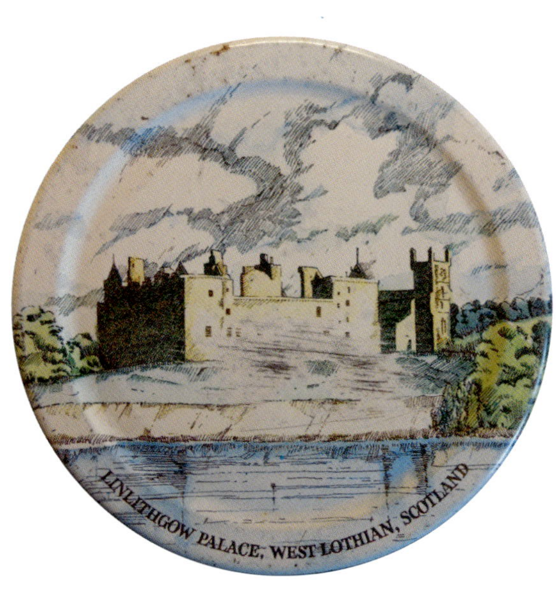

Wall hanging by Liz Beetham

(Lower left)

Edible architecture by Margaret Hamilton

(Upper right)

Model of St Peter's Church by Andrew Anderson

(Lower right)

Linlithgow Civic Trust celebrated its 40th birthday party with a cake created by Margaret Hamilton of Lanark, based on the Scottish Episcopal Church of St Peter's in the High Street of Linlithgow. This amazing little church, completed in 1928, set back from the High Street, and looking across to the loch, is Byzantine in style with Celtic details. Inside the church the unusual façade is included in a delicate wall hanging by Liz Beetham and as a small model of the church by Andrew Anderson.

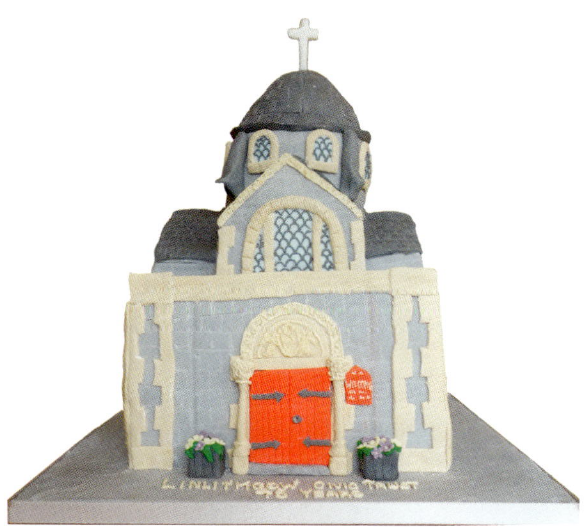

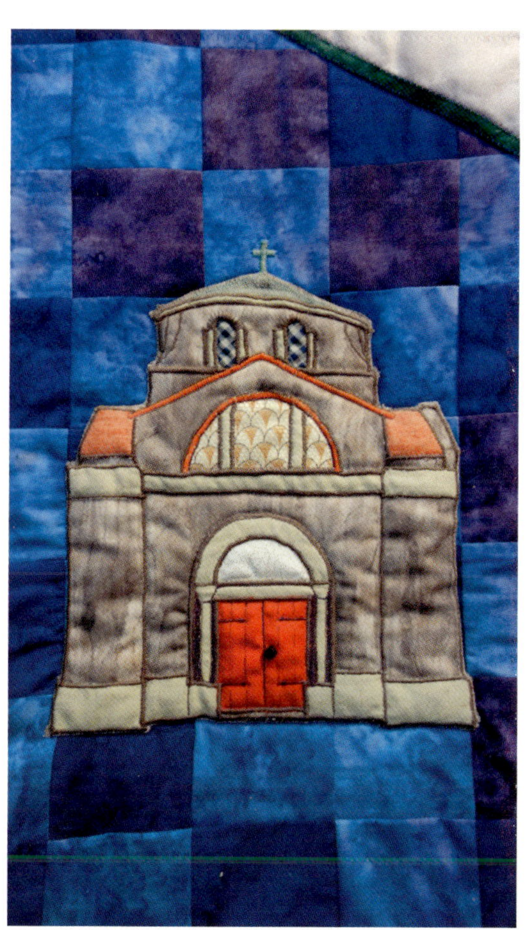

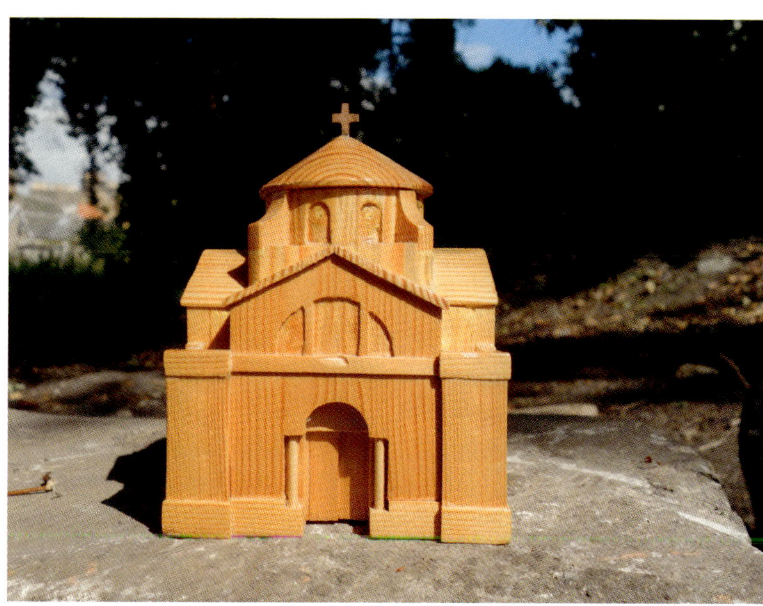

The Avon Viaduct by James Duncan Ltd
© Image by Paul Gavin Photography
(Below)

Linlithgow Palace and Loch by James Duncan Ltd
© Image by Paul Gavin Photography
(Opposite)

The company name of James Duncan Ltd is not widely known outside those with an interest in historic ceramic tile applications. It first appeared in Glasgow post office directories around 1877-78, as 'Duncan, James, Mosaic, Encaustic and Geometrical Tile Layer and Art Tile Merchant, 106 West Campbell Street, Glasgow'. The company was responsible for pictorial and ornamental tile work for churches, schools, public buildings, dairies, fishmongers and butchers. Clean and hygienic interiors were made possible with the use of ceramic tiles.

An excellent example, in first class condition, survives at the shop of T. D. Anderson, butcher at 165 High Street Linlithgow. The pictorial panels are set in distinctive scroll work framed with thistles and roses. It is apparent that generations of butchers have appreciated the quality of the work at Linlithgow and taken care to preserve it. The ceramic scenes, finished in 1912, are signed 'J.D. Ltd' – the work of James Duncan of Glasgow.

Two major scenes of Linlithgow are depicted. First are the sheep grazing by the loch in front of the palace. Also illustrated are the church and the Burgh Halls. The flora around the loch are beautifully captured in the coloured six-inch tiles. It would appear that James Duncan worked closely with a company in Staffordshire called T. & R. Boote of Burslem, where it is likely that the manufacturing took place. The second scene depicts cows grazing beneath the Avon railway viaduct. Around the shop are wall friezes of the heads of bulls.

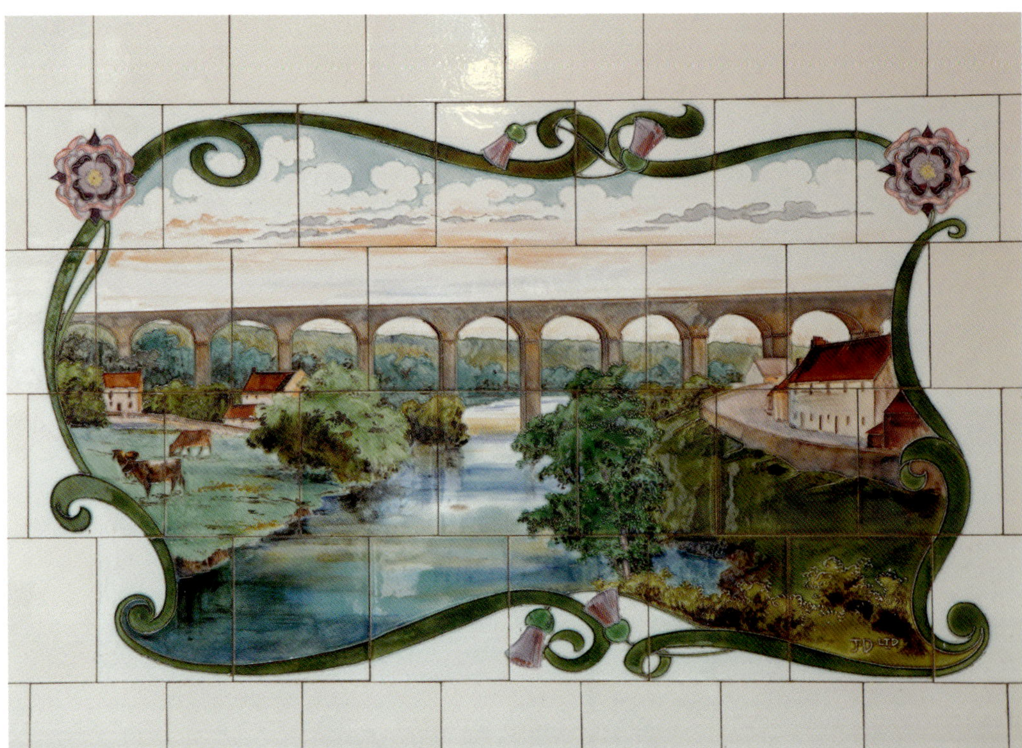

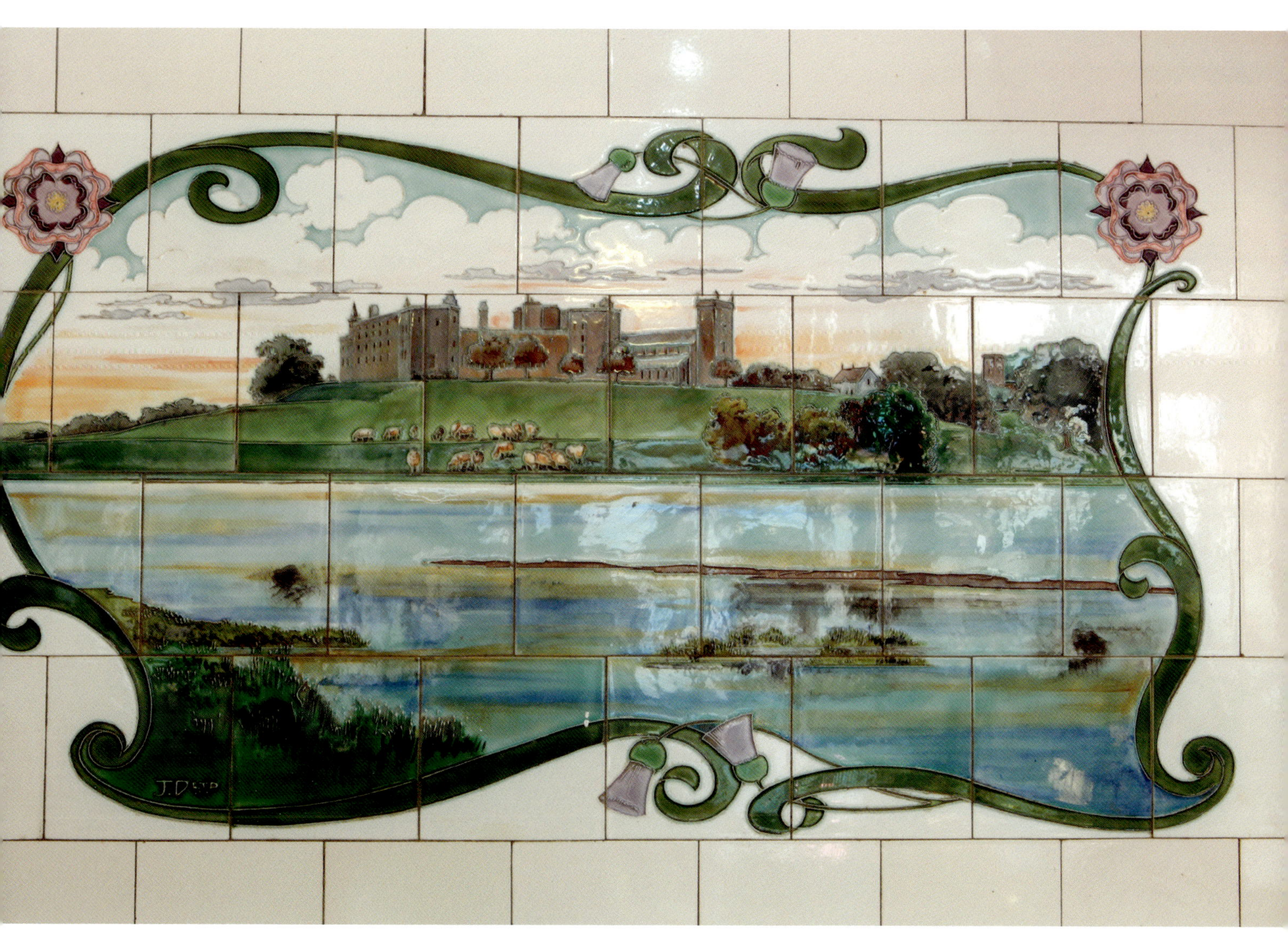
J.D

Blue and white earthenware plate by J. Clews
© National Trust / Karen George
(Below)

Royal Doulton Linlithgow plate by J. Hughes
Private collection
(Opposite)

In common with other attractive locations, Linlithgow has featured in the production of high quality earthenware products. Royal Doulton produced vases, hand painted by their artist, J. Hughes, around 1910. A century before that, the company of William Mason produced colourful glazed earthenware plates based on Turner's painting of the loch from the east as described previously.

Another example is the fine blue and white earthenware plate, below, by J. Clews with canted corners. It has a transfer printed border depicting flowers with foliage on a plain blue background. The central scene shows several locals in front of the east entrance of the palace. On the reverse side is inscribed 'Palace of Linlithgow' and 'Clews Warranted Staffordshire'. This plate is displayed at the National Trust property of Llanerchaeron in Ceredigion, Wales.

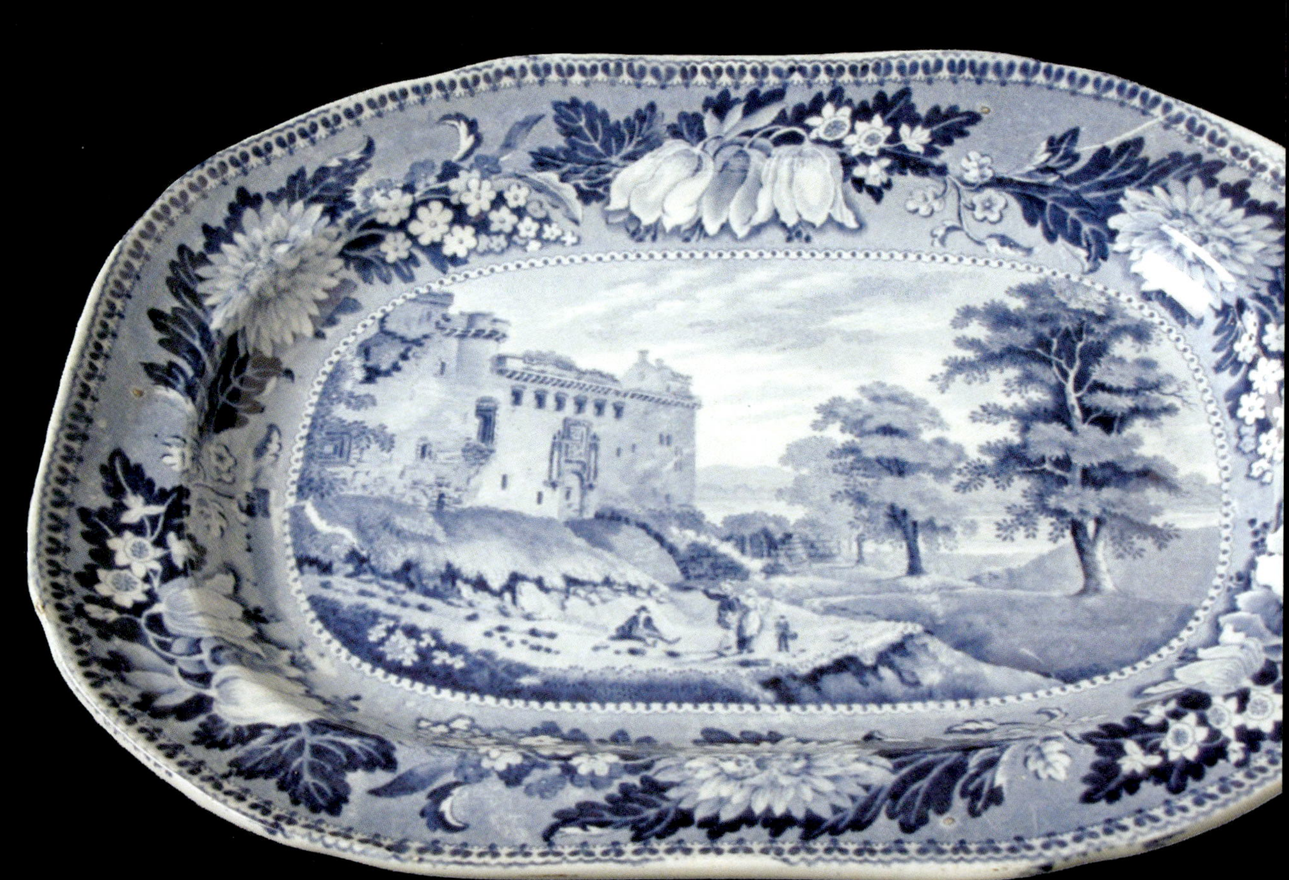

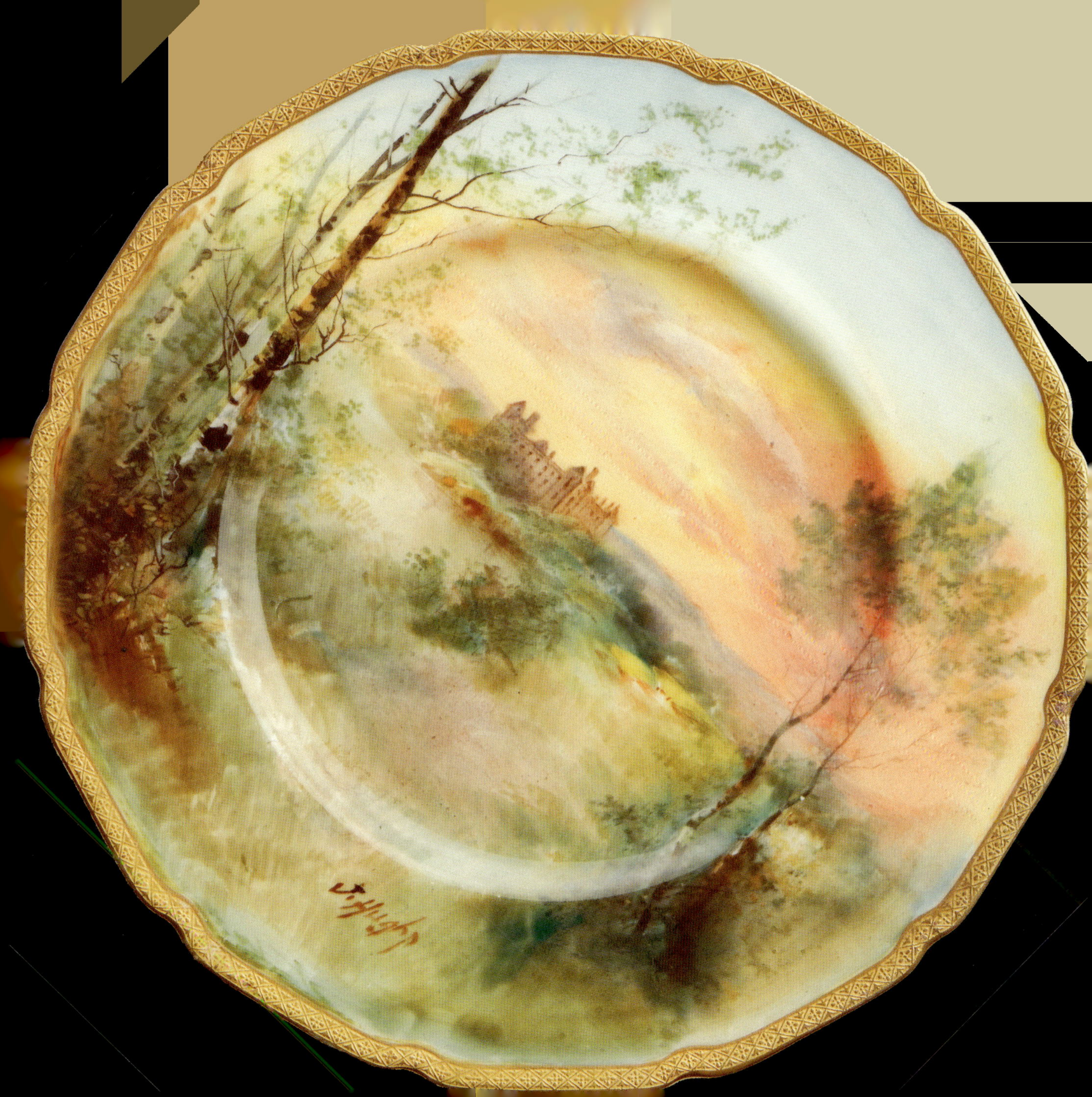

Part of the old mercat cross
© Linlithgow Heritage Trust
(Below left)

Black bitch sculpture on the gable wall at West Port, Linlithgow
© West Lothian Council
(Below right)

Earlier in the book, reference was made to a black hound. There are various stories of the origin of this dog but the legend that is most commonly told is of a criminal sentenced to a slow death tied to an oak tree on an island in the loch. To the puzzlement of the town's people, the prisoner thrived. With scrutiny it was discovered that the man's black greyhound bitch, under the cover of darkness, had been carrying food for her master. Her loyalty was 'rewarded' by also being tied to the tree.

Many depictions of the hound appear in the town. A selection of representations are illustrated. Some show the hound with two, three or four feet on the ground. Some images omit the island. Some indicate an oak tree, others a more generic tree. Some show the dog facing the right, most face to the left. The following is a selection of the author's favourites in various materials.

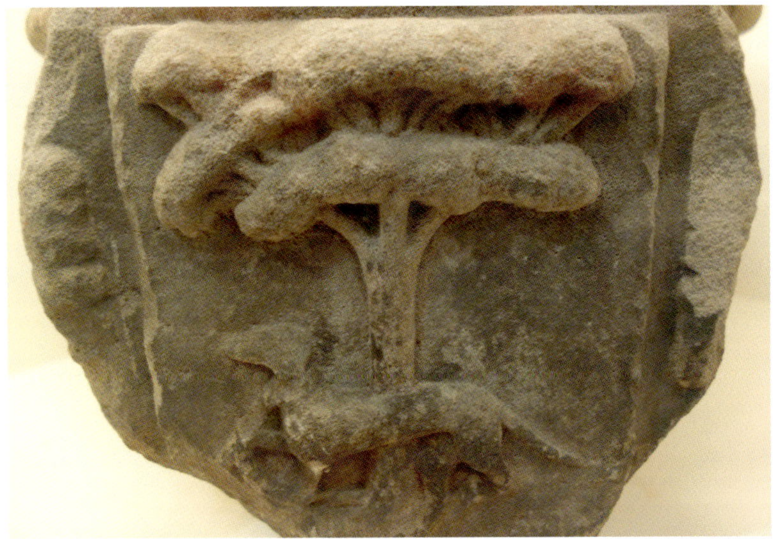

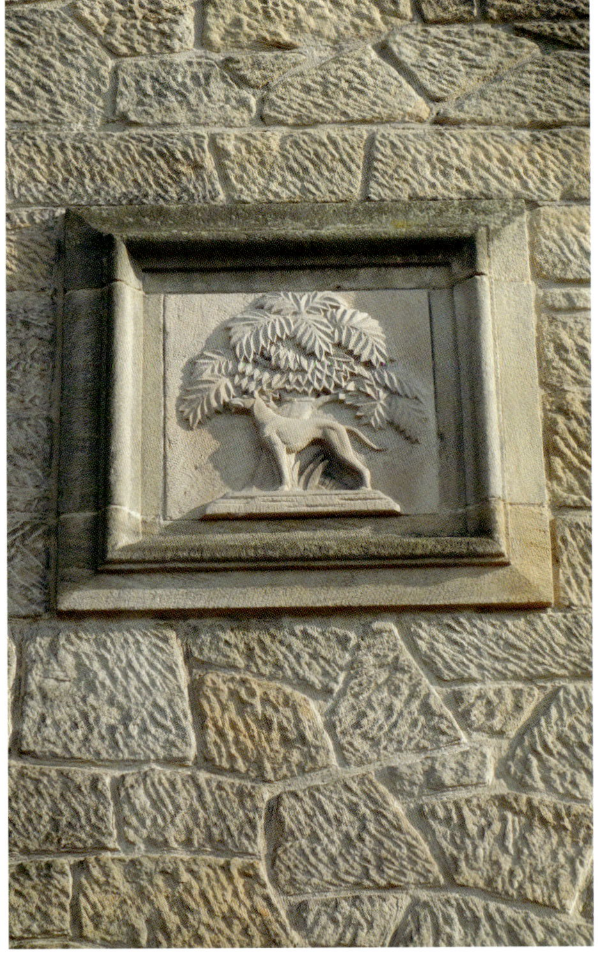

Top of the emblem of the Linlithgow finger post
© West Lothian Council
(Top left)

March stone on Linlithgow Bridge
© Court of the Deacons of the Ancient and Royal Burgh of Linlithgow
(Top right)

Winchester bushel dry measure with attached plaque carrying the arms and name of Linlithgow
Courtesy of Dumfries and Galloway Museums Service, Stranraer Museum
(Lower left)

Black bitch symbol on the provost's lamp, outside Tam Dalyell House
© West Lothian Council
(Lower right)

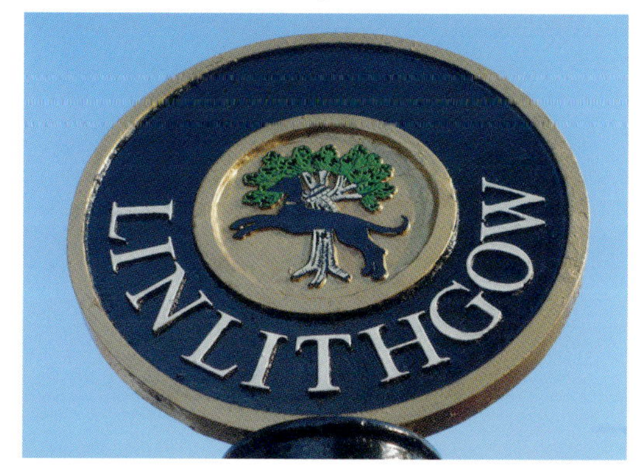

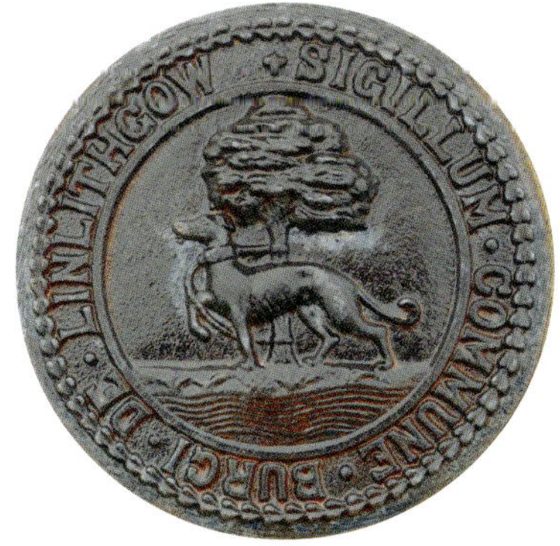

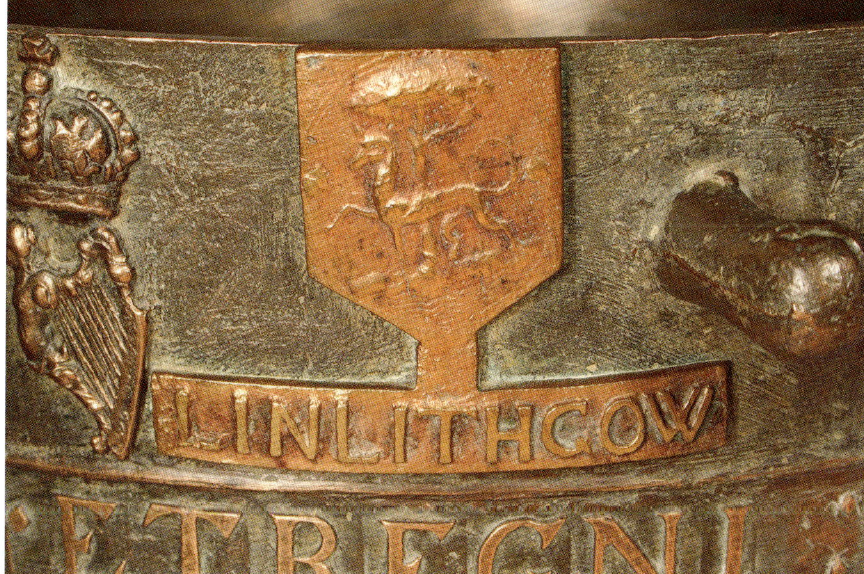

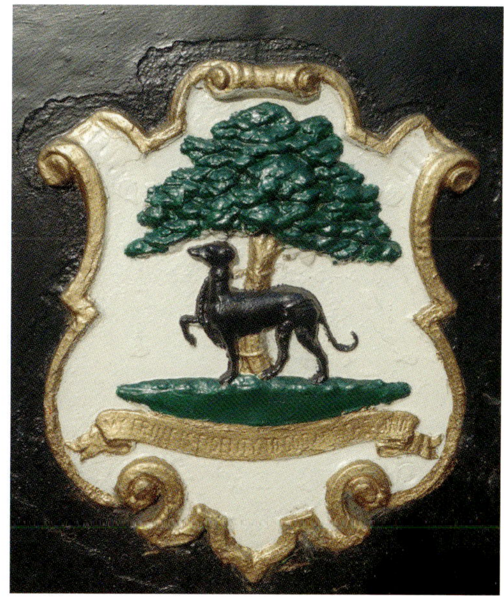

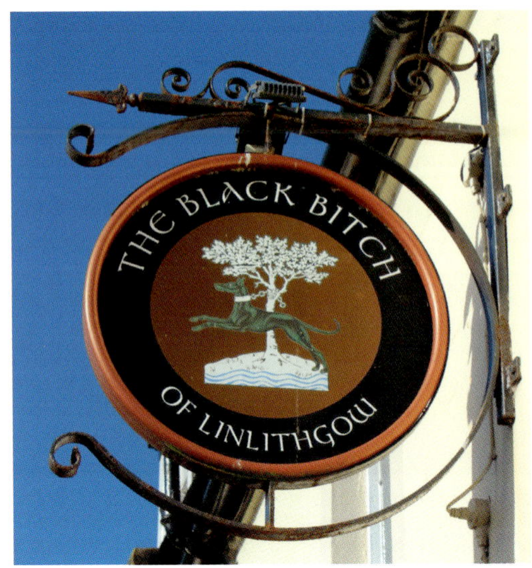

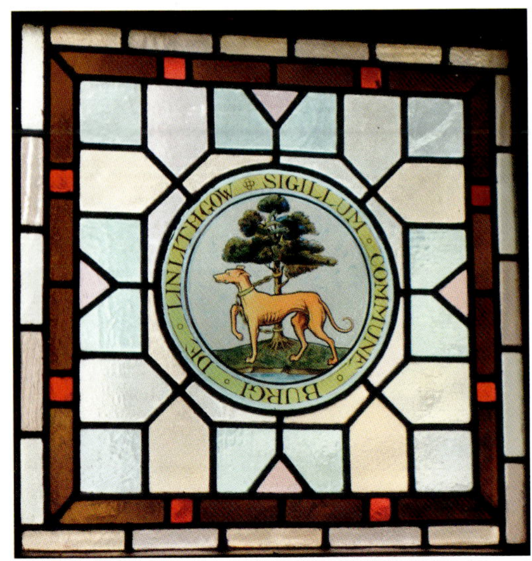

Sign hanging outside the Black Bitch Tavern
© Calum Smith photographer
(Above left)

Stained glass of the black bitch at Poldrait House, Linlithgow
Courtesy of John Yuille, Poldrait House, Linlithgow
© Christopher Long photographer
(Above right)

The 'black bitch' legend is not well-known outside Linlithgow, but Tam Dalyell, MP for the town over many years, was pleased to call himself a 'black bitch', having been born in the town, as does Alex Salmond, a former First Minster of Scotland. The 'black bitch' term may be not considered politically correct and may confuse visitors from other countries, but on the other hand, the current proprietor of the Black Bitch Tavern, Robert Lowe, in a recent community magazine article said that he notices lots of visitors taking photos of the signs outside.

Outside the royal burgh, for the sharp-eyed, there are a number of visual images of the black bitch, most notably in Edinburgh. A carved stone column survives, but now significantly eroded, at Melville Drive, in the Meadows, left over from the 1886 International Exhibition of Science, Art and Industry, in Edinburgh. The column has place names engraved on it and a band with carved plaques on it. One plaque has the name Linlithgow on it and a picture of a certain dog under a tree.

In the Nicolson Street gardens, in Edinburgh, is the Brass Iron Founders' pillar. It features the biblical character, Tubal Cain, the legendary founder of brass and iron-making skills. The pillar is decorated with the coats of arms of old Scottish burghs, on shields arranged vertically. The side facing the street includes Linlithgow. The monument was commissioned for the same 1886 Exhibition by the Edinburgh and Leith Brass Founders. Following the exhibition, the pillar was moved from the Meadows to its present location.

The arms of the royal burgh of Linlithgow are included in the frieze painted by William Hole around 1898 in the central hall at the Scottish Portrait Gallery, in Edinburgh.

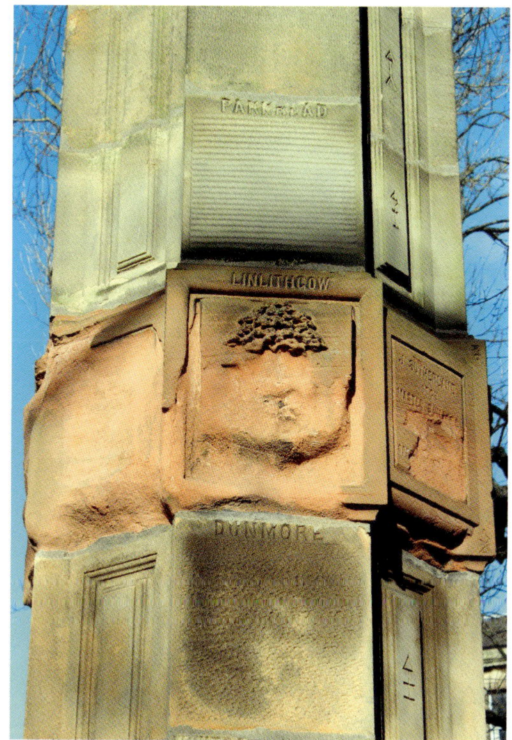

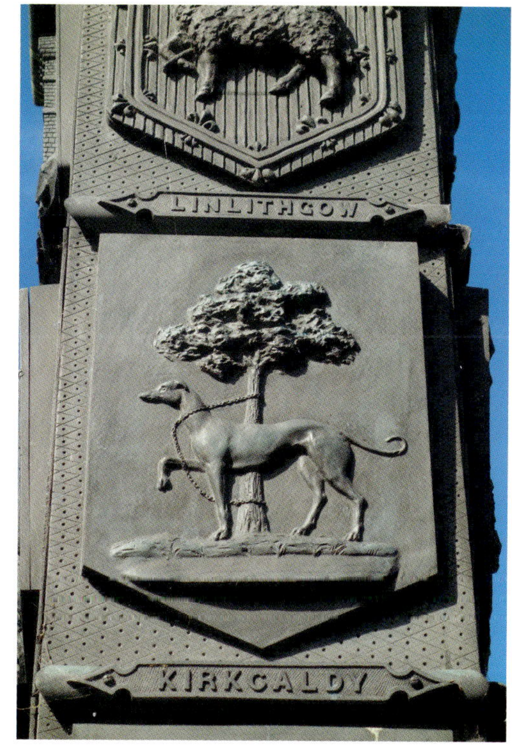

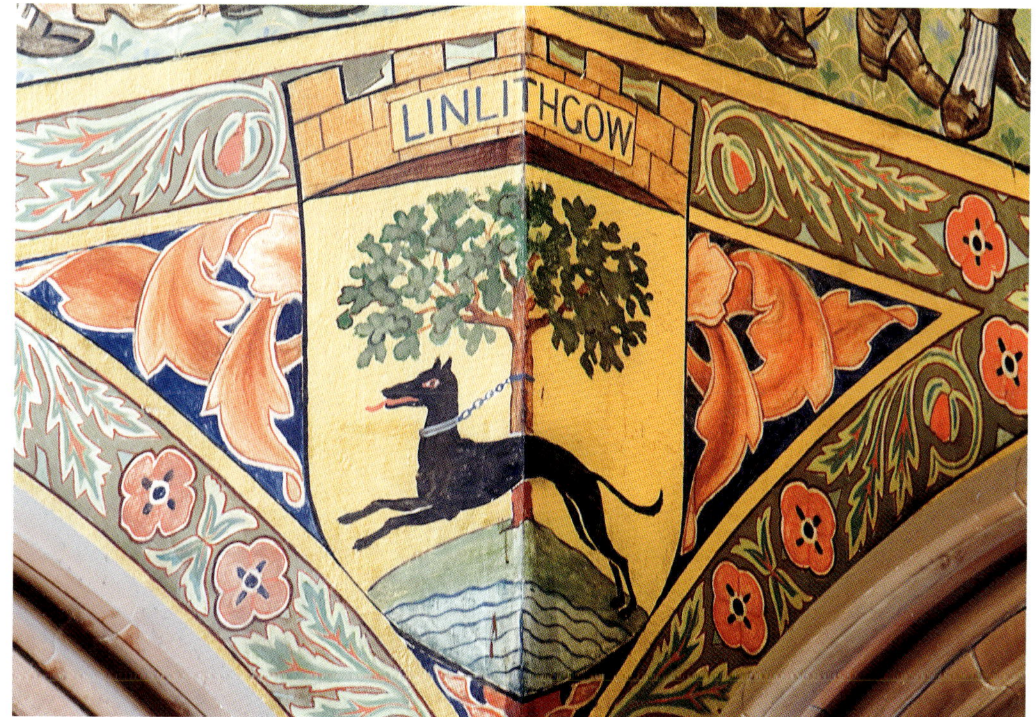

The stone column with black bitch symbol in Melville Drive, Edinburgh
© Calum Smith photographer
(Top left)

Brass Iron Founders' Pillar, Edinburgh, with black bitch insignia
© Calum Smith photographer
(Top right)

The town insignia at the Scottish Portrait Gallery, Edinburgh
© Linlithgow Coat of Arms, William Brassey Hole, National Galleries of Scotland.
Keith Hunter
(Right)

Banner of the Court of Deacons
© Court of the Deacons of the Ancient and Royal Burgh of Linlithgow
© Christopher Long photographer
(Right)

Logo of Linlithgow Golf Club
© Linlithgow Golf Club
© Christopher Long photographer
(Below)

Deacon's chain
© Court of the Deacons of the Ancient and Royal Burgh of Linlithgow
© Christopher Long photographer
(Lower right)

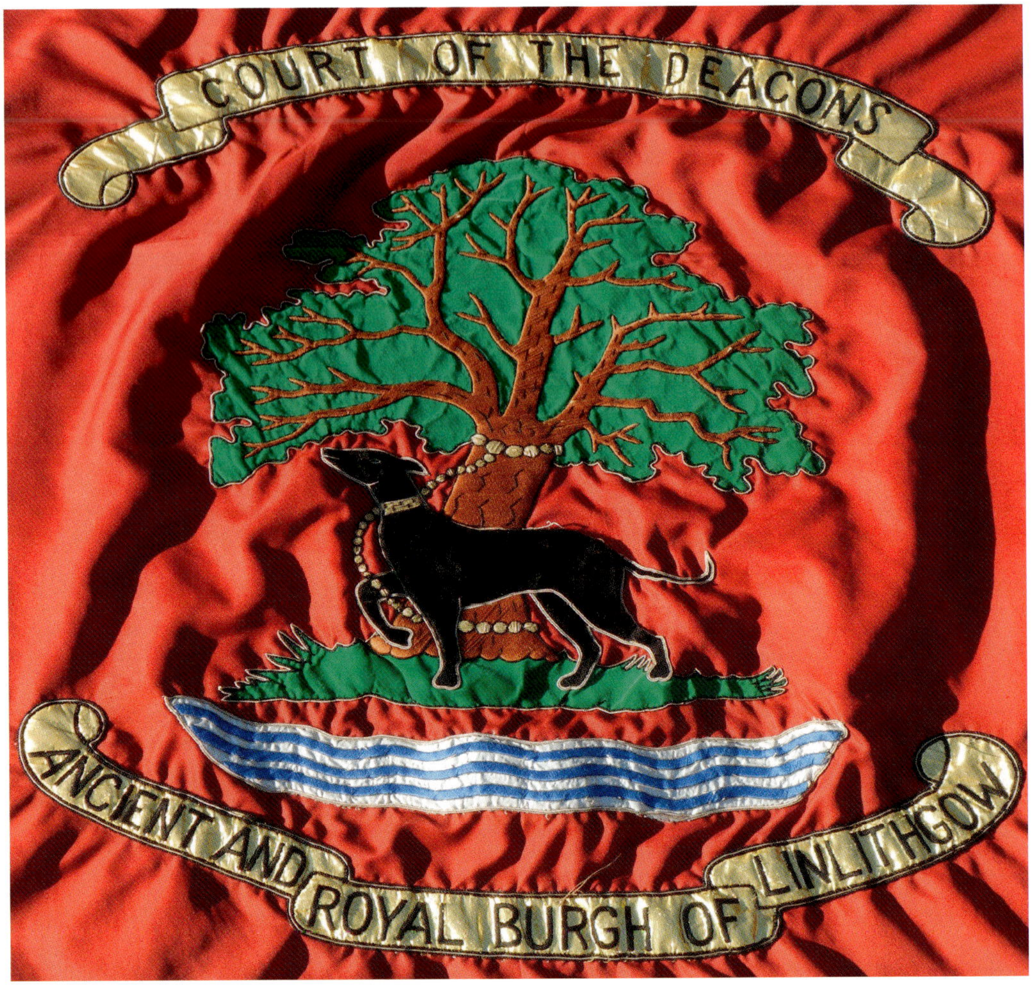

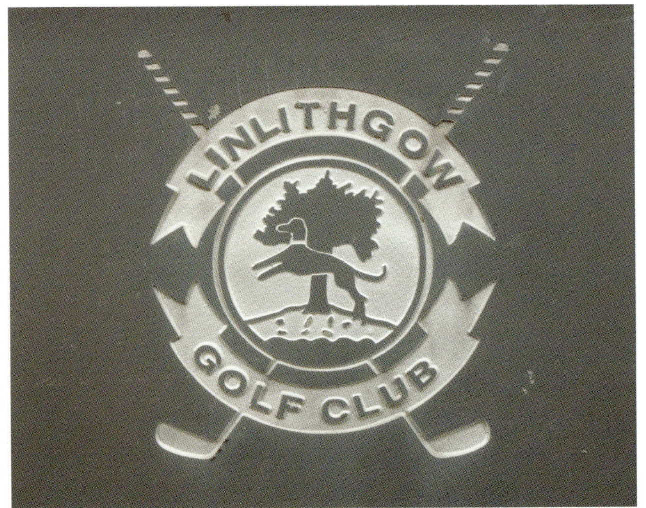

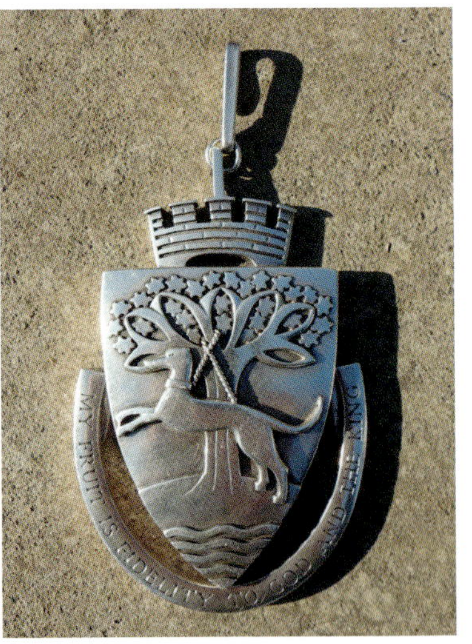

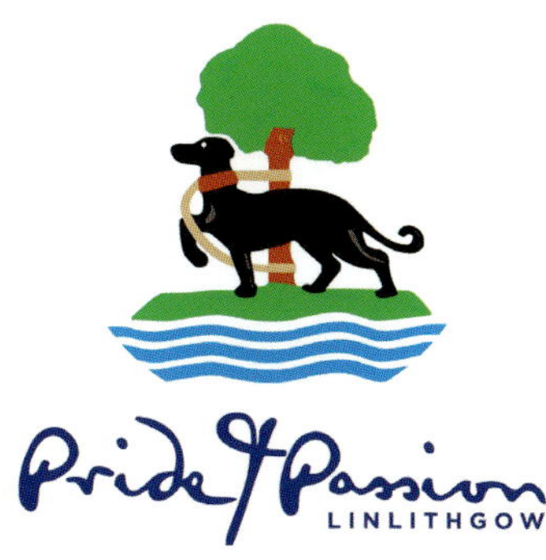

Logo of Pride and Passion Linlithgow
© Pride and Passion Linlithgow
(Above)

The coat of arms of Linlithgow and Linlithgow Bridge Community Council
Courtesy of Linlithgow and Linlithgow Bridge Community Council

Many Linlithgow organisations and businesses today use the black bitch symbol. Some examples are: the Court of the Deacons of the Ancient and Royal Burgh of Linlithgow, Linlithgow Golf Club and Pride and Passion Linlithgow.

Scotland's town councils were abolished in 1975 and the old two-sided Linlithgow town seal, as displayed at each of the many town entrances to Linlithgow, was replaced in 2017 by a new seal by the Lord Lyon. The Lord Lyon regulates matters heraldic in Scotland and further to the petition by the Linlithgow and Linlithgow Bridge Community Council the Lord Lyon granted a new coat of arms to an agreeable design fitting for a statutory community council. The seal, hand painted on vellum, was presented to the Linlithgow and Linlithgow Bridge Community Council in the Bailie Hardie Hall with invited community representatives. The new seal features St Michael killing a serpent and holding a shield displaying the black bitch tied to a tree with water below.

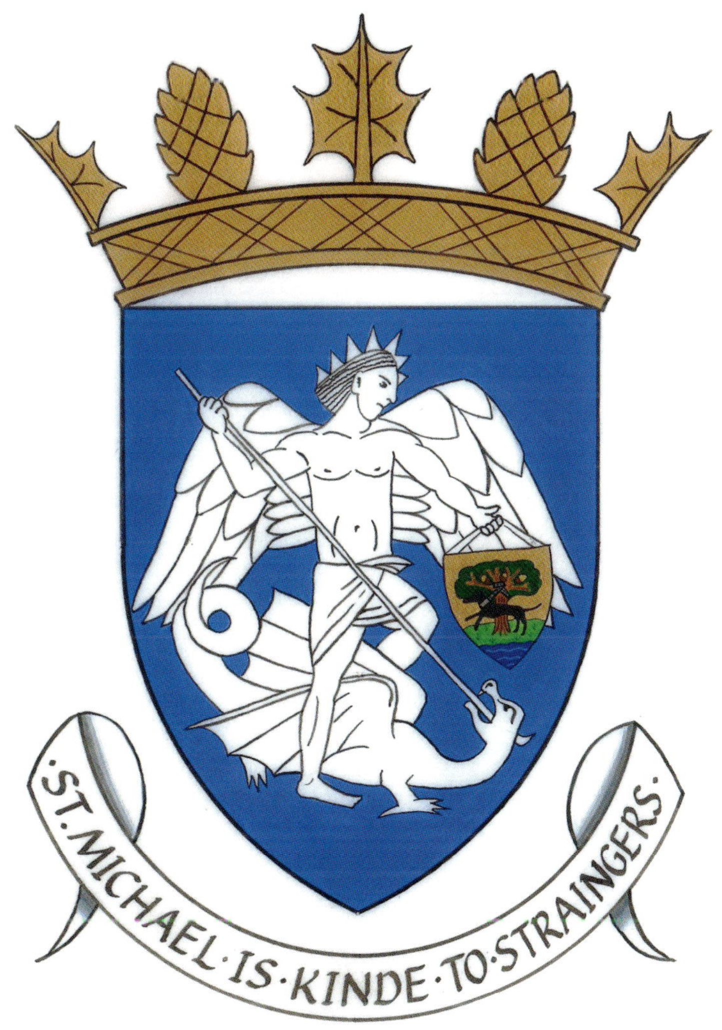

The figure of Archangel Michael holding a shield with the town's coat of arms and base inscribed "1720 Saint Michael is kind to straingers."
© Calum Smith photographer
(Below)

Stained glass of St Michael in St Michael's Parish Church
© Gordon Young photographer
(Far right)

Stained glass of St Michael in St Michael's R.C. Church
© Christopher Long photographer
(Centre)

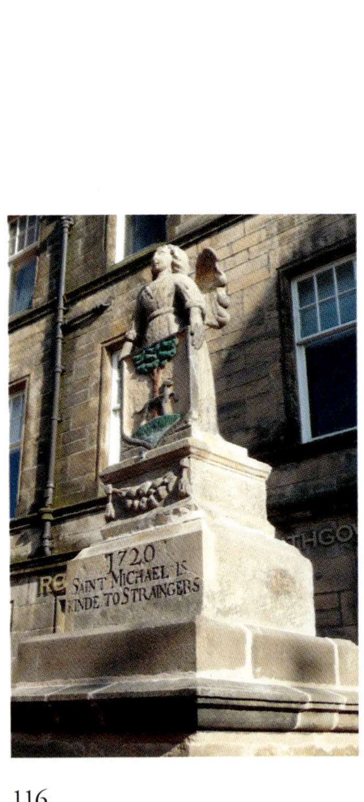

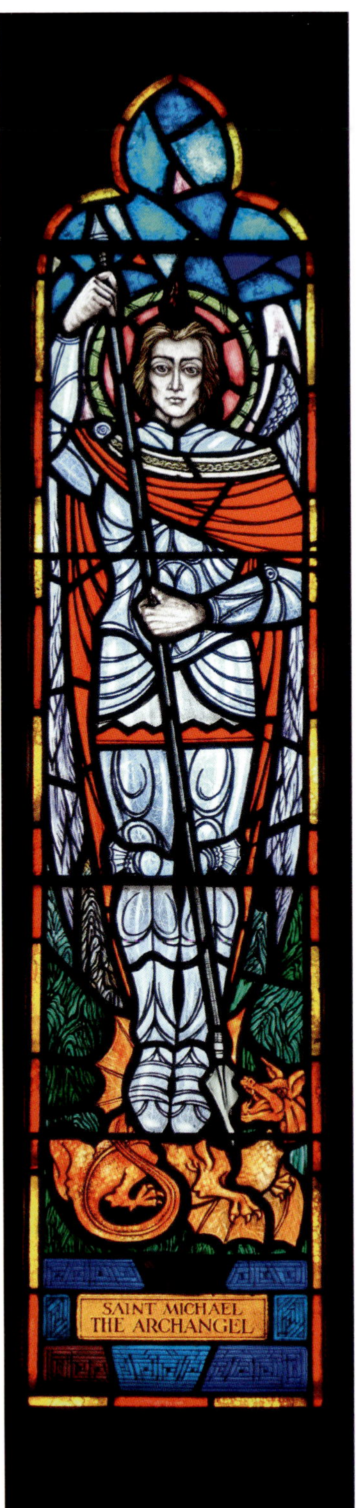

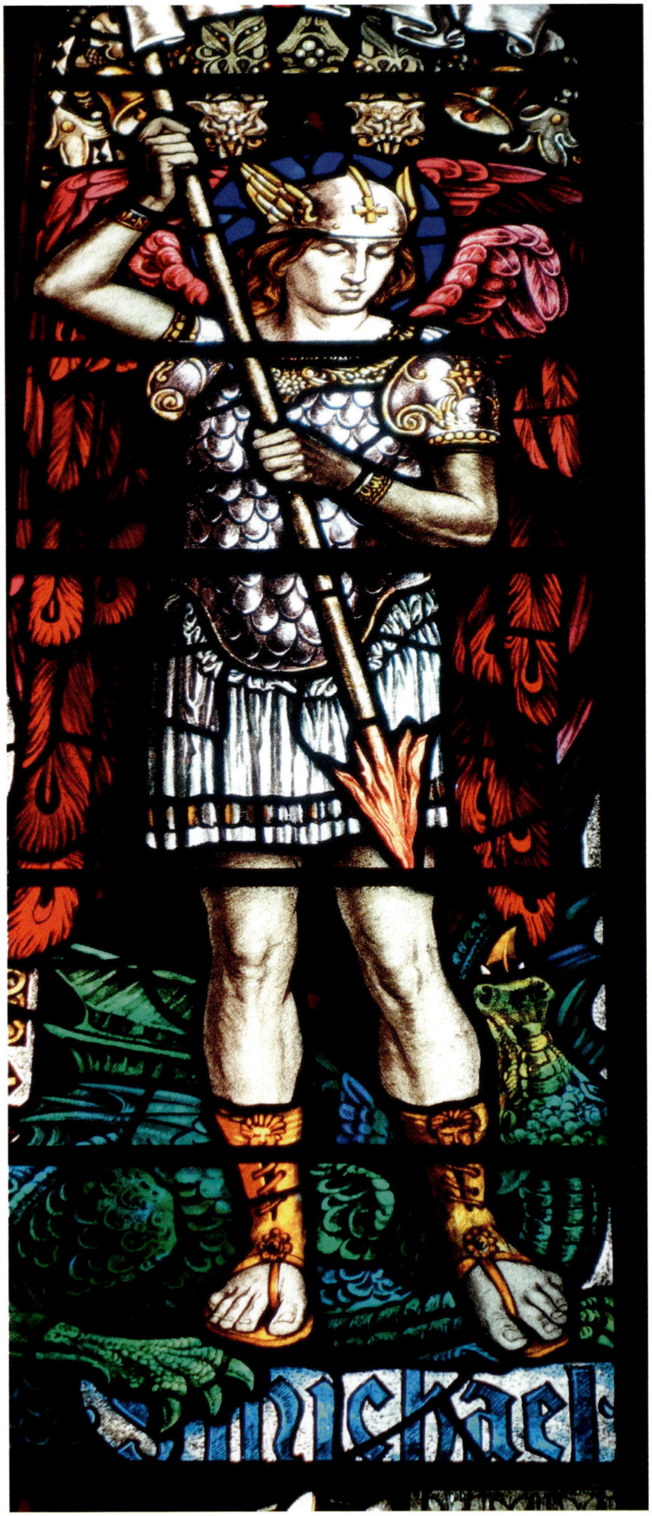

Many churches in Europe are dedicated to St Michael. Illustrations show him killing serpents and dragons. It is uncertain when the first mention was made of St Michael being the patron saint of Linlithgow.

On the east side of Linlithgow High Street is the statue of St Michael which marks the location of one of the many wells in the towns. Carved by an unknown sculptor, the inscription in the stone reads 'St Michael is Kinde to Straingers' and it is dated 1720.

The parish church at the top of Kirkgate contains representations of the saint in stone, wood, stained glass and textiles, in different locations within the church. Outside, high up in the stonework on the west end of the church, is a survivor of the Reformation when the other sculptures, similarly housed in carved niches, were destroyed. The town war memorial is located in the Queen's Aisle, within the parish church. It was unveiled in 1921 and is constructed of the local Kingscavil stone and features St Michael, the patron saint of the town is also the patron saint of soldiers. Here he is about to kill a very human-looking serpent. St Michael also features in a wood carving over the communion table in the east end of the church, in a fine oak chair in the choir featuring the killing of another serpent; in glorious red and gold in the choir carpets, manufactured by Templetons of Elderslie; as well as in strong colours in the stained glass on the south window. This contrasts to a very different glass image of St Michael in the nave of St Michael's Roman Catholic Church, the latter designed by Pugin and Pugin and dedicated in 1893 to Mary, Queen of Scots.

St Michael's statue in St Michael's Parish Church © Gordon Young photographer (Below left)

The war memorial in the east end of the Queen's Aisle at St Michael's Parish Church © Calum Smith photographer (Below right)

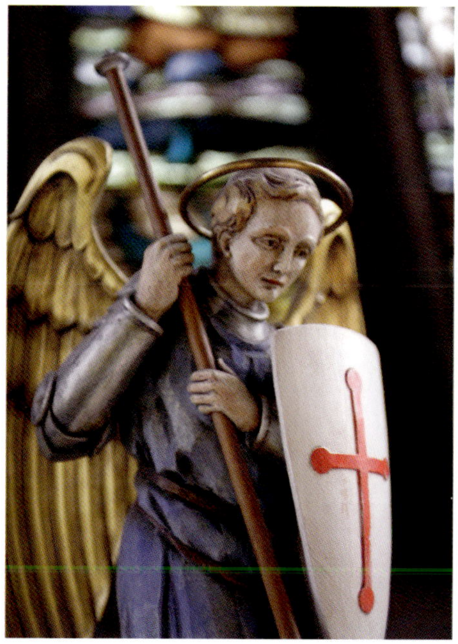

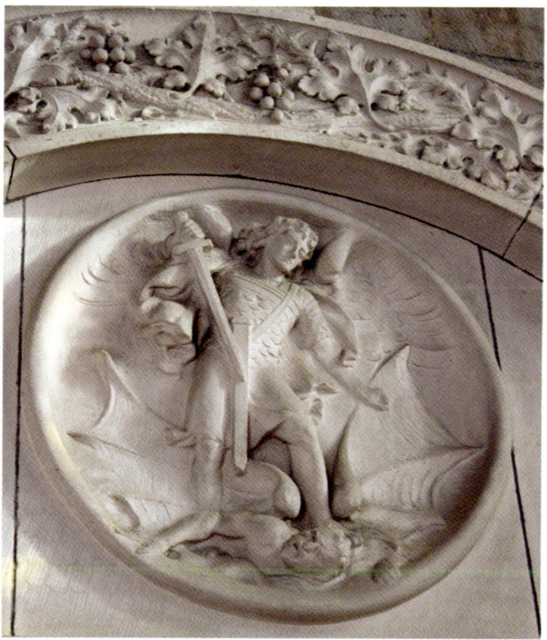

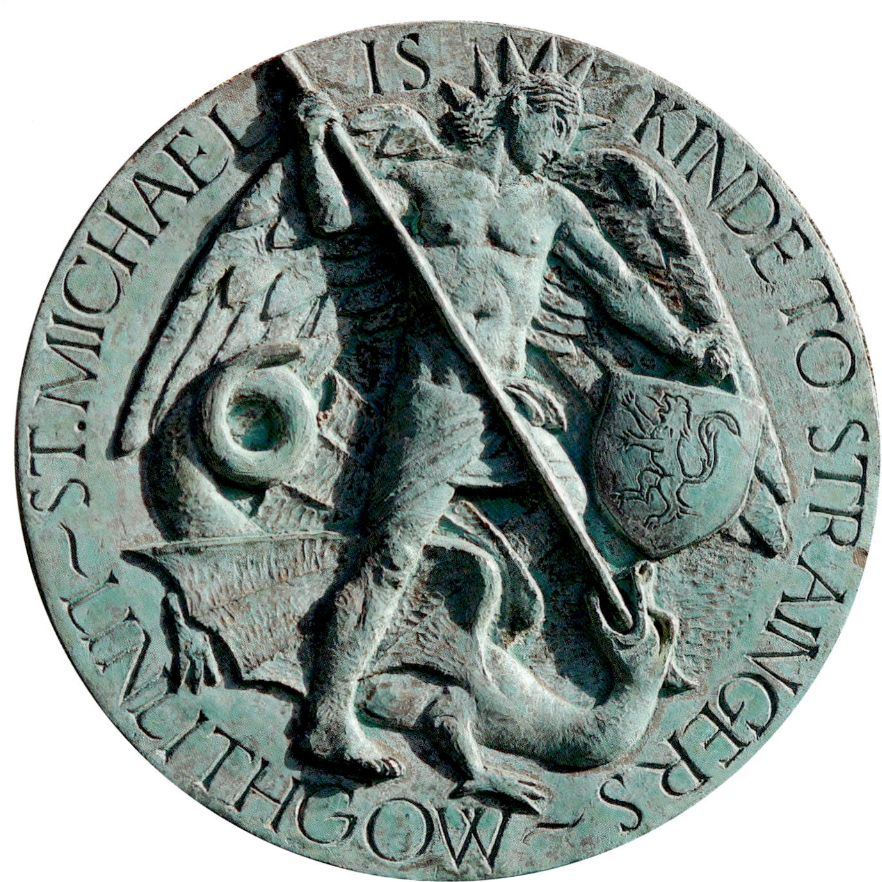

Town trail sign by Tim Chalk
© Tim Chalk
Commissioned by Linlithgow Town Management Group
© Calum Smith photographer
(Above)

Linlithgow's Town Management Group commissioned Tim Chalk, in 2009 to design a town plaque to mark buildings of merit and interest along the new town trail. It, too, features the image of St Michael the archangel.

Roads, canal, railway and motorway thread their way through Linlithgow and between the Airngarth Hill to the north and the hill of Cockleroi to the south. Visitors may view the distinctive spire of St Michael's Parish Church sitting high on the Kirkgate.

As we have seen, on page 39, Slezer depicted the stone crown spire. The original stone spire was removed in 1821 because it was thought to be in imminent danger of collapse. For 140 years the tower had no spire. There were no accurate records of the original crown so the late Very Rev. Dr. David Steel decided to replace it with a new crown characterised by lightness and bold design. Designed by Geoffrey Clarke, the spire offered a modern interpretation of the crown of thorns placed on the head of Christ.

As a symbol, townsfolk either love it or loathe it. Some have thought it resembled a rocket about to take off while Tam Dalyell said 'my mother who liked the Rev. D. Steel, (as Kathleen and I did), was appalled by the construction of the Crown of Thorns, as I was and still am.' Others see the new spire as a symbol of hope and inspiration as does the author. Indeed for many it has become a symbol of the town.

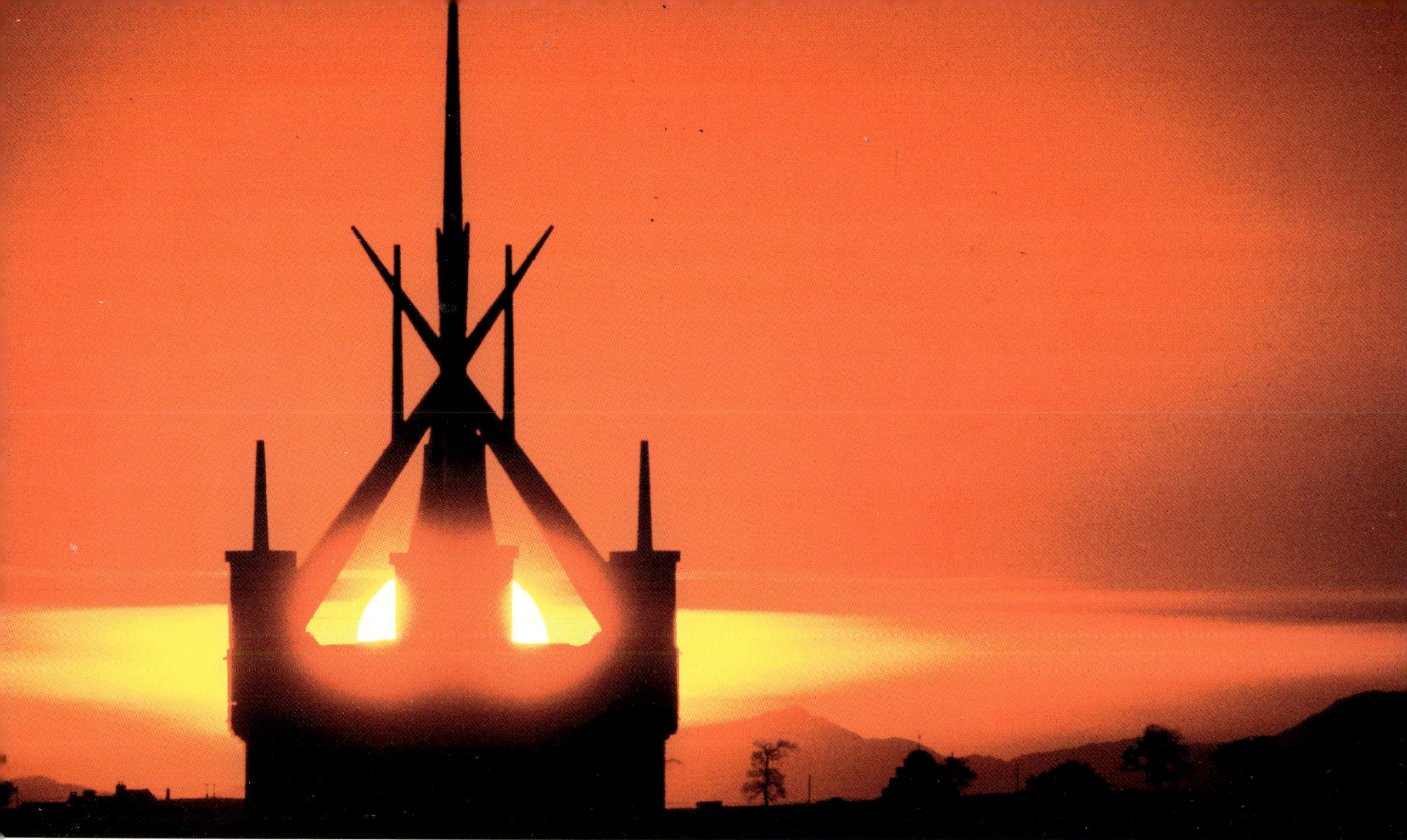

The setting sun precisely framed behind the distinctive steeple
© Christopher K. Mylne BA FRPS
(Above)

Chris Mylne, (1927–2018), naturalist and photographer, took four years to plan his image of the orb of the sun setting behind the spire. He explained to Rebecca Bell in the Black Bitch Magazine, the challenge he had set himself: 'First of all I had to wait for (and not miss), the right sunset. It couldn't be too bright as this would create flare in the lens pointing directly at the sun, but it still had to be bright enough to use the full circle of the sun to good effect and carefully positioned - exactly filling one of the triangles. Trials with lenses of various focal lengths soon established that my most powerful (600mm telephoto lens) was the best one for the job, for which a sturdy tripod was essential for a steady, sharply focussed composition. I found a site on steeply sloping ground above and to the east of the canal basin offering exactly what I needed – a position where the camera could be aligned squarely on to the tower and at exactly the right height above it, where the sun could curve down from about eleven o'clock into the triangle. My options were fairly narrow as only an orange or even red sun would avoid causing flare at a magnification of twelve times. The window of opportunity was clearly only a few weeks in October when the curved descent of the sun's orb followed a track where it was possible to be in exactly the right place to get the chance to make an exposure. It was also weather permitting.'

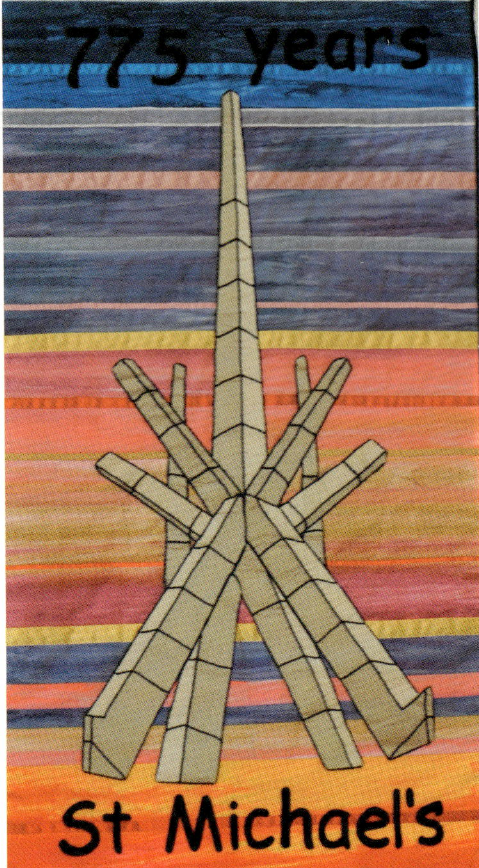

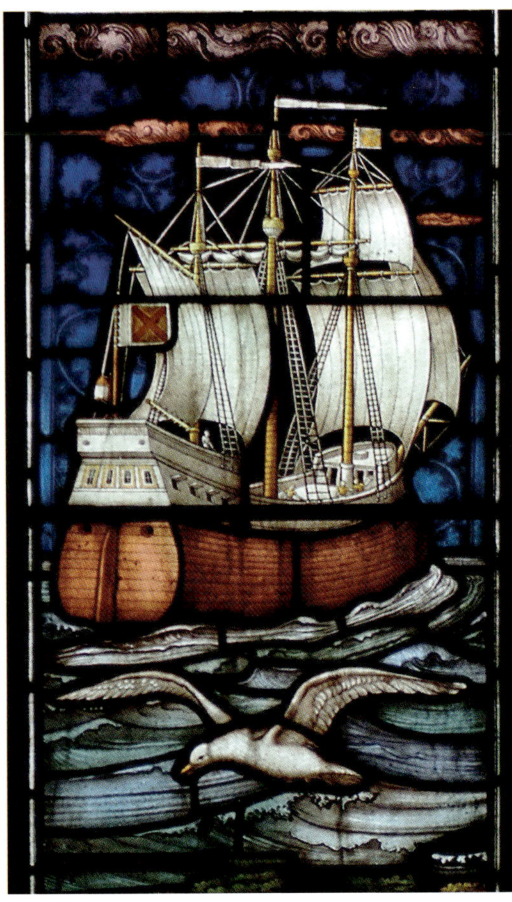

Wall hanging of the spire
© Original artwork by Katie Marshall. Wall hanging by the Church Banner Group, led by Valerie Spence
© Stephen Blake photographer (Above left)

The Wyville Thomson Memorial Window © Gordon Young photographer (Above right)

The Pentecost Window by Crear McCartney, 1992
© Gordon Young photographer (Opposite)

The spire has also been caught vividly by Katie Marshall of Linlithgow in her collage 'The Spire' using cardboard, acrylic paint and pens for the spire and paint and card for the background. In the 2017 Faith and Fabric exhibition she remarked that 'the composition shows that even against a vibrant sky, it is the spire that steals the show.' A textile interpretation of the composition has now been made and it hangs in St Michael's Parish Church.

Behind is the equally colourful Pentecost Window, installed in 1992 by the Friends of St Michael's to mark the 750th anniversary of the church. Twelve tongues of fire burst out to touch the traditional symbols of the apostles, beneath the butterfly wings and peacock feathers representing the risen Christ.

The artist was Crear McCartney (1931-2016) who studied at Glasgow School of Art. The church exhibits stained glass of an exceptional standard depicting biblical themes and commemorating local individuals. Of note is the magnificent Wyville Thomson memorial window located in the apse. Thomson, born in Linlithgow, was an explorer who charted the world's oceans in HMS Challenger from 1872-76.

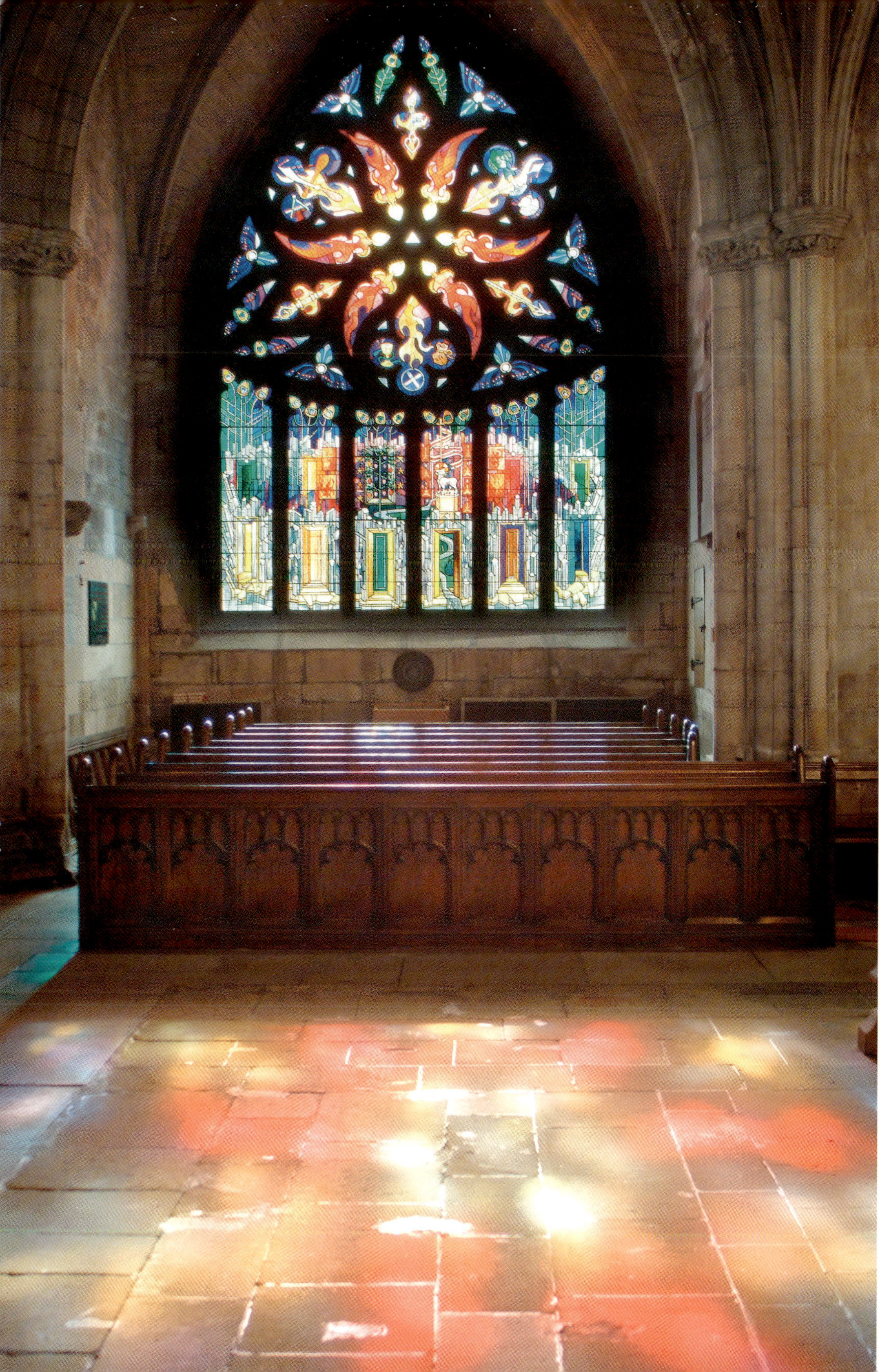

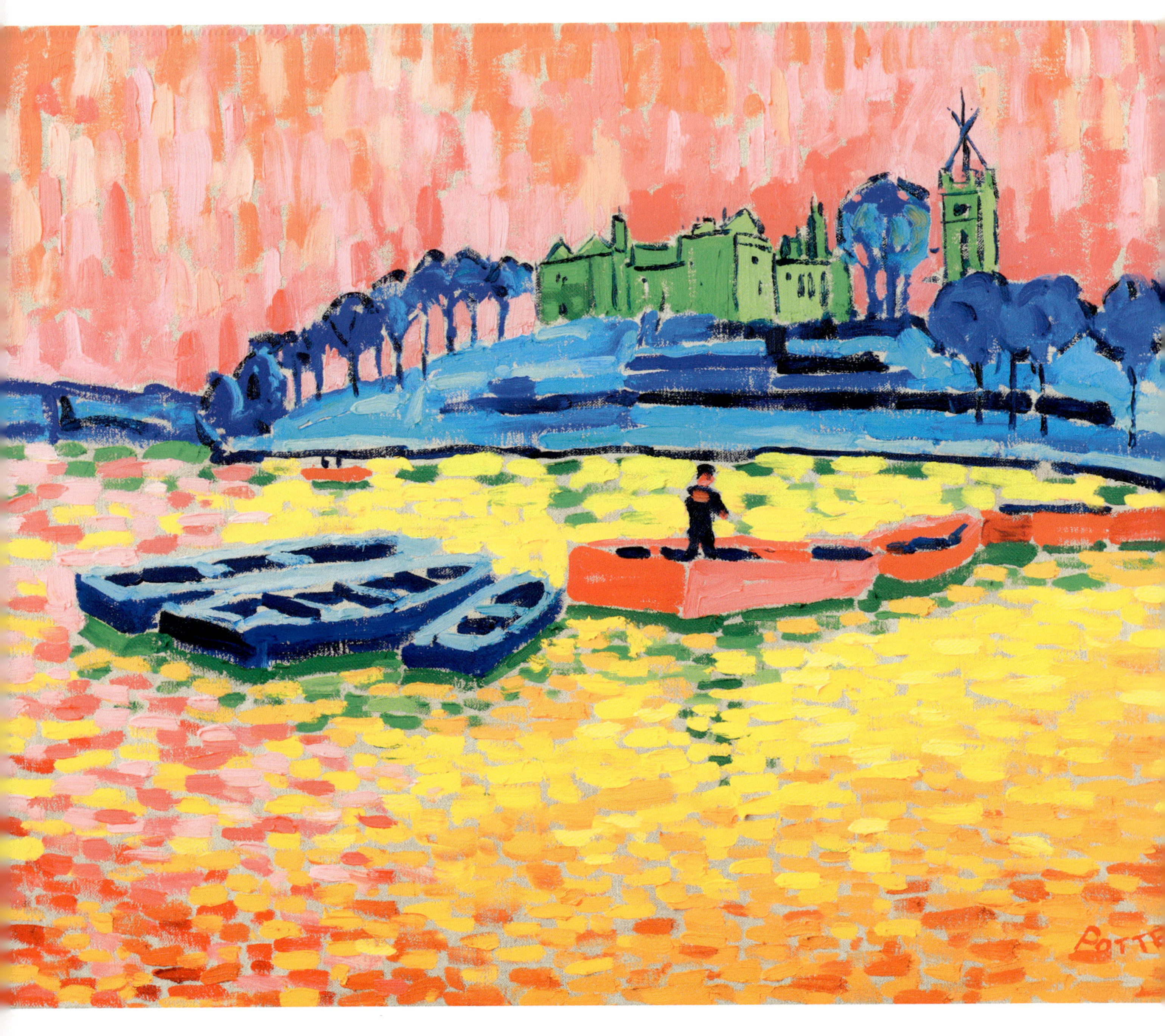

FIVE

Looking at Linlithgow Today

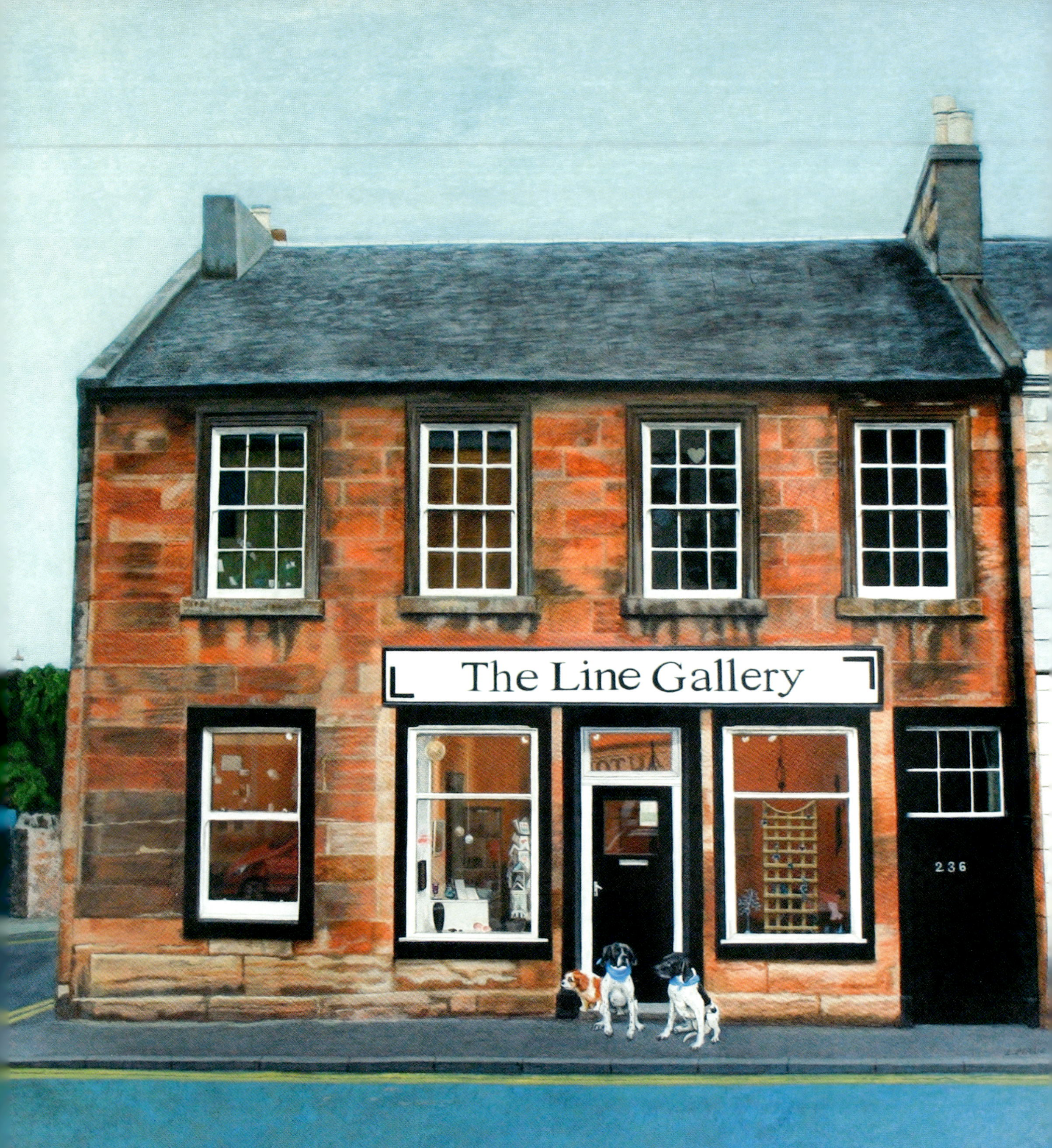
The Line Gallery
236

Linlithgow Palace, by James Potter
© James Potter
(On page 122)

The Line Gallery by Lorna Pirrie
© Lorna Pirrie
(Opposite)

Artists, from many disciplines, continue to look at Linlithgow and draw inspiration. The work of a few are illustrated on these pages.

Lorna Pirrie, whose work is illustrated opposite, captures well the front of 238 High Street, Linlithgow, the Line Gallery. She has exhibited several times at the gallery, and here paints the end of the terrace and the street edged by yellow lines, dogs and all.

The Line Gallery is a dynamic, contemporary gallery and has been promoting modern artists, new and established, old and young for many years. Gail Boardman and Elisabet Thorin command much respect amongst artists of today as they encourage a new generation.

At the start of this section is reproduced, in bold colours, the oil painting, 'Linlithgow Palace' by artist James Potter with the familiar shapes of palace and parish church. James is a self-taught artist who grew up in West Sussex and now lives in Edinburgh who has painted many commissioned portraits, as well as having been an official war artist in Bosnia. He considers himself first and foremost a plein air painter and he believes that only when the artist is within the landscape and surrounded by it can he truly study the subject matter.

In contrast is Sarah Felton Lewis, overleaf, whose delicate penwork has drawn the outline of no fewer than 19 buildings, familiar as well as less well-known, throughout the town, from the dovecote to the Burgh Halls.

The art gallery in the Burgh Halls, run by the Community Arts section of West Lothian Council organises a wide offering of national and international art and has included exhibitions of many notable artists, including Alan Davies, Michael McVeigh and James Cumming.

Writer and researcher, Wendy Ball, prepared the publication, 'Out In The Open. Public Art in West Lothian,' published in 2012, which covered the numerous works of public art in the West Lothian area, including eight in Linlithgow, all of which are featured in this book.

Art continues to play an important role in the life of the secondary and primary schools as evidenced by the vibrant external wall mosaic at Linlithgow Primary School. The project was carried out by teachers at the school who led parent helpers and pupils. The sun shines over the town and notable local buildings such as the churches of St Ninian's Craigmailen and the familiar Byzantine-inspired St Peter's Church, featured earlier in this book. The eight mosaic panels are linked with a band of figurative children with linked, outstretched arms and a sky interspersed with clouds. The 'Victoria' boat plies along a very blue Union Canal.

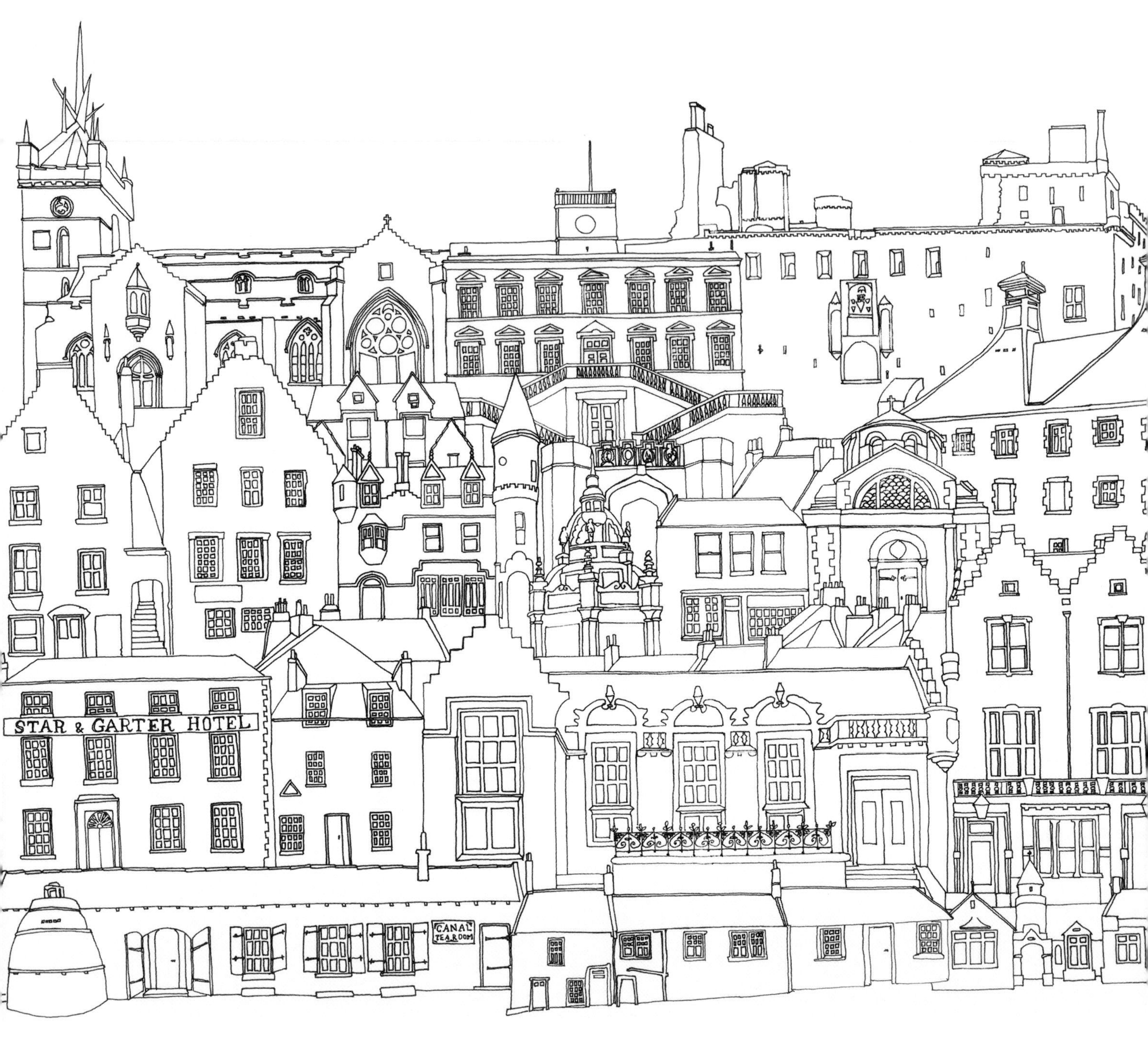
STAR & GARTER HOTEL
CANAL
TEA ROOM

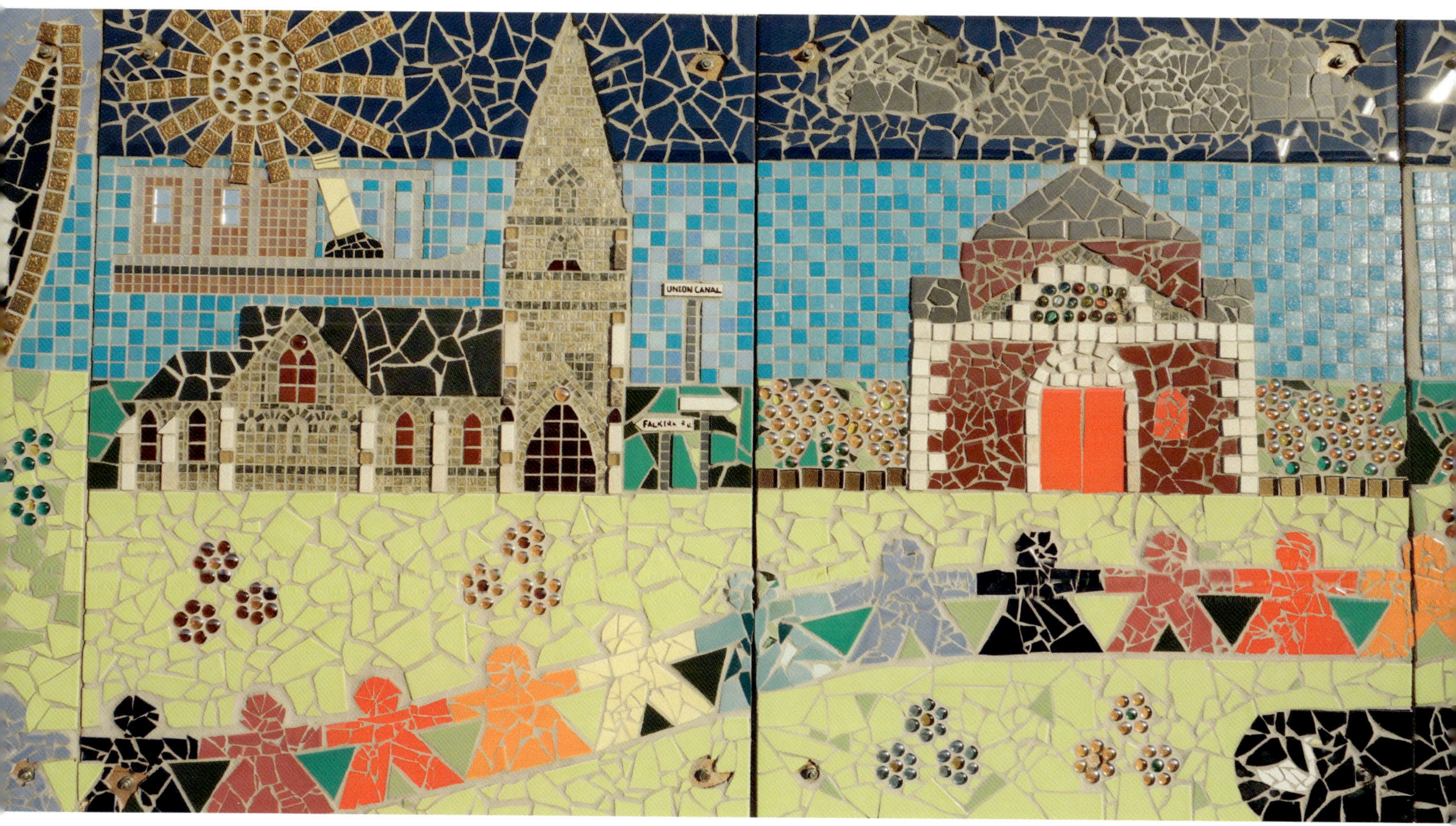

The buildings of Linlithgow by Sarah Felton Lewis
© Sarah Felton Lewis
(Opposite)

Linlithgow in mosaic by staff, parents and pupils of Linlithgow Primary School
© West Lothian Council
© Christopher Long photographer
(Above)

The changing High Street scene has been recorded by today's artists. This includes the former 'Marynka' restaurant by Glasgow architectural painter and illustrator Adrian McMurchie. Born and educated in Glasgow, Adrian graduated in graphic design. Most of his work is of an architectural nature, depicting buildings and cityscapes. He illustrated the restaurant reviews for the Sunday Herald from 2000-11. Evonne Little has captured the spirit of the smallest shop in the town, A Wee Mindin', a traditional sweetshop and gift shop, located in a unique 16th century High Street building, Hamilton's Land. Another High Street building, illustrated by the author, is the former Royal Bank of Scotland at 55 High Street. Local artist, Morag Stevenson, has prepared a series of small shopfronts, some of which are illustrated here. Artist Leo du Feu grew up in the town and attended Linlithgow Academy. He first exhibited in the Line Gallery in Linlithgow, winning the Royal Scottish Society of Painters in Watercolour's Alexander Graham Munro Travel Award 2008, the Royal Over-Seas League Commonwealth Travel Scholarship 2010 and the Bet Low Trust Award in 2013. Illustrated here is a sunset over the St Magdalene's distillery.

The former Marynka Restaurant, 57 High Street Linlithgow by Adrian McMurchie
© Catriona Staddon
(Right)

A Wee Mindin', 48 High Street, Linlithgow by Evonne Little
© Yvonne Sherratt
(Below left)

The former Royal Bank of Scotland, 55 High Street Linlithgow
© Christopher Long
(Below right)

The Do It Yourself Shop, 167 High Street and Granary Café, 102 High Street, Linlithgow, by Morag Stevenson
(Opposite)

St Magdalene's, Linlithgow by Leo du Feu
© Leo du Feu
(Opposite)

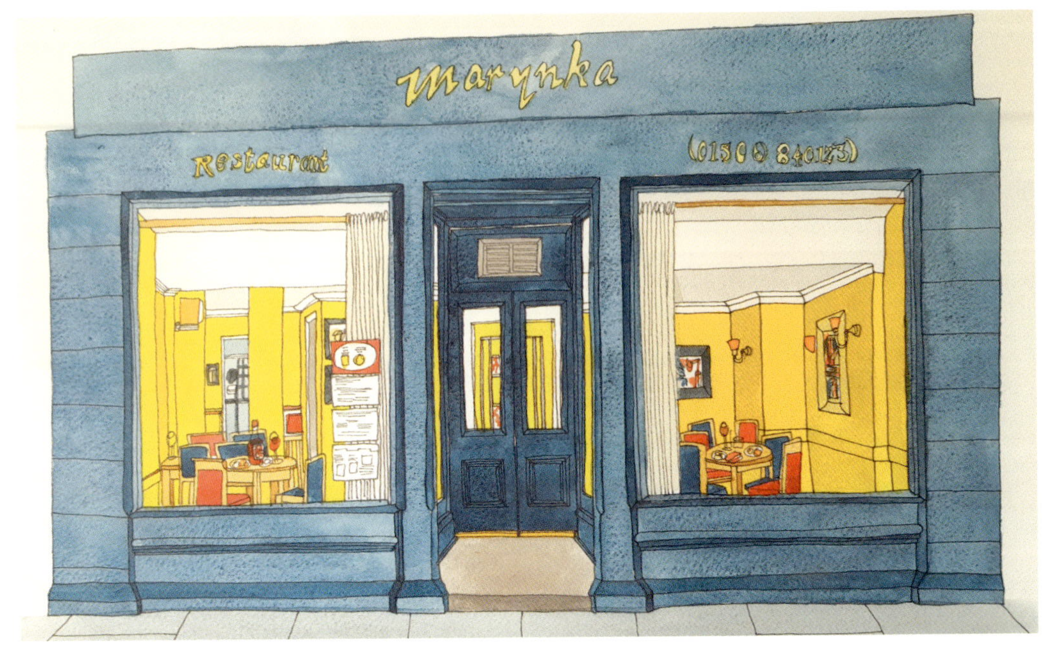

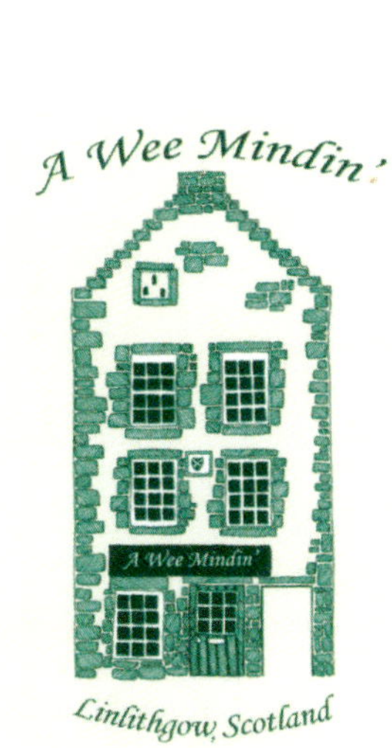

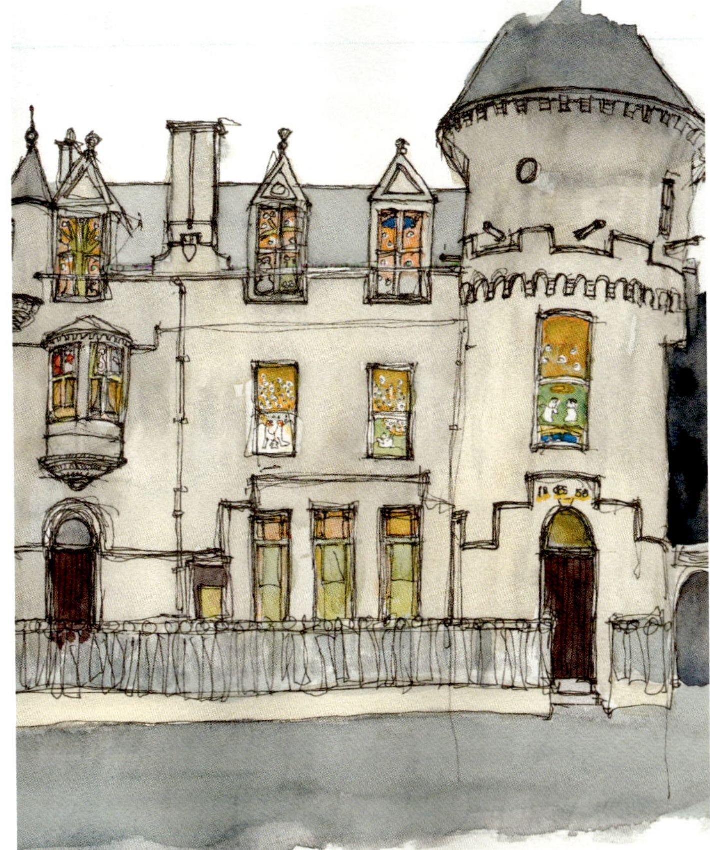

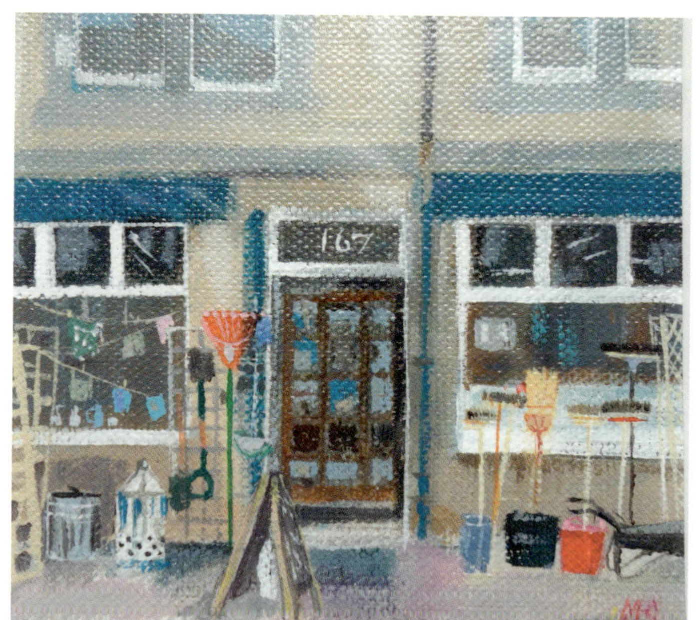
167

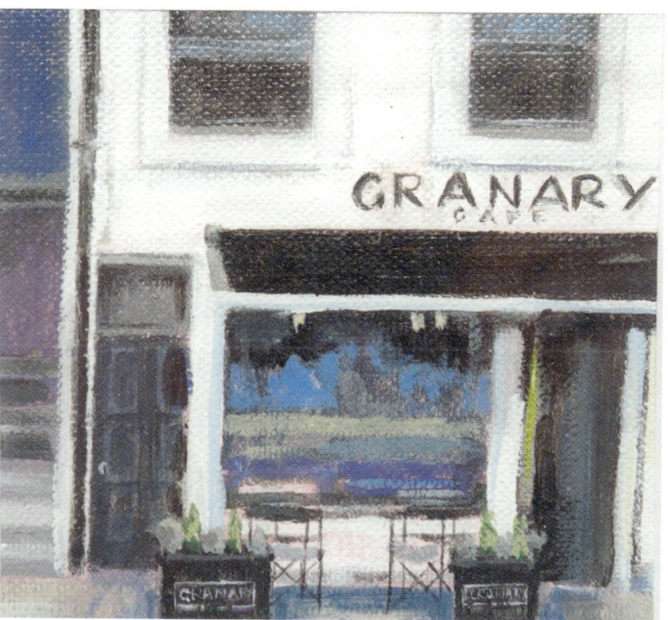
GRANARY

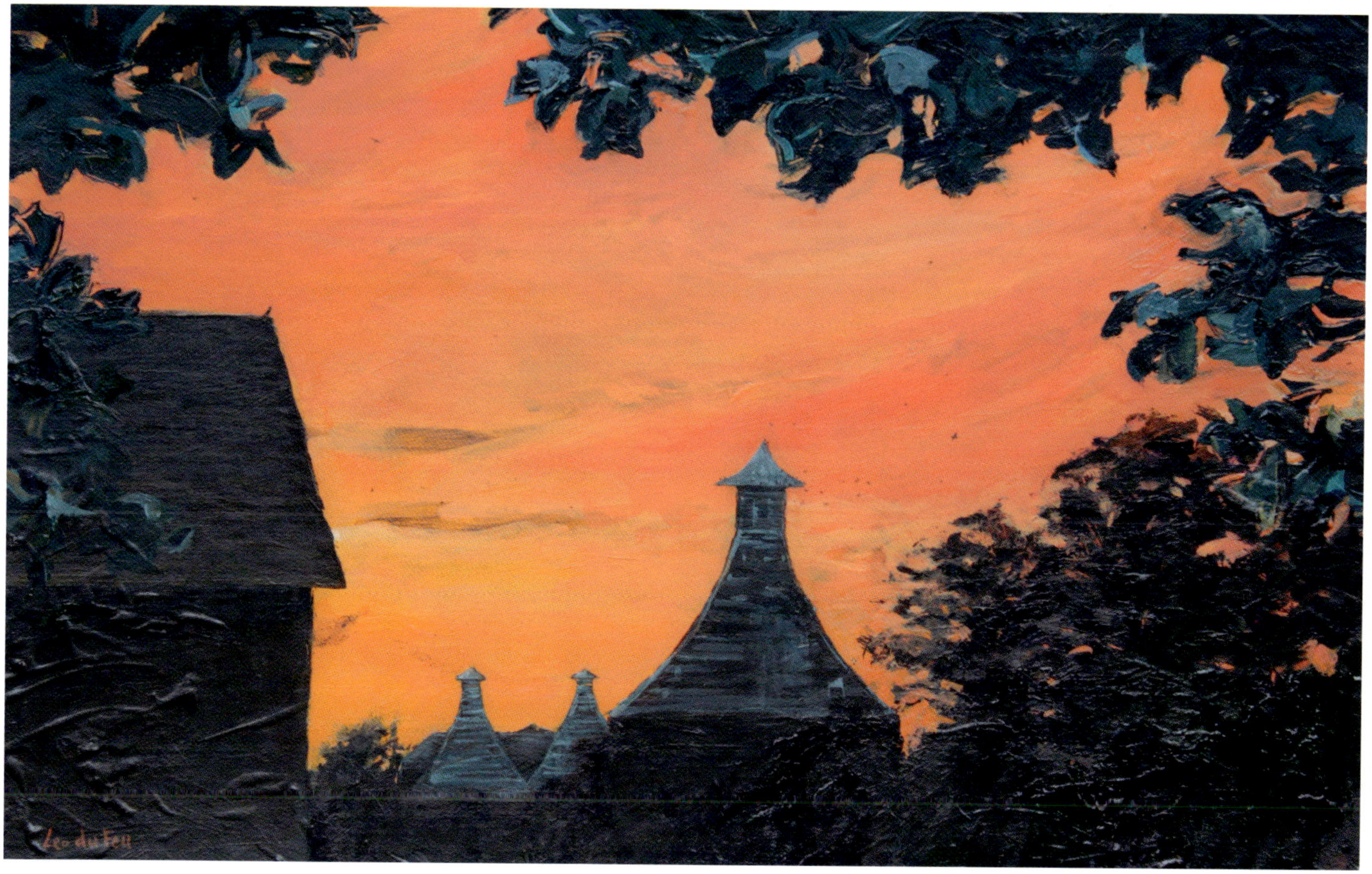

December Day, Linlithgow by John Forgan
© John Forgan
© Paul Gavin Photography (Below)

John Forgan's vibrant 'December Day, Linlithgow' was commissioned by Alan Steel Asset Management and hangs in their offices. While training for winter Olympic ice skating, John took up painting and sketching. He focuses on the towns and cityscapes of Edinburgh and the Lothians, including Linlithgow, as well as the many East Neuk fishing villages.

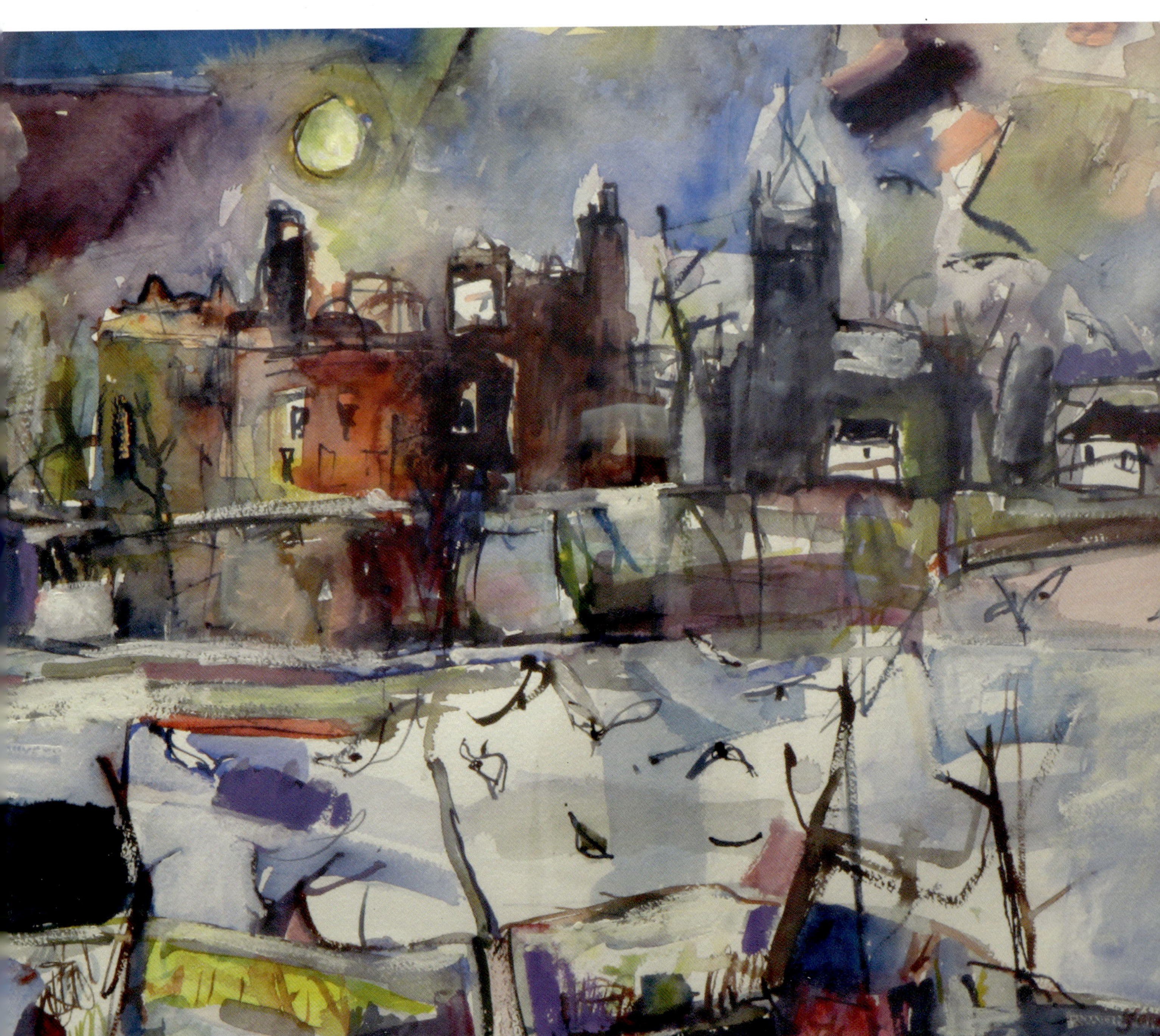

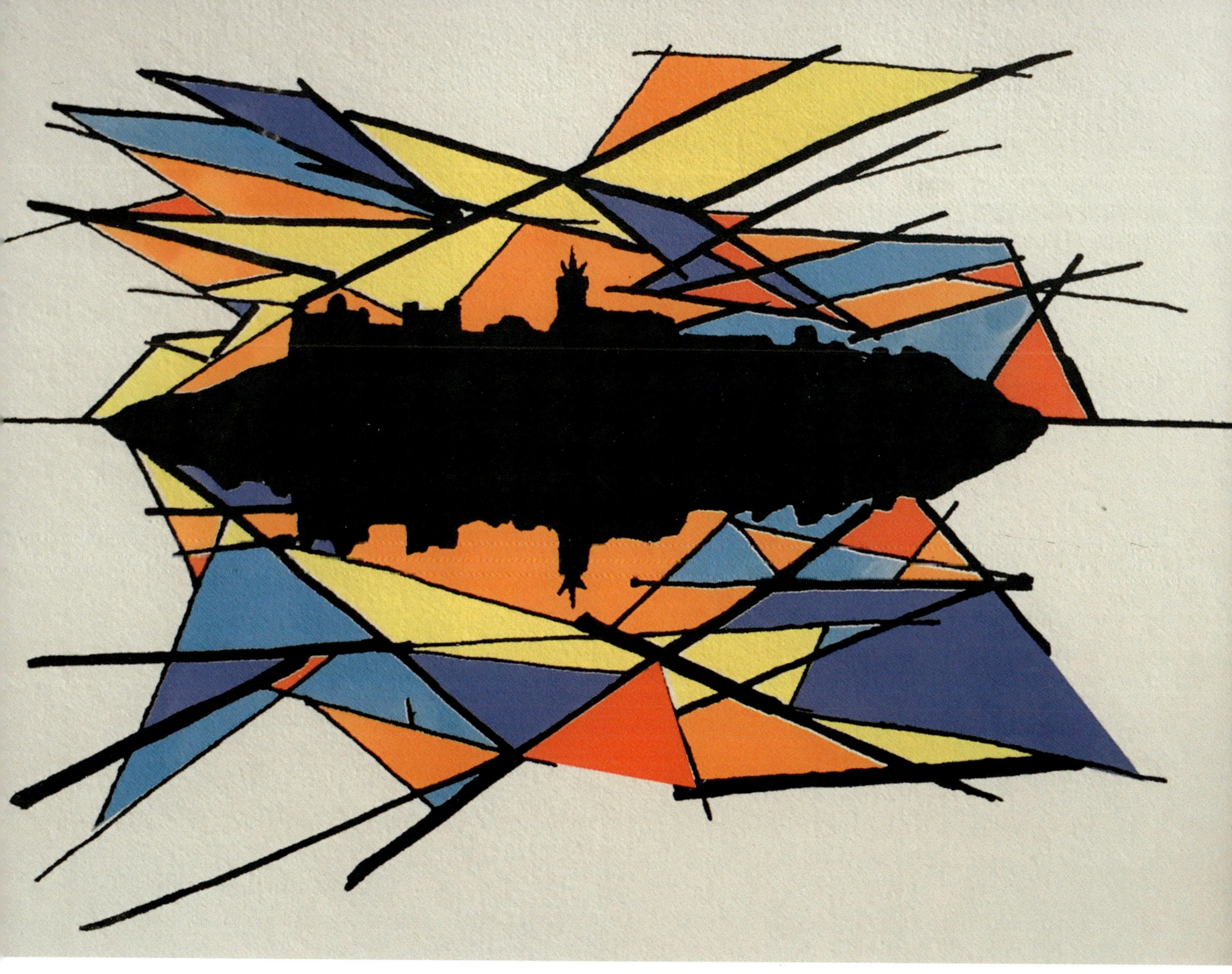

Reflections of the Palace by Douglas Cook
© Douglas Cook
(Above)

Douglas Cook is a young Linlithgow artist who graduated from the University of Dundee. At the Art, Design & Architecture Degree Show in 2017 he exhibited a painting of the landscape between the Falkirk Wheel and Edinburgh in his linear fashion. His dazzling image of the town concludes this section.

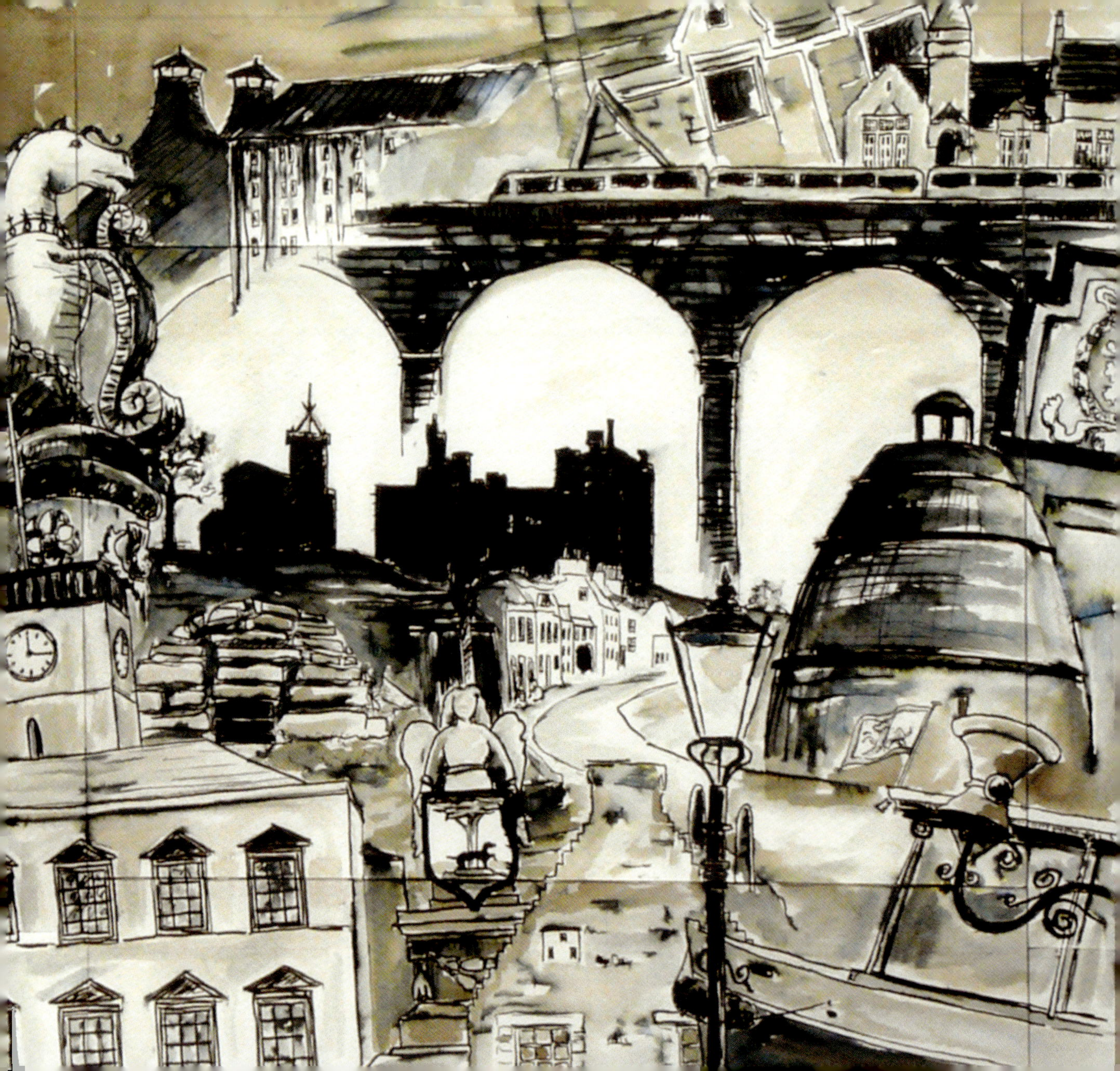

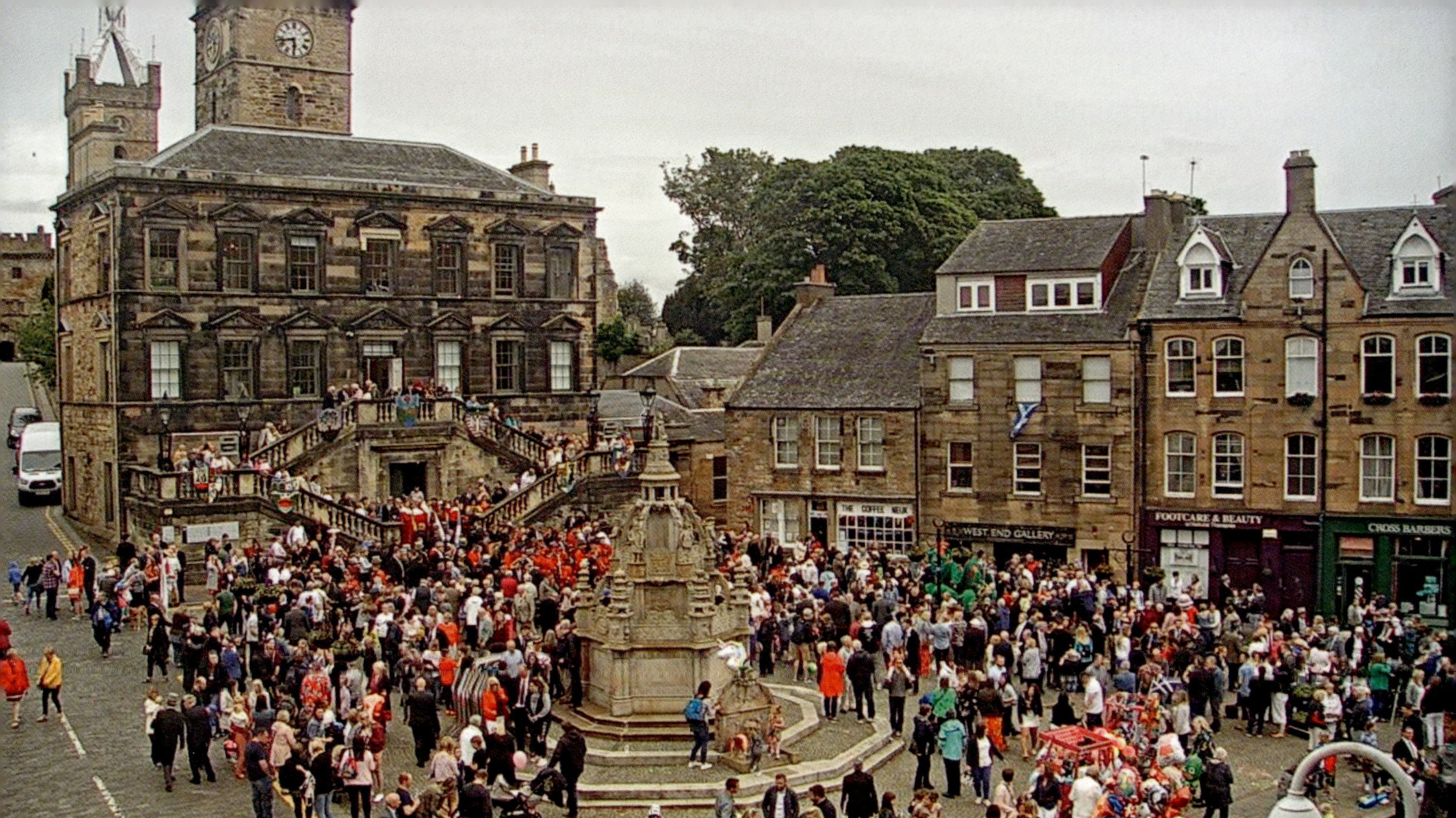

Conclusion

Marches Day 2018 from the webcam overlooking the Cross (Above)

Historic Linlithgow by Leo du Feu
© Leo du Feu
(Opposite)

This book started with a picture looking down at Linlithgow taken from a camera on a drone. Webcams are everywhere. Whether walking past the Cross or kayaking down the canal, you are being looked at, even if you are unaware of it.

The final image is from the webcam that features participants of the annual Marches Day who have paraded three times between the West Port and the Cross Well, in front of the marvellous stage set of the Palace, Parish Church, Burgh Halls and the Cross Well.

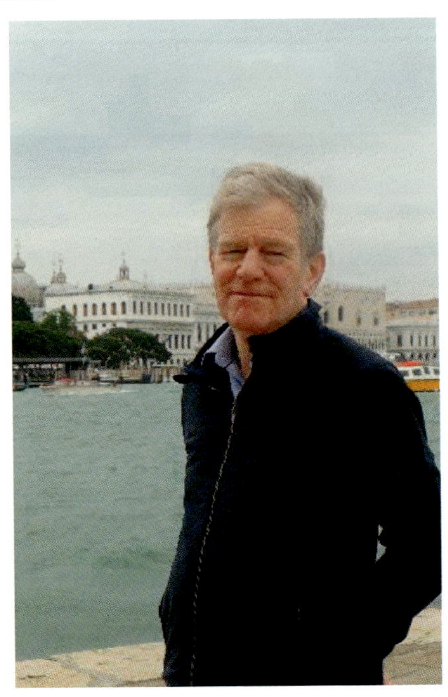

Biography

Christopher Long worked for many years as an architect in local and central government in Scotland after studying architecture in Canterbury, Kent. He has lived for over 20 years in Linlithgow, many of these serving as chair of Linlithgow Civic Trust, now part of Linlithgow Burgh Trust. He combines family interests with hill walking, painting as well as service to the community with the Rotary Club of Linlithgow Grange.
His favourite places are Venice and… Linlithgow.

Bibliography

Ball, Wendy E, *Out in the Open, Public Art in West Lothian*, 2012, West Lothian Council Community Arts

Cadell, Henry M. T*he Rocks of West Lothian; An Account of the Geological and Mining History of the West Lothian District,* 1925, Oliver & Boyd

Campbell, Ian, *Linlithgow's 'Princely Palace' and its Influence in Europe*, 1994, Edinburgh University Press, Architectural Heritage, Volume 5, Issue 1, Edinburgh

Cavers, Keith, *A Vision of Scotland. The Nation Observed by John Slezer 1671 to 1717,* 1993, HMSO Edinburgh

Collie, James, *The Royal Palace of Linlithgow, Illustrated*, 1847, J. Weale, London, Adam and Charles Black, Edinburgh and J. Smith & Son, Glasgow

Dennison, Patricia and Coleman, Russel, *Historic Linlithgow*, 2000, Historic Scotland in association with Scottish Cultural Press.

Dennison, Patricia; Eydmann, Stuart; Lyell, Annie; Lynch, Michael; Stronach, Simon, *Painting the Town, Scottish Urban History in Art*, 2013, The Society of Antiquaries of Scotland, Edinburgh

Dunbar, John G. *Scottish Royal Palaces*, 1999, Tuckwell Press, East Lothian

Ferguson, John, *Ecclesia Antiqua or The History of an Ancient Church (St. Michael's, Linlithgow)*, 1905, Oliver & Boyd, Edinburgh

Ferguson, John, *Linlithgow Palace, Its History and Traditions,* 1910, Oliver & Boyd, Edinburgh

Firth, Jack, *James Cumming, An Appreciation,* 1995, The Mercat Press, in association with The Scottish Gallery, Edinburgh

Fraser, Antonia, *Mary, Queen of Scots,* 1969, George Weidenfeld & Nicolson Ltd, London

Gristwood, Sarah, *This Ill Fated Queen,* 24th January 2004, Book Review in the Guardian Newspaper

Grogan, Elaine, *Beginnings: Charles Rennie Mackintosh's Early Sketches,* 2002, Architectural Press in association with the National Library of Ireland

Hannavy, John, *A Moment in Time, Scottish Contributions to Photography 1840-1920,* 1983, Third Eye Centre Ltd, Glasgow

Jaques, Richard and McKean, Charles, *West Lothian, An Illustrated Architectural Guide,* 1994, The Rutland Press, Edinburgh

Jamieson, Bruce, *A 15th century Christmas at Linlithgow Palace,* 21st December 1979, Linlithgow Journal & Gazette, Linlithgow

Jamieson, Bruce, editor, *Recording Linlithgow's Street Carvings,* (undated), Linlithgow Civic Trust

Jamieson, Bruce, Old Linlithgow, 1998, Stenlake Publishing, Ayrshire

Kallus, Veronica, *St Giles' Cathedral Edinburgh,* 2010, Heritage House Group, Norfolk

Lennie, Lindsay, *Scotland's Shops,* 2010, Historic Scotland, Edinburgh

Lennie, Lindsay, *The Tiled Shops of James Duncan Limited,* 2009, Journal of the Tiles & Architectural Ceramics Society, Volume 15

Mylne, Robert S. *The Master Masons to the Crown of Scotland and their Works,* 1893, Scott & Ferguson and Burgess & Company, Edinburgh

Simpson, Roddy, *Hill & Adamson's Photographs of Linlithgow,* 2002, West Lothian History & Amenity Society, Linlithgow

Simpson, Roddy, *Thresholds*, 2018, Published by Roddy Simpson, Edinburgh

Smailes, *Helen, A Portrait Gallery For Scotland, The Foundation, Architecture and Mural Decoration of the Scottish National Portrait Gallery 1882-1906*, 1985, Trustees of the National Galleries of Scotland, HMSO, Edinburgh

Smith, Ron, *Linlithgow Architecture & History of a Scottish Royal Burgh*, 2010, Linlithgow Civic Trust, Linlithgow

Steel, David and Paterson, Ian, *The Parish Church of Linlithgow St Michael's*, 2004, St Michael's Parish Church, Linlithgow

Tabraham, Chris and Cox, Adrian, *Linlithgow Palace*, 2010, Historic Scotland, Edinburgh

The Times, article regarding the unveiling of the Green Man statue, 6th October 1911, page 9

Wallace, Gordon, *See For Yourself*, 2016, Unicorn Publishing Group Ltd, London

Wallace, Gordon, *Singing Softly to the Light, The Biography of Mary Louise Coulouris*, 2015, Unicorn Publishing Group Ltd, London

Wormald, Jenny, *Mary, Queen of Scots, A Study in Failure*, 1988, George Philip

Websites

www.artuk.org

www.canmore.org.uk

www.capitalcollections.org.uk

https://digital.nls.uk/slezer/theatrum-scotiae.html

www.etsy.com

http://www.linlithgowcommunitymagazine.co.uk

www.linlithgow.info/visit-linlithgow/webcams-linlithgow

www.liverpoolmuseums.org.uk/walker/collections/highlights/item-238710.aspx

https://maps.nls.uk/towns

www.parliament.uk/art

www.tate.org.uk/art/research-publications/jmw-turner/joseph-mallord-william-turner-linlithgow-palace-r1132059

Index